Constitutional Policing

Striving for a More Perfect Union

Michael A. Hardy
EDITOR

Cover design by ABA Design

The materials contained herein represent the opinions of the authors and/or the editors and should not be construed to be the views or opinions of the law firms or companies with whom such persons are in partnership with, associated with, or employed by, nor of the American Bar Association or the Section of State and Local Government Law, unless adopted pursuant to the bylaws of the Association.

Nothing contained in this book is to be considered as the rendering of legal advice for specific cases, and readers are responsible for obtaining such advice from their own legal counsel. This book is intended for educational and informational purposes only.

© 2023 American Bar Association. All rights reserved.

No part of this publication may be reproduced, stored in a retrieval system, or transmitted in any form or by any means, electronic, mechanical, photocopying, recording, or otherwise, without the prior written permission of the publisher. For permission, complete the request form at www.american bar.org/reprint or email ABA Publishing at copyright@americanbar.org.

Printed in the United States of America.

27 26 25 24 23   5 4 3 2 1

ISBN 978-1-63905-304-9

A catalog record for this book is on file with the Library of Congress.

Discounts are available for books ordered in bulk. Special consideration is given to state bars, CLE programs, and other bar-related organizations. Inquire at Book Publishing, ABA Publishing, American Bar Association, 321 N. Clark Street, Chicago, Illinois 60654-7598.

www.shopABA.org

Contents

Foreword   v
Zachary W. Carter

About the Editor   ix

About the Authors   xi

Introduction: A More Perfect Union   xvii
Michael A. Hardy

PART I
Foundations

Chapter 1
Qualified Immunity   3
Wylie Stecklow

Chapter 2
Administrative Complaints against Police   21
Rita McNeil Danish

Chapter 3
Accountability of Police as Public Employees   37
James Hanks

Chapter 4
What Is Constitutional Policing?   69
Royce Russell

PART II
Effecting Positive Changes
Toward a More Perfect Union

Chapter 5
Contemporary Civilian Oversight of Law Enforcement   95
Sharon R. Fairley

Chapter 6
Pattern or Practice Investigations and Consent Decrees   129
Michael A. Hardy

Chapter 7
Litigating Police-Civilian Encounters   151
William Harmening

Chapter 8
Transforming Policing: Lessons from New York City   173
Donna Lieberman, with Johanna Miller, Lee Rowland,
Chris Dunn, Michael Sisitzky, and Jared Trujillo

Afterword
The Most Perfect Union Protects and Serves Us All   197
Jelani Jefferson Exum

Index 203

Foreword

Zachary W. Carter

Criminal justice reform in this country is a perpetual work in progress—not unlike our journey *toward a more perfect union*. Particularly as it pertains to police/community interactions, criminal justice reform never occurs (or fails to occur) in a vacuum. Rather, reforms are inspired by high-profile incidents, affected by the prevailing political climate, and influenced by scientific and technological advances that establish objective facts and provide important insights into human psychology and behavior.

The pace of progress in achieving reform of police practices has always correlated closely with the availability of evidence that convincingly establishes that violations of constitutional rights by police have in fact occurred. In the not-too-distant past, this presented a substantial challenge. After all, allegations of police abuse of authority arise most often in the context of confrontations between police and racial minorities residing in impoverished communities. Much of the public has tended to credit the accounts of the police over the accounts of these civilians, particularly in the absence of incontrovertible evidence.

A paradigm-shifting event occurred in March of 1991, when millions of Americans viewed a video recording a Black man, Rodney King, being brutally beaten, without apparent justification, by officers of the Los Angeles Police Department. The acquittal of these officers in state court sparked outrage on the part of a public that had virtually witnessed the police assault firsthand.

Over the succeeding three decades, video cameras have become a ubiquitous presence at police/civilian confrontations. Cell phones place a camera in every pocket. Police departments around the country have broadly accepted body-worn cameras and dashcams as necessary to 21st-century policing. Street surveillance cameras, both private and municipal, are everywhere. Consequently, encounters between police and civilians that in an earlier age would likely be reduced to "he said, she said" credibility contests now yield videos, of varying degrees of completeness and quality, that permit the public to form its own opinions concerning the confrontation in question. The outcomes of video-informed incidents vary, as illustrated by the cases of Eric Garner, Michael Brown, and George Floyd. But few now doubt that police violations of constitutional rights in fact occur. The debate now centers on whether a particular incident is evidence of a pattern or practice of constitutional violations by a specific police department, particularly where a community of color is concerned.

What video has achieved in providing objective evidence of constitutional violations during police/civilian street encounters, DNA evidence has achieved in establishing that violations of constitutional rights by police have in fact resulted in wrongful convictions for serious, often capital crimes.

The hundreds of DNA-based exonerations achieved by the Innocence Project over the past few decades have required the criminal justice system to reconsider accepted wisdom in two broad areas.[1] First, those exonerations challenged the belief that only guilty persons confess, a notion so stubbornly entrenched in our criminal justice system that it is embedded in our rules of evidence as an exception to the hearsay rule. Second, DNA exonerations challenged the reliability of widely accepted police practices in securing eyewitness identifications. The DNA-based exonerations of defendants convicted based on erroneous eyewitness identifications were the catalyst for research into what factors contributed to those mistakes. The result has been wholesale changes to longstanding eyewitness identification procedures, including and especially procedures affecting the conduct of lineups.[2]

Criminal justice reform, particularly police reform, rarely occurs without a factual foundation, sometimes achieved through negotiation and consensus, and sometimes externally imposed as findings by a court. The principal vehicles through which critical facts and advances in science have been established in court and revealed to the public are litigation and policy advocacy.

This book, aptly titled *Constitutional Policing: Striving for a More Perfect Union*, has two broad objectives. The first is to develop and articulate policy positions that can support a manner of policing that is at the same time effective and respectful, that embraces the community as partners in achieving public safety, and that intrudes in the lives of the people it serves only to the extent necessary to keep them safe. The second is to provide practical guidance to litigators confronting laws, regulations, and contractual provisions that present obstacles to proving constitutional violations in courts of law, holding individual officers and government institutions accountable, and making the evidentiary case necessary to support operational reforms. This book further provides useful insights into the challenges presented by the defense of qualified immunity, the obstructive provisions of police union contracts, the conduct of Department of Justice pattern and practice investigations, and the role of administrative oversight agencies in investigating allegations of police misconduct.

As we emerge from a disruptive pandemic and confront the consequent national increase in crime, the political environment is challenging for advocates of police reform and other criminal justice reforms. It will require effective policy and legal advocacy to establish once and for all that, for example, one state's bail reform initiative cannot possibly account for a national crime wave, and that a pandemic that at its worst sickened and killed thousands of Americans each week discouraged the kind of personal human interaction fundamentally necessary for police/community engagement and proactive, crime prevention–oriented policing. These and other possible breakthroughs in fact-based understandings as a basis for popular consensus can be as consequential as the impact video and DNA evidence had on public consciousness in prior years.

This book provides guidance and tools to advocates engaged in this important undertaking, and in that, it does a great service.

Endnotes

1. The Innocence Project was founded in 1992 by Barry C. Scheck and Peter J. Neufeld. To date, the organization as achieved 375 exonerations based on DNA evidence. https//innocenceproject.org.

2. *See Eyewitness Identification Reform*, INNOCENCE PROJECT, https://innocenceproject.org/eyewitness-identification-reform.

About the Editor

Michael A. Hardy, Esq., is a native New Yorker, born and raised in Bedford-Stuyvesant, Brooklyn-New York. He is a graduate of New York Law School and currently serves as Executive Vice President and General Counsel to the National Action Network, Inc. (NAN). Mr. Hardy attended undergraduate school at Carleton College in Northfield, Minnesota, and completed his secondary school education at the Northfield Mount Hermon School in Massachusetts.

Mr. Hardy is admitted to the Bar of the State of New York; the Supreme Court of the United States, and each of the Federal District Courts within the State of New York.

Mr. Hardy is a founding member of NAN and has served as counsel to NAN and Rev. Al Sharpton for over 25 years. He co-hosts with Rev. Sharpton NAN's live weekly rally and radio broadcast that is heard on WLIB 1190 AM and broadcast nationally on the Impact TV Network. As NAN's Executive Vice President and General Counsel, Mr. Hardy manages its day-to-day operational and legal affairs. He hosts a monthly free legal clinic at NAN's House of Justice where community members can address basic legal questions with participating lawyers. "Legal Night" happens on the last Thursday of every month at the House of Justice.

Mr. Hardy has been in the forefront of key civil rights and police misconduct cases including the matters of Eric Garner, Noel Polanco, Sean Bell, Abner Louima, Amadou Diallo, Fermin Arzu, Ousmane Zongo, and many others. He led the legal efforts for all of NAN's major civil disobedience actions to date, highlighted by his representation of the approximately 1,200 persons who were arrested during the 1999 Amadou Diallo protests at One Police Plaza in New York City. In April 2014, New York Governor Andrew M. Cuomo appointed Mr. Hardy as a member of the Commission on Youth, Public Safety and Justice, which resulted in raising the age of criminal liability in New York from 16 to 18 years old. Mr. Hardy participated in the U.S. Department of Justice's creation of the Clemency Project, where the Obama administration began an effort to release low-level drug offenders sentenced to life or near-life prison sentences under mandatory sentencing guidelines that would not be applicable today. In April 2022, Mr. Hardy was appointed to a special panel for the New York Metropolitan Transit Authority to review and make recommendations on issues of public safety, equity, and fare evasion.

Mr. Hardy's primary areas of practice include civil rights litigation, criminal defense litigation, not-for-profit organizations, and employment matters. While in private practice he was lead counsel in several high-profile cases, such as the infamous mother/son murder trial of Santé and Kenny Kimes, upon which several books and television movies were based. He also had the distinct honor of arguing a matter before the late great U.S. Supreme Court Justice Thurgood Marshall. In 1988, along with attorney John Zwerling of Alexandria, Virginia, he participated in one of the first cases to challenge the Foreign Intelligence Surveillance Act (FISA) wiretaps of American citizens, long before 9/11 when FISA became a household word. In 1986, he was a candidate for New York State Attorney General.

Mr. Hardy has written numerous editorials for several news publications and authored a series of editorials under the general title of "Equal Justice" for the *Huffington Post*. He co-authored a voting rights article for the *Touro Law Review* titled "Let All Voters Vote: Independents and the Expansion of Voting Rights in the United States," 35 Touro L. Rev. 649 (2019). Prior to beginning his law practice, Mr. Hardy was one of the editors of the *National Alliance* newspaper, a national political weekly that focused on social justice, electoral, and democratic reform issues. His career has been profiled in the *New York Times*, *New York Law Journal*, and *Village Voice*, among others.

Mr. Hardy can be reached at hardy@nationalactionnetwork .net.

About the Authors

Zachary W. Carter is an attorney who most recently served as Corporation Council for the City of New York. His prior positions in public service include United States Attorney for the Eastern District of New York, U.S. Magistrate Judge, New York City Criminal Court Judge, and Executive Assistant District Attorney at the Brooklyn DA's Office. Mr. Carter has served on the boards of the Vera Institute of Justice, the New York University (NYU) School of Law, and the Brennan Center. He was a partner at the law firm of Dorsey & Whitney. Mr. Carter is a graduate of Cornell University and the NYU School of Law. He currently serves as Chairman of the Board of Directors of the Legal Aid Society of New York.

Sharon R. Fairley is a graduate of the University of Chicago Law School and has taught there since 2015. She became a Professor from Practice in 2019. Her academic research and writing focus on criminal justice reform with an emphasis on police accountability. Before joining the University of Chicago Law School, Ms. Fairley spent eight years as a Federal Prosecutor with the U.S. Attorney's Office for the Northern District of Illinois, investigating and trying criminal cases involving illegal firearms possession, narcotics conspiracy, bank robbery/murder, murder for hire, and economic espionage, among other criminal acts. She also served as the First Deputy Inspector General and General Counsel for the City of Chicago Office of the Inspector General. In December 2015, following the controversial officer-involved shooting death of Laquan McDonald, Ms. Fairley was appointed to serve as the Chief Administrator of the Independent Police Review Authority, the agency responsible for police misconduct investigations. She was also responsible for creating and building Chicago's Civilian Office of Police Accountability.

James Hanks is a retired shareholder with the Des Moines, Iowa, firm of Ahlers & Cooney, P.C. The firm represents a large number of local government bodies, including cities, counties, airports, special use districts, school districts, community colleges, and area education agencies. For 12 years, Mr. Hanks represented the Governor of the State of Iowa in labor negotiations on behalf of the Executive Branch of the State, including negotiations with the State Police Officers Council. The principal emphasis of his practice was in employment, local government, and educational law; in the course of his career, he negotiated over 1,000 collective bargaining agreements. Mr. Hanks is a Phi Beta Kappa graduate and was a Rhodes Scholar nominee of the University of Iowa. He received his law degree with high distinction from the College of Law of the University of Iowa. Mr. Hanks is past Chair of the Council for the American Bar Association Section of State and Local Government Law, and he received a Lifetime Achievement Award from the section in 2022. He is also past Chair of the Council of School Attorneys for the National School Boards Association and, in 2018, received the Lifetime Achievement Award from the council. In his 43 years of practice, Mr. Hanks was a presenter on a variety of governmental and employment topics to more than 25 national and state organizations. He is the author of several publications of the American Bar Association Section of State and Local Government Law including *School Bullying* (first edition, 2012; second edition, 2015) and the editor of and a contributing author for *School Violence: From Discipline to Due Process.*

William Harmening is a retired Illinois law enforcement officer and former professor of forensic psychology at Washington University in St. Louis. He has authored numerous textbooks in the areas of criminal justice and forensic psychology and has consulted as an expert witness in over 200 police use of force cases in 35 states, including the cases of Michael Brown in Ferguson,

Missouri, and George Floyd in Minneapolis, Minnesota. Mr. Harmening is a 1994 graduate of the University of Illinois at Springfield (M.A. Psychology) and a 1982 graduate of the Illinois State Police Academy. He now lives near Nashville, Tennessee.

Jelani Jefferson Exum is Dean and Philip J. McElroy Professor of Law at the University of Detroit Mercy School of Law. She is a nationally recognized expert in sentencing law and procedure. Before joining academia, Dean Jefferson Exum served as a law clerk for the Honorable James L. Dennis, U.S. Circuit Judge for the Fifth Circuit Court of Appeals, and the Honorable Eldon E. Fallon, U.S. District Judge for the Eastern District of Louisiana. Prior to joining the Detroit Mercy Law faculty, she was a Professor of Law and Associate Dean for Diversity and Inclusion at the University of Toledo College of Law, Associate Professor at the University of Kansas School of Law, and Visiting Associate Professor at the University of Michigan Law School. Dean Jefferson Exum has also been a Forrester Fellow and Instructor in Legal Writing at Tulane Law School. She serves on the Deans Advisory Committee of the ABA Legal Education Police Practices Consortium. She is also a member of the Editorial Board of the *Federal Sentencing Reporter*, and her work has been featured on prominent sentencing blogs, such as *Sentencing Law and Policy*. Dean Jefferson Exum mainly writes in the area of sentencing law and policy, but her research interests also include comparative criminal law and procedure, policing, and the impact of race on criminal justice.

Donna Lieberman has been Executive Director of the New York Civil Liberties Union (NYCLU) since December 2001. Under Ms. Lieberman's leadership, the NYCLU has expanded the scope and depth of its work, using litigation, advocacy, and state-wide organizing to promote civil rights and civil liberties. Among the NYCLU's many accomplishments during her tenure are protecting the right to counsel, reforming stop and frisk and solitary confinement, repealing the 50a secrecy law for law enforcement, representing Edie Windsor to win marriage equality, expanding abortion rights, winning voting rights in East Ramapo school board elections, overhauling conditions in the psychiatric emergency rooms in Kings County Hospital Center, and founding the Education Policy Center and the Teen Activist Program. Under her leadership, the NYCLU is widely recognized as the state's leading voice for freedom, justice, and equality, advocating for those whose rights and liberties have been denied. Ms. Lieberman began her public interest legal career as a criminal defense lawyer in the South Bronx office of the Legal Aid Society, and she later served as Executive Director of the Association of Legal Aid Attorneys. For a decade, Ms. Lieberman served on the faculty of the Urban Legal Studies Program at City College. She joined the NYCLU in 1989 and was the Founding Director of its Reproductive Rights project.

Rita McNeil Danish, a highly accomplished attorney, transformational leader, and community changemaker, possesses more than 30 years of professional legal experience across a range of industries and business sectors. Ms. McNeil Danish serves clients as the Founder and Principal of JD2 Strategists, LLC, and she is currently a Partner and the DEI Strategic Business Partner at Taft Law LLP. In both roles, she diligently supports and provides counsel to municipalities and small and minority- and women-owned businesses. Through collaboration and communication, Ms. McNeil Danish engages elected officials, community stakeholders, and business leaders to find a foundation of unity on which to build systems that deliver safer communities and justice for all. While her professional contributions to DEI, MWBE, and community advocacy are prolific and significant, her unique set of skills is often why she is sought after to contribute to boards, including her recent five-year appointment to the Ohio Civil Rights Commission. Additionally, she serves on the boards of the National Civic League and the Ohio Chamber of Commerce and as the National Board Chair for Women for Economic and Leadership Development. Ms. McNeil Danish is licensed in Ohio, Illinois, and the U.S. Supreme Court.

Royce Russell is the Principal of R-SQUARE, ESQ. PLLC. He specializes in false arrest/police brutality (section 1983 civil rights violations), criminal defense, immigration, contracts, employment law, and trademark. For 18 years, he was a Partner at Emdin & Russell, LLP. Mr. Russell represented individuals in federal and state court, from criminal investigations to trials, and represented victims of police brutality/false arrest (section 1983 civil rights violations). Most notably, he represented the families of Ramarley Graham, who, at 18 years old, was shot to death by New York Police Department (NYPD) officers, and Kawaski Trawick, killed by NYPD officers as he stood in his apartment cooking, and Renise Hinton, who was catcalled and then arrested and groped because she did not respond to a police officer's sexual advances. Dedicated to justice and reform from an early age, once Mr. Russell graduated from Hofstra University School of Law, he began his law practice as an Assistant District Attorney in the Bronx, New York, under the first African-American District Attorney, Robert Johnson. DA Johnson's leadership and multifaceted approach to preventing crime through community outreach were invaluable to Mr. Russell. He has sought to serve and represent those lost to the justice system so often. To enhance that goal, Mr. Russell co-founded a mentoring program named Hoop Brothers that combined academics and athletics to assist in the development of at-risk high school students. Hoop Brothers partnered with the Legal Aid Society to allow assistant district attorneys to pair with high school student mentees to assist them with academic and life challenges. When this program ended, Mr. Russell continued to serve his community by conducting workshops and speaking engagements with organizations such as Fathers in the Hood, National Action Network Legal Night, and Jack and Jill of America, Inc. He served as the co-host of *Legally Speaking*, which aired on WWRL 1600 AM, and as a legal analyst for Tru TV, Fox News, ABC, MSNBC, CNN, BronxNet TV, On Point Radio, NY 1, and Hot 97's Street Soldiers. Currently, he is the co-host of *Speaking Legally . . . Where the Legal Meets the Cultural*, which airs every Wednesday on www.Facebook.com/RSQUAREESQ2.

Wylie Stecklow has been one of New York City's leading civil rights lawyers for more than 20 years and has a long history of working with community organizations and individuals for police accountability. Mr. Stecklow is a past President of the Southern District of New York Chapter of the Federal Bar Association, past National Chair of its Civil Rights Law Section, and an adjunct Professor at Fordham Law School (his alma mater). He is the 2021 recipient of the Sarah T. Hughes Civil Rights Award, and in 2022 he joined the Second Circuit Civic Education Committee. Mr. Stecklow is a founding member of the National Action Network's Legal Rights Nights and for the past 20 years has been litigating police policies and practice concerning the constitutional rights of protesters and photographers. He has litigated section 1983 cases involving First Amendment rights in New York, Maryland, and Iowa and tried constitutional cases to verdict in various state and federal courts. His firm was retained by the Occupy Wall Street General Assembly in 2011, where he organized pro bono representation for over 200 Occupy arrestees, and he has continued to litigate civil rights claims relating to the policing of Occupy. Currently Mr. Stecklow is co-counsel to two of the consolidated cases in the litigation in the Southern District of New York (SDNY) arising from the summer of George Floyd protests, *In Re New York City Policing During Summer 2020 Demonstrations*, along with the New York State Attorney General, New York Civil Liberties Union, Legal Aid Society, Davis Wright Tremaine, and many excellent civil rights counsel that collectively are seeking to reform the New York Police Department to ensure constitutionally compliant protest policing. He is the founder of the well-respected biennial Civil Rights Étouffée (CLE) in New Orleans and Chair of the Federal Bar Association of the SDNY's Rule of Law Award that has honored Bryan Stevenson (2016), Hon. John Lewis (2019), and Hon. Justice Sonia Sotomayor (2022).

Introduction

Michael A. Hardy

The United States finds itself at a crossroad when it comes to issues of equity and fairness in criminal justice matters and particularly policing in 21st-century America. The rise of the Black Lives Matter movement and the explosion of wrongful deaths in civilian and police encounters have turned the nation's attention to look more closely at the body of laws, rules, and regulations that govern police/community interactions.

The nation has also been in the grip of the Covid-19 pandemic, which has been harsh in its impact around the world. Millions have lost their lives to it, and it has had significant economic and social impacts in the United States and throughout its states and cities.[1] The result has been a significant uptick in crime. Communities have spoken loudly to address the predatory nature of many of the crimes that have infested their communities.[2]

Without doubt, a dynamic has been created where constitutional policing is critically important. Guidance, confidence in the institutions that protect and serve, and security in believing that all persons will be equally protected before the law have to be ascertained. As we go to publication with this book, the nation was shocked by the January 2023 incident of the Memphis, Tennessee Police beating an unarmed Tyre Nichols to death.

Practitioners in this field are confronted with having to litigate and advocate in the difficult area of policing. This book looks to provide a litigation road map in the area of policing and civilian/governmental oversight of policing.

The nation has come a long way in terms of policing since the mid-19th century when most modern urban police departments were founded. Gone are many of the unregulated acts that police were able to do in these early years. Federal, state, and local governments and the courts had to play catch-up to ensure that police authorities were properly regulated, and that the

U.S. Constitution's Bill of Rights was applicable to these critical engagements between policing authorities and the civilians they have jurisdiction over.

The march of time has brought us to an era when cameras are everywhere and are capturing everything. These images are then almost instantly available to the world through virtual technology. Nowhere has this impact been felt more than in the area of police-civilian interactions.

These modern technologies play a significant role in policing because the basic notions and expectations that police are here to "protect and serve" are brought into the light of our nation's bedrock belief that we are a nation and a "government of the people, by the people, for the people." But we arm police with both the authority to seize our liberty and weapons to take our lives.

We have constructed this book into two parts. *Part I: Foundations* consists of four chapters. *Part II: Effecting Positive Changes toward a More Perfect Union* also has four chapters.

Chapter 1 examines the issue of qualified immunity. Qualified immunity is a rule constructed by the U.S. Supreme Court that states that "[G]overnment officials performing discretionary functions generally are shielded from liability for civil damages insofar as their conduct does not violate clearly established statutory or constitutional rights of which a reasonable person would have known."[3] No issue has commanded the attention of our lawmakers, our police officers and other first responders, and the public at large like qualified immunity. It is one of the main issues currently under consideration by the U.S. Congress.[4] Many have argued that qualified immunity more than any other factor has contributed to unconstitutional policing and to the destabilizing of police civilian/community relations. On the other hand, many in the ranks of policing and first responders argue that it is their shield against abuse of process and security in performing their duties in a lawful manner. Chapter 1 seeks to guide litigators, lawmakers, and the general public in this most determinative and controversial area of policing.

Chapter 2 engages the administrative process of seeking accountability of police officers and utilizing the checks and balances that exist to ensure the process of policing remains true to its task of protecting and serving public constituents. It examines the current procedures used in internal affairs reviews of alleged police misconduct or corrupt practices. The chapter also examines the value and transparences that come with independent and/or civilian review agencies that address the often-raised questions about police policing themselves.

Chapter 3 examines police unions and labor law aspects of reform. The critical issue of reform is tied to the significant influence police unions and labor laws have on the ability to create reform without extensive and costly litigation. Few will argue the fact that police remain among the most important and protected public employees throughout the nation.

Many have said that the jewels of the American Constitution are the first ten amendments known as the Bill of Rights. Those amendments provide the protections of our individual rights and guard us against governmental overreach and abuse, issues that are crucial to ensuring that policing happens within the confines of not only our state and local laws that may be applicable but also the U.S. Constitution. Chapter 4 specifically examines the issues of excessive force and the checks and balances over police conduct afforded by the First and Fourth Amendments.

Part II: Effecting Positive Changes toward a More Perfect Union is not just an aspiration. It comes about through deep commitment to upholding the ideals of this nation that has created a belief by most that we can always be better than we currently are. We live with faith that this nation can provide possibilities and a secure future to all its citizens.

The issues of racial profiling and police brutality rushed to the forefront during the presidency of Barack Obama. In response, the president convened a study of policing in the 21st century. That report focused on issues from trust and legitimacy to officer wellness and safety.[5]

Chapter 5 reviews the developments in civilian oversight and examines the changing legal landscape in policing on issues of civilian oversight.

Chapter 6 examines the U.S. Department of Justice's (DOJ's) role in policing oversight. There is no doubt that the DOJ has had and should have in the future a significant role in advancing issues regarding the policing of Americans. The DOJ was created in the aftermath of America's Civil War in 1870.[6] It was specifically tasks with protecting the newly granted rights of emancipated slaves and preventing the spread of terror from the Ku Klux Klan. Consistent with this history was the passage of 42 U.S.C. § 14141 in reaction to the 1991 Los Angeles police officers' beating incident of Rodney King. Section 14141 (re-codified at 34 U.S.C. § 12601) is commonly referred to as "pattern or practice cases" and authorizes the DOJ to investigate law enforcement agencies that engage in unconstitutional practices in systemic patterns. Chapter 6 examines the DOJ's pattern or practice investigations when policing agencies have gone wrong.

It is often said that necessity is the mother of invention, and Chapter 7 fully examines this in the context of policing. The use of police body cameras, citizen/bystander videography, facial recognition, and social media has revolutionized litigating police/civilian encounters or other enforcement engagements. How these tools are being integrated into policing and enforcement is having a significant impact. Can we believe what we see, or is what we see what we are told? This is at the core of the landscape change in litigating police and civilian encounters. The chapter also examines the use of experts in police litigation and the urgency regarding the standards that are acceptable in qualifying experts.

Chapter 8 examines evolving issues in policing through the lens of developments in New York City. This chapter highlights the integrated nature of police-community engagement and why reform is essential. It suggests six areas of our daily interactions with police that need to be examined: police presence in our schools, interactions in mental health situations, the militarized command structure, broken windows policing, vice squads, and police discipline.

Dr. Martin L. King Jr. once said that "the arc of the moral universe is long but it bends toward justice."[7] Both our *Foreword* and *Afterword* describe the long road this nation has been on to be a nation of laws that respects the highest principles of justice and the challenging paths we have to travel to recognize that.

We must always remember the preamble to the Constitution of the United States: that we come together as a nation to "form a more perfect Union . . . promote the general Welfare and secure the Blessings of Liberty to ourselves and our Posterity." While we may never be a perfect union, we can never cease in our efforts to form a more perfect union, and nowhere does this matter more in the 21st century than in the relationship between the police and the people they are sworn to protect and serve. Former Chief Judge of the U.S. Supreme Court Earl Warren captured this necessity the most when he wrote in *Spano v. People of the State of New York*,[8] "that the police must obey the law while enforcing the law; that in the end life and liberty can be as much endangered from illegal methods used to convict those thought to be criminals as from the actual criminals themselves." It is our hope that this book will help practitioners to effectively address issues of constitutional policing in the decades to come.

Endnotes

1. Covid Data Tracker, CENTERS FOR DISEASE CONTROL AND PREVENTION, https://covid.cdc.gov/covid-data-tracker/#datatracker-home.

2. https://en.wikipedia.org/wiki/Killing_of_Tyre_Nichols.

3. Harlow v. Fitzgerald, 457 U.S. 800, 818 (1982).

4. H.R.1280: George Floyd Justice in Policing Act of 2021.

5. OFFICE OF COMMUNITY-ORIENTED POLICING SERVICES, DEPARTMENT OF JUSTICE, FINAL REPORT OF THE PRESIDENT'S TASK FORCE ON 21ST CENTURY POLICING (May 2015).

6. *History of the Department of Justice*, U.S. DEPARTMENT OF JUSTICE, https://www.justice.gov/history.

7. Dr. Martin Luther King Jr., "Remaining Awake Through a Great Revolution." Speech given at the National Cathedral, March 31, 1968.

8. Spano v. New York, 360 U.S. 315, 320–321 (1959).

PART I

Foundations

Chapter 1

Qualified Immunity[1]

Wylie Stecklow

Introduction

President Abraham Lincoln issued the Emancipation Proclamation in 1863, declaring that "all persons held as slaves are and henceforward shall be free." But in the years that followed, white militia who sought to continue white supremacy by threatening and killing Black Americans dominated law enforcement in the southern United States. It was cited in a recent district court decision that in Shreveport, Louisiana, more than 2,000 Black people were killed in 1865 alone.[2] In 1866, there were riots in Memphis and New Orleans, with more than 30 African-Americans murdered in both cities.[3] That same year, the Ku Klux Klan was formed in a law office in Pulaski, Tennessee. The Klan spread across the South, murdering, lynching, and instilling fear in its wake. In response, the U.S. Congress enacted numerous pieces of civil rights legislation, including the "Ku Klux Klan Act of 1871,"[4] (KKK Act) that "targeted the racial violence in the South undertaken by the Klan, and the failure of the states to cope with that violence."[5] Section 1 of the KKK Act became 42 U.S.C. § 1983. However, it was not until the Supreme Court decision in 1963 in *Monroe v. Pape* that section 1983's purpose was acknowledged: "to interpose the federal courts between the States and the people, as guardians of the people's federal rights."[6]

The law became known as the private attorney general statute because it allows attorneys to file constitutional violations against municipalities, regardless of the dollar amount of damages. If the attorney proves the constitutional violation, the client recovers the damages and the attorney recovers lodestar attorney fees—hours expended at the normal and customary hourly rate in the community.

The intent of the law was to incentivize attorneys to take on small constitutional violations and not allow limited damages to block the doors of the courthouse for important constitutional claims from being litigated. The practice of civil rights law is not often one that is entered for the tens of hundreds of dollars that lawyers might earn. These cases are difficult to win consistently. Qualified immunity may take a claim where liability and misconduct are proven and still make it a losing case with no recovery for litigant or attorney. If qualified immunity is allowed to make these cases unwinnable, fewer of these cases will be able to be filed and the original intent of the legislation will be defeated.

A Direct Line from Reconstruction to Jim Crow to Qualified Immunity

In the dozen years that followed the end of the civil war, America entered the Reconstruction era. From 1865 to 1877, Congress followed the abolishment of slavery with civil rights to present the newly freed slaves with rights as citizens. Initially, Congress passed the Civil Rights Act of 1866, which provided a definition of citizenship and provided equal protection for all citizens. After President Andrew Jackson vetoed the law, Congress passed the bill the second time with a veto-proof majority. Subsequently, Congress passed the Thirteenth Amendment (abolishment of slavery), Fourteenth Amendment (birthright citizenship, due process, equal protection), and Fifteenth Amendment (protection of the right to vote).[7] In the same time frame, white supremacist groups terrorized Black Americans throughout the South in order to subjugate these new citizens. As local and state governments refused to provide protection against this illegal conduct, the killing and terrorizing of Black Americans continued.

The KKK Act of 1871 was followed by the Civil Rights Act of 1875, which provided the right to serve on a jury and equal access to all public places such as hotels, restaurants, theaters, and train stations. However, the Supreme Court struck down these congressional efforts to support Black Americans. In 1883, the Supreme Court ruled that the aspect of the civil rights acts that provided for actions by private individuals regarding lynchings and other mob-type conduct concerned state action, not private action.[8] The same year, the Supreme Court declared the Civil Rights Act of 1875 to be unconstitutional (which protected individuals against discrimination in accommodations, public transport, and theaters), stating that the Fourteenth Amendment could not reach private conduct.[9] In the next decade, a low point in Supreme Court jurisprudence arrived with the decision of *Plessey v. Ferguson,*[10] in which the Court held that state-mandated segregation laws did not violate the equal protection clause of the Fourteenth Amendment.

In 1961, a suit filed against the City of Chicago and members of its police department for civil rights violations found its way to the Supreme Court after being dismissed by the trial court and the Seventh Circuit. While the Court ruled that municipal liability did not exist,[11] the Court held that the individual police officers could face suit by private individuals, writing that Congress passed section 1983 "to give a remedy to parties deprived of constitutional rights, privileges, and immunities by an official's abuse of his position."[12] In 1967, private civil rights litigation again came to the Supreme Court in a case that was filed in response to the arrests of 15 clergy including 3 Black priests during the summer of 1967 at a bus station in Jackson, Mississippi, for a breach of the peace as part of the Mississippi Freedom Rides through the Deep South. The criminal charges were dismissed by the appellate court, and a lawsuit followed against the police for these arrests utilizing title 42, section 1983 of the 1871 KKK Act. The trial court found in favor of the police. The Fifth Circuit ruled that the underlying criminal statute was unconstitutional but that the police did not know the statute was unconstitutional, so there could be no liability against them for enforcing the law.

The Supreme Court then birthed the concept of qualified immunity, holding that the officers could not be held liable if they acted in good faith, finding probable cause under a statute they believed to be valid.[13]

Qualified Immunity as a Legal Defense

Qualified immunity is an affirmative defense.[14] To establish the affirmative defense, the defense must provide evidence to support one of two findings. Trial courts that make such findings, and appellate courts that review them, can examine either of the issues first.[15]

To determine whether qualified immunity applies in a given case, the reviewing court must determine (1) whether a public official has violated a plaintiff's constitutionally protected right and (2) whether the particular right that the official has violated was clearly established at the time of the violation. Only if both elements are met will qualified immunity be defeated.

To complicate matters a little, the federal circuits do not agree on who carries the burden of proof once a defendant pleads the qualified immunity defense (and there are even inconsistent decisions within the same circuit). While the law in some circuits shifts the burden to the plaintiff to prove the qualified immunity defense does not apply,[16] other circuits hold conversely that the burden remains with defendants.[17] The Supreme Court does not seem concerned about clearing up this confusion, as it has denied certiorari in two cases in which allocation of the burden of proof was at issue.[18] It is important to note that qualified immunity does not apply to municipal liability and does not apply to claims for declaratory or injunctive relief.[19]

It has often been described that qualified immunity is not just an immunity against judgment but a protection against the burdens of suit and discovery as well. Therefore, defense motions seeking protection of qualified immunity can be filed as part of a motion to dismiss, a summary judgment, or part of special interrogatories presented to a jury after liability has been found by the jury. Moreover, each of these requests for qualified immunity protection comes with rights to appeal, interlocutory and post-trial. It is important to note that the filing of these motions and appeals has been identified as the cause of significant delays in litigation that serve to deprive families and individuals of justice. Additionally, the length of time these suits will be pending coupled with the costs of filing these motions and appeals begs the question of whether the ability to seek qualified immunity multiple times in a singular lawsuit actually serves to defeat the intended protection against the burdens of suit.

Evolution of the Qualified Immunity Standard

Initially, whether liability would exist for law enforcement misconduct was a one-pronged analysis, had the plaintiff asserted a violation of a constitutional or statutory right under current law. This rule allowed that the defense were entitled to immunity if they had acted in good faith under the law, as it existed, at the time of the conduct in question. The courts would not hold police officers liable for enforcing the law on the books. Understandably, law enforcement must be able to have a good faith belief that the laws that were passed were constitutional in order to perform their job of enforcing the law. Yet, in 1982, the Burger Court decided that qualified immunity should be available beyond when law enforcement was simply enforcing the law on the books. In *Harlow v. Fitzgerald*, the Supreme Court created a second prong to the qualified immunity protection. If the first prong was met, the plaintiff asserted a violation of a constitutional or statutory right under current law, the examining court would also have to decide whether the right or law that was violated was clearly established in the jurisdiction. Thereafter, even if the police misconduct violated someone's constitutional rights, the immunity would still protect against liability if the right that was violated was not clearly established in the jurisdiction in which the violation occurred.[20]

The Burger Court continued to enlarge and reinforce the shield of qualified immunity. In 1986, the Supreme Court issued an opinion that stretched the standard further, to now include "protection to all (law enforcement officer conduct) but the plainly incompetent."[21] The Supreme Court had created this immunity and stretched, pulled, and played at it until it now had expanded its scope and lowered the bar for police misconduct that would be immune from federal liability to all errors and misdeeds by all law enforcement officers but the plainly incompetent.

The Rehnquist Court identified that the two-prong analysis had to be examined in a specific order. The initial inquiry would be whether the police officer's conduct violated a constitutional or statutory right. If that question was answered in the affirmative, the next question would be whether the right was clearly established in the context of the case.[22]

The Roberts Court has consistently widened the qualified immunity protection, and even undid the rigid order requirement of *Saucier*, in a manner that would impact and hinder the clear establishment of rights in this country. In 2009, the Supreme Court decision in *Pearson v. Callahan* held that the two-prong analysis of qualified immunity did not have a rigid order; either factor could be analyzed first.[23] This served to ensure that many issues would avoid being "clearly established" as the district courts would not have to analyze the right that was violated and determine whether it was a valid constitutional or statutory right. The district or circuit court could jump to the clearly established analysis and hold that it need not determine if a constitutional right had been violated if it identified that no such right was clearly established. Therefore, these decisions would no longer be the basis for clearly establishing a right. Prior to *Pearson*, a case could decide that a constitutional right was violated but had not been clearly established previously. From the date of that decision forward, that right would be considered clearly established. Now, these lower courts could simply state that whatever right may or may not have been violated, it was not clearly established and, therefore, it need not reach whether the plaintiff had correctly articulated a valid constitutional or statutory violation. The Roberts Court then augmented the standard once again by instructing the lower courts that they must not define "clearly established" with a high level of generality. Over the next decade, the Court regularly revisited this commentary when reversing circuit denials of qualified immunity.[24]

What Does "Clearly Established" Mean?

The Second Circuit identified that a right can be treated as clearly established if "decisions by this or other courts clearly foreshadow a particular ruling on the issue, even if those decisions come from courts in other circuits."[25] In that case, the circuit court looked to the New York State Court of Appeals in the absence of circuit and Supreme Court precedent regarding whether it had been clearly established (or clearly foreshadowed) that law enforcement must be able to articulate a reasonable suspicion that a felony arrestee is hiding contraband inside a body cavity before a visual body cavity search would be authorized. The First Circuit has held that sister circuit law may be sufficient to clearly establish a proposition of law.[26] The Tenth Circuit agrees that there are ways for rights to be clearly established beyond Supreme Court precedence[27] but does not believe that law enforcement training about a specific right (civilians have a First Amendment right to record officers in public) clearly establishes the right for those same law enforcement officers.[28]

Qualified immunity became the rule rather than the exception, with its expansive scope requiring a plaintiff to prove not only the unconstitutional conduct of the officer but also that the law was clearly established prior to the incident supported by a prior court ruling that was factually consistent and perhaps identical to the current case.[29] The Supreme Court has reviewed 30 qualified immunity cases between inventing the defense in 1967 and 2021, finding in favor of law enforcement in all but two of them.[30] Unsurprisingly, this provided protection for some incredibly bad misconduct.

Examples of Application of Qualified Immunity That Defies Decency and Rational Conduct of Law Enforcement

There are numerous examples of decisions granting qualified immunity to police officers under facts that simply belie logic and societal standards. One horrendous example in the Second Circuit protected a corrections officer who fondled the genitals of an inmate for no legitimate purpose.[31] An example from the Tenth Circuit involved a hospitalized man suffering from pneumonia and confusion who was non-violent but refused to return to his hospital room. The police tased, tackled, and killed Johnny Leija by pinning him on the ground and straddling his back while handcuffing him, thereby starving his already compromised lungs of oxygen. A jury awarded significant sums to his family, but the Tenth Circuit granted the officers qualified immunity, reversed the jury verdict, and directed dismissal of the case.[32] A class of parole violators, whose concurrent sentences were unconstitutionally transformed into consecutive sentences, causing them to be held in prison long past their lawful maximum release dates, brought suit. The action was dismissed on qualified immunity grounds, even though the Court described the defense conduct as "abhorrent and absurd."[33]

A naked, emotionally disturbed person who claimed to be G-d was tased repeatedly by officers in front of his home until he died. The police had been called to the location by the individual's mother. In granting the officers qualified immunity, the circuit court held that although it was clearly established that non-violent, non-fleeing subjects should be free from multiple tasings, such law was not "clearly established" regarding a naked, aggressive person with no weapons.[34]

Qualified immunity has been applied in claims surrounding expressive speech activity, including a Fourth Amendment violation involving a two-hour suspicionless and warrantless detention of demonstrators where the court found no probable cause and denied the defense claim of a "special needs search" doctrine. Still, the Second Circuit granted qualified immunity to the defendant officers due to lack of binding precedent.[35]

In the excessive force setting, the Fifth Circuit granted qualified immunity to an officer who had pepper-sprayed an inmate in the face without provocation, because the appeals court had not yet adjudicated a case involving a correction officer's unprovoked use of pepper spray.[36] Even when there was a finding of malice and excessive force used by an officer, the Ninth Circuit reversed and vacated a jury verdict, granting qualified immunity to an officer who had injured a college student, armed with a water balloon, by violently throwing him to the ground. The court narrowly interpreted the issue and failed to find clearly established precedence where a comparable use of force was exercised. However, counsel reviewing the decision have explained that the circuit court would have denied qualified immunity had the student been accused of felonious activity, as the excessive force would have been clearly established, but not for a lesser, misdemeanor act ("physical resistance or obstruction").[37]

The Judiciary Strikes Back against Qualified Immunity (while Continuing to Follow Its Precedence)

Perhaps, with the immaculate conception of qualified immunity coupled with the tortured logic used to employ it in various cases, it is not surprising that even members of the bench have objected to its existence. There has been a rising chorus both in courts of law and in the court of public opinion to abolish qualified immunity. On the Supreme Court, Justices Sotomayor and Thomas have each inserted dicta in decisions expressing their dissatisfaction with qualified immunity. In 2018, Justice Sotomayor, in a dissent joined by Justice Ginsburg, stated that the Supreme Court's "one-sided approach to Qualified Immunity transforms the doctrine into an absolute shield for law enforcement officers, gutting the deterrent effect of the Fourth Amendment." Going even further, the dissent set out that qualified immunity "tells officers that they can shoot first and think later, and it tells the public that palpably unreasonable conduct will go unpunished."[38] Two years later, Justice Thomas wrote in a rare opinion denying certiorari:

> There likely is no basis for the objective inquiry into clearly established law that our modern cases prescribe. Leading treatises from the second half of the 19th century and case law until the 1980s contain no support for this "clearly established law" test. Indeed, the Court adopted the test not because of "general principles of tort immunities and defenses," but because of a "balancing of competing values" about litigation costs and efficiency,
>
> Regardless of what the outcome would be, we at least ought to return to the approach of asking whether immunity "was 'historically accorded the relevant official' in an analogous situation 'at common law.'" *Ziglar, supra,* at ___, 137 S. Ct. 1843, 198 L. Ed. 2d 290 at 323 (opinion

of Thomas, J.) The Court has continued to conduct this inquiry in absolute immunity cases, even after the sea change in Qualified Immunity doctrine. We should do so in Qualified Immunity cases as well. (Internal citations omitted).

I continue to have strong doubts about our §1983 Qualified Immunity doctrine. Given the importance of this question, I would grant the petition for certiorari.[39]

Criticism of qualified immunity is not restricted to justices on the Supreme Court. Circuit court judges have recently joined the fray. Judge Calabresi, concurring in a Second Circuit opinion concerning the suppression of a gun that was found by police without any articulable suspicion, stated that

[In most of these] cases in which the hunch or the stereotype was wrong, an honest person was humiliated, searched, and all too often maltreated . . . lead[ing] to distrust and even hatred of the police, with dire consequences. . . . There may well be hundreds of situations in which searches like the one before us today turned up nothing. But surely no more than a handful will get to court. And even these will almost always get decided against the innocent "searchee" on Qualified Immunity.

All this might not matter if courts knew, directly and emotionally, from personal experience, the stories of those unnecessarily, improperly, and humiliatingly searched. But we judges, and our families and friends, are not likely to be the ones whom the police decide to search on a hunch. We are not likely to be stopped for failing to signal. And we are most unlikely to be made to spread eagle, even if stopped.[40]

In June 2020, Judge James A. Wynn of the Fourth Circuit Court of Appeals took the extraordinary step of publishing an op-ed in the *Washington Post* titled "As a Judge, I have to follow the Supreme Court. It should fix this mistake." Judge Wynn wrote that

[t]he Supreme Court's creation and expansion of Quali-fied Immunity—and its ongoing refusal, thus far, to reconsider it—not only diminishes the law's intended effect; it also harms individuals who are booted out of court before they can ever bring claims of excessive force before a jury. And it strains the separation of powers. By creating a defense unmoored from the text, the Supreme Court has undermined Congress's intent to provide remedies to those whose rights have been violated.[41]

District Court Judge Carleton W. Reeves, sitting in the Southern District of Mississippi, recently published an opinion granting qualified immunity but excoriating the court-created immunity:

The Constitution says everyone is entitled to equal protection of the law—even at the hands of law enforcement. Over the decades, however, judges have invented a legal doctrine to protect law enforcement officers from having to face any consequences for wrongdoing. The doctrine is called "Qualified Immunity." In real life it operates like absolute immunity. . . . Tragically, thousands have died at the hands of law enforcement over the years, and the death toll continues to rise. Countless more have suffered from other forms of abuse and misconduct by police. Qualified Immunity has served as a shield for these officers, protecting them from accountability. . . . But let us not be fooled by legal jargon. Immunity is not exoneration. And the harm in this case to one man sheds light on the harm done to the nation by this manufactured doctrine.

As the Fourth Circuit concluded, "This has to stop."

[J]udges took a Reconstruction-era statute designed to protect people *from the government*, added in some "legalistic argle-bargle," and turned the statute on its head to protect the government *from the people*. . . . [E]very hour we spend in a § 1983 case asking if the law was "clearly established" or "beyond debate" is one where we lose sight of why Congress enacted this law those many years ago: to hold state actors accountable for violating federally protected rights [. . .]

Let us waste no time in righting this wrong.[42]

Strange Bedfellows

The issues that surround qualified immunity have created an environment where individuals and organizations that would often be on opposite sides find themselves working together to defeat the ever-expanding coverage of qualified immunity. One example can be seen in an amicus brief that was filed to support a writ of certiorari in a religious freedom case involving prison accommodations. The Second Circuit ruled in favor of the inmate but then granted qualified immunity to the prison officials. The amici curie included 15 groups who self-identified in their brief as "15 Cross-Ideological Group dedicated to ensuring accountability and restoring the public's trust in Law Enforcement and promoting the rule of law." These groups included what would be termed conservative groups such as the Alliance Defending Freedom and Law Enforcement Action Partnership; libertarian groups including the Cato Institute, Institute for Justice, and Second Amendment Foundation; and progressive groups including the American Association for Justice, ACLU, MacArthur Justice Center, National Association of Criminal Defense Lawyers, and National Police Accountability Project.

After 50 years of qualified immunity jurisprudence, how did qualified immunity become a hot topic at the virtual watercoolers and cocktail parties in 2020 and 2021?

In July 2019, at a presidential primary debate, Secretary Julian Castro spoke to a national audience about his stance on criminal justice reform. He stated that to ensure police accountability, he suggested a national use of force standard and an end to qualified immunity. One year later, with the horrible and well-publicized murder of George Floyd at the hands of Minnesota police officer Derek Chauvin, questions about this officer and his accountability were not answered until a jury returned a guilty verdict on April 20, 2021.[43] Protesters took to the street demanding more police accountability and talking about ending qualified immunity. Both state and federal legislatures took note.

Protests, Legislation, and Lawsuits: Recent Inroads against Qualified Immunity at the State and National Levels

It is said that great change in society does not flow directly from litigating cases in court, protesting in the streets, or seeking changes in legislation; it comes when all of these have been toiling in separate ways seeking to effectuate change until a groundswell of support explodes in society. In our recent history, this moment occurred in the aftermath of the George Floyd killing in March 2020.

The protests that began across the country, and the world, became the groundswell that may finally bring change to qualified immunity. Federally, in the wave of protests and the strength of the Black Lives Matter movement, two different bills were created to end qualified immunity: the End Qualified Immunity Act (H.R. 7085) (which did not make it out of committee) and the more expansive George Floyd Justice in Policing Act of 2020 (H.R. 7120) (which passed the U.S. House of Representatives twice but was never brought to a vote in the U.S. Senate). However, at least two state legislatures have already acted to end qualified immunity in their states by creating state statutes that provide for constitutional claims and attorney fees while disallowing qualified immunity.

In June 2020, the Colorado legislature passed Senate Bill 20-17, the Law Enforcement Integrity and Accountability Act, which was signed into law by Governor Jared Polis.[44] The act included major police reforms including a ban on chokeholds, body-worn camera requirements in the state, and an avenue for state claims for constitutional violations of rights, similar to section 1983, however, without the availability of qualified immunity. Interestingly, the act requires the municipality to indemnify the officer in any such suit and if the officer is deemed to have acted in bad faith, there is a requirement for individual liability (to a maximum of $25,000) for any damages awarded to a plaintiff.

In April 2021, New Mexico passed House Bill 4, the New Mexico Civil Rights Act.[45] Governor Lujan Grisham soon signed the bill into law. The statute provides for a state claim for the deprivation of "rights, privileges or immunities" provided under the New Mexico Constitution. The New Mexico Civil Rights Act allows for a claimant to file a lawsuit seeking actual damages, injunctive relief, reasonable attorney fees, and litigation expenses. Moreover, in any claim brought pursuant to the act, qualified immunity is prohibited as a defense.

While New York State legislature was unable to get a qualified immunity bill passed in 2020 or 2021 or 2022, the New York City Council passed a bill that amended the Administrative Code allowing for a city claim to be filed in any court of competent jurisdiction for a Fourth Amendment violation (excessive force, unlawful arrest/detention) and providing for attorney fees while disallowing qualified immunity.[46]

In a showing that the wind of change may be sweeping through qualified immunity, the Supreme Court issued a few decisions[47] that may indicate it is ready to "recalibrate" its qualified immunity jurisprudence.[48] In *Taylor v. Riojas*, the Supreme Court provided for a little humanity into the qualified immunity standard.[49] In reversing the circuit issuance of qualified immunity, the Court opined that the particularity required of the facts underlying the clearly established standard must also consider a morality and common sense that would indicate whether (mis) conduct was constitutional or not. The facts of that case are horrendous: an inmate held in a solitary confinement without a mattress or a working toilet, and a stuffed drain that allowed sewer water to come up and out of the drain, filling the floor of the cell with feces-filled water. Only time will tell if these newer Supreme Court decisions are an isolated moment in Supreme Court jurisprudence or if the Court has looked out its windows, observed the protests on the streets, and read the writing on the wall.

Why Is the End of Qualified Immunity Not Enough?

Qualified immunity applies to individual officers but not municipalities. Cities and towns do not need qualified immunity, as section 1983 liability can extend to the municipality only through a *Monell* claim, not through respondeat superior. As such, the removal of qualified immunity, without ensuring that the municipality will cover the damages owed by its law enforcement officers, would be a hollow victory. Therefore, the end of qualified immunity must also see a requirement of either indemnification for each officer or respondeat superior liability; otherwise, the end of qualified immunity will serve to provide even further protection to these cities and officers and not achieve accountability or justice for those harmed by law enforcement.

Endnotes

1. Acknowledgment is made that the basis for this chapter began as an article that appeared in the NEW YORK STATE BAR ASSOCIATION JOURNAL: Wylie Stecklow, *Qualified Immunity: Is the End Near?* 93 NY STATE BAR ASSOCIATION J. 22 (Jan/Feb 2021).

2. Jamsion v. McClendon, 2020 U.S. Dist. LEXIS 139327, at *19 (S.D. Miss. 2020).

3. For a more complete history of the violence in the post-slavery United States and the failures of reconstructionism, see the Equal Justice Initiative's report on lynching in America. *Lynching in America: Confronting the Legacy of Racial Terror*, LYNCHING IN AMERICA, https://lynchinginamerica .eji.org/report/.

4. While this article focuses on section 1983 of the Civil Rights Act, claims against state actors, and qualified immunity in those claims, section 1985 has been interpreted to allow claims against private actors for Thirteenth Amendment violations when the claim involves "badges and incidents of slavery." In 1984, attorney Morris Dees, co-founder of the Southern Poverty Law Center, obtained a $7 million judgment against the KKK for the lynching murder of Michael Donald, essentially bankrupting the KKK. *The 1981 Lynching that Bankrupted an Alabama KKK*, HISTORY, https://www.history .com/news/kkk-lynching-mother-justice. A similar suit based on section 1985 was led by Michael Bloch, Roberta Kaplan, and Karen Dunn, among others, against white supremacists and white supremacist groups following

the violence in Charlottesville, Virginia, at the "Unite the Right" rally in 2017. The verdict in that suit was for $25 million, but on a different claim as there was a hung jury on the section 1985 claim. Will Carless & Kevin McCoy, *Jury awards plaintiffs $25 million in lawsuit against white supremacists behind violence at Charlottesville 'Unite the Right' rally*, USA TODAY (Nov. 23, 2021), https://www.usatoday.com/story/news/nation/2021/11/23/charlottesville-unite-the-right-trial-verdict/8685316002/. Unfortunately, in 2023, this verdict was drastically reduced by the trial judge. Allison Dunn, *Attorneys Mull Appeal after $24M Punitive Damages Award in Charlottesville Case Is Capped at $350K*, Law.com (Jan. 4, 2023), https://www.law.com/2023/01/04/attorneys-mull-appeal-after-24m-punitive-damages-award-in-charlottesville-case-is-capped-at-350k/.

5. Jamison v. McClendon, 2020 U.S. Dist. LEXIS 139327 (S.D. Miss. 2020).

6. Haywood v. Drown, 556 U.S. 729, 735 (2009).

7. *Reconstruction*, HISTORY, https://www.history.com/topics/american-civil-war/reconstruction.

8. U.S. v. Harris, 106 U.S. 629 (1883).

9. "The Civil Rights Cases," Stanley v. US, Ryan v. US, Nichols v. US, Singleton v. Memphis & Charleston R. Co, 3 S. Ct. 18 (1883).

10. 163 U.S. 537 (1896).

11. This aspect of the *Monroe* case was later overruled by *Monell v. Dept. of Social Services of NYC*, 436 U.S. 658 (1978).

12. Pierson v. Ray, 386 U.S. 547 (1967).

13. *Id.*

14. Gomez v. Toledo, 446 U.S. 635 (1980) (since qualified immunity is a defense, the burden of pleading it rests with the defendant).

15. Pearson v. Callahan, 555 U.S. 223 (2009).

16. Daugherty v. Sheer, 891 F.3d 386 (D.C. Cir. 2018); Felarca v. Birgeneau, 891 F.3d 891 (9th Cir. 2018); Rivera-Corraliza v. Morales, 794 F.3d 208 (1st Cir. 2015); Becker v. Bateman, 709 F.3d 1019 (10th Cir. 2013); Mannoia v. Farrow, 476 F.3d 453 (7th Cir. 2007); Crosby v. Monroe County, 394 F.3d 1328 (11th Cir. 2004); Gardenhire v. Schubert, 205 F.3d 303 (6th Cir. 2000); Pierce v. Smith, 117 F.3d 866 (5th Cir. 1997).

17. Outlaw v. City of Hartford, 884 F.3d 351 (2d Cir. 2018); Halsey v. Pfeiffer, 750 F.3d 273 (3d Cir. 2014); Henry v. Purnell, 501 F.3d 374 (4th Cir. 2007); Moreno v. Baca, 431 F.3d 633 (9th Cir. 2005); DiMarco-Zappa v. Cabanillas, 238 F.3d 25 (1st Cir. 2001).

18. Anderson v. City of Minneapolis, 2020 U.S. LEXIS 3220 (June 15, 2020); Corbitt v. Vickers, 2020 U.S. LEXIS 3152 (June 15, 2020).

19. Joanna C. Schwartz, *How Qualified Immunity Fails*, 127 YALE LAW J. 2 (Oct. 2017).

20. Harlow v. Fitzgerald, 457 U.S. 800 (1982).

21. Malley v. Briggs, 475 U.S. 335, 341 (1986).

22. Saucier v. Katz, 533 U.S. 194 (2001).

23. Pearson v. Callahan, 555 U.S. 223 (2009).

24. City & County of San Francisco v. Sheehan, 575 U.S. 600, 613 (2015) ("We have repeatedly told courts—and the Ninth Circuit in particular—not to define clearly established law at a high level of generality.").

25. Sloly v. Van Bramer, 945 F.3d 30, n.6 (2d Cir. 2019).

26. Irish v. Fowler, 979 F.3d 65 (1st Cir. 2020).

27. Ullery v. Bradley, 949 F.3d 1282 (10th Cir. 2020).

28. Frasier v. Evans, 992 F.3d 1003 (10th Cir. 2021).

29. The Sixth Circuit standard requires that the prior ruling be in a published opinion in that circuit, making the expanding even more the application of qualified immunity, to protect obviously improper and unconstitutional conduct. McCoy v. Alamu, 950 F.3d 226, 233 n.6 (5th Cir. 2020).

30. Robert Barnes, *Supreme Court asked to reconsider immunity available to police accused of brutality*, WASHINGTON POST (JUNE 4, 2020), https://www .washingtonpost.com/politics/courts_law/supreme-court-asked-to-recon sider-immunity-available-to-police-accused-of-brutality/2020/06/04 /99266d2c-a5b0-11ea-b473-04905b1af82b_story.html

31. Crawford v. Cuomo, 721 Fed. Appx. 57 (2d Cir. 2018) (even though the officer's intentional contact with an inmate's genitalia that served no penological purpose and was undertaken with the intent to gratify the officer's sexual desire was repugnant and intolerable, because the unconstitutional nature of the officer's abuse was not clearly established in 2011, qualified immunity was properly recognized); Shannon v. Venettozzi, 749 F. App'x 10, __ (2d Cir. 2018) (same inappropriate genitalia touching granted qualified immunity even though the conduct alleged in the amended complaint is reprehensible both then and now; when it occurred in 2011, precedent did not establish that such conduct was clearly unconstitutional).

32. Aldaba v. Pickens, 844 F.3d 870 (10th Cir. 2016).

33. Sudler v. City of N.Y., 569 U.S. 1018, 133 S. Ct. 2777 (2013).

34. De Boise v. Taser Int'l, Inc., 760 F.3d 892 (8th Cir. 2014).

35. Berg v. Kelly, 897 F.3d 99 (2d Cir. 2018).

36. McCoy v. Alamu, 950 F.3d 226, 228 (5th Cir. 2020).

37. Shafer v. Padilla, 868 F.3d 1110 (9th Cir 2017).

38. Kisela v. Hughes, 138 S. Ct. 1148 (2018).

39. Baxter v. Bracey, 140 S. Ct. 1862 (2020).

40. United States v. Weaver, 975 F.3d 94, 109 (2d Cir. 2020).

41. James A. Wynn Jr., *As a judge, I have to follow the Supreme Court. It should fix this mistake*, WASHINGTON POST (June 12, 2020), https://www.washing tonpost.com/opinions/2020/06/12/judge-i-have-follow-supreme-court-it -should-fix-this-mistake/.

42. Jamison v. McClendon, 2020 U.S. Dist. LEXIS 139327 (S.D. Miss. 2020) (much of the historical information of this article was taken from this opinion).

43. Mike Hayes et al., *Derek Chauvin Guilty in Death of George Floyd*, CNN. COM (Apr. 21, 2021), https://www.cnn.com/us/live-news/derek-chauvin -trial-04-20-21/index.html.

44. Russell Berman, *The State Where Protests Have Already Forced Major Police Reform*, THE ATLANTIC (July 17, 2020), https://www.theatlantic.com /politics/archive/2020/07/police-reform-law-colorado/614269/.

45. *Gov. Lujan Grisham ratifies Civil Rights Act*, OFFICE OF GOVERNOR (Apr. 7, 2021), https://www.governor.state.nm.us/2021/04/07/gov-lujan -grisham-ratifies-civil-rights-act/.

46. NY City Admin. Code, ch. 8, *available at* https://codelibrary.amlegal.com/codes/newyorkcity/latest/NYCadmin/0-0-0-5270.

47. Taylor v. Riojas, 141 S. Ct. 52 (2020); Tanzin v. Tanvir, 141 S. Ct. 486 (2020); McCoy v. Alamu, 141 S. Ct. 1364 (2021).

48. Patrick Jaicomo & Anya Bidwell, *Recalibrating Qualified Immunity: How Tanzin v. Tanvir, Taylor v. Riojas, and McCoy v. Alamu Signal the Supreme Court's Discomfort with the Doctrine of Qualified Immunity*, 112 J. Crim. L. & Criminology 105 (2022).

49. Taylor v. Riojas, 141 S. Ct. 52 (2020).

Chapter 2

Administrative Complaints against Police

Rita McNeil Danish

Introduction

The need for a reliable and trustworthy review of police conduct seems more and more relevant in today's world. The steady stream of news stories alleging police misconduct fills traditional news outlets and social media. Growing mistrust in law enforcement is routinely remarked upon and discussed. This has focused attention on the availability of administrative processes to investigate or review alleged police misconduct.

An advantage or benefit to an administrative review process is that it is an alternative to litigation. While there are certainly incidents that shock the conscience, the majority of complaints against law enforcement may not justify the expense and burden of litigation. Citizens seeking redress, even if it is only an explanation and acknowledgment of the incident, have the option of an administrative remedy. This remedy is, at a minimum, the review of the incident through an administrative process that examines complaints against law enforcement officers.

Administrative review varies depending on the context. For the purposes of police conduct, policies and procedures specifically, administrative review is the formal mechanism that investigates and generates consequences for misconduct. The consequences may range from reprimand to discharge from employment for a police officer and policy change for the law enforcement agency. Civilians who interact with police officers usually can initiate an administrative review through a complaint process, or a law enforcement agency may initiate the review through an internal complaint process or automatically when an incident results in serious injury or death. A citizen filing a complaint can expect to receive acknowledgment of the complaint and be informed of the outcome of the review, although this does not always occur. Depending on the circumstances, the citizen may be formally interviewed or may simply provide a statement. The best outcome is that the review process is transparent and the civilian, along with the public, understands how the final determination was reached, even if there is not universal consensus as to its fairness. The worst outcome is that the review process is cloaked in secrecy and the outcome, if it is fully known at all, is viewed with suspicion and frustration by the complaining civilian, the public, or both. The most common outcome, of course, is somewhere in the middle, with the complaining citizen learning of the outcome of the investigation and there is too little explanation regarding the conclusion reached. In addition, police officers often have appeal rights independent of the administrative review process, through either union contracts or local law, that can alter or set aside the discipline.

The administrative review processes that exist today fall into two broad categories: internal affairs review and independent agency review. As their names suggest, one review occurs primarily within a law enforcement agency, and the other involves individuals from outside the law enforcement agency in the review of the conduct. Internal affairs review is the more traditional, the more well-known, and, increasingly, the process most often criticized. Independent citizen review is growing in usage, and perhaps popularity, but comes in varying forms that also vary in their perceived effectiveness.

The value of this administrative review process is that it can be initiated at no cost to a complainant or may be self-initiating as the result of a serious incident that automatically triggers an investigation or review. As noted, there is a place for litigation in reviewing police misconduct, yet it consumes time, money, and resources that the eventual damage award may not offset. The administrative review process usually applies to every allegation of misconduct, regardless of its severity. It provides standardized access to a complaint and review process. There are also remedies available that litigation may not produce. Litigation has not been shown to result in change to the organizational structure that fostered the misconduct.[1] The administrative review process can result in discipline, up to and including termination of employment. As part of the review, policies, procedures, and training may be examined, and those may be updated or amended. The complainant may receive an opportunity to be heard and an explanation, even if unsatisfactory, for the conduct of law enforcement during the incident. Lastly, the administrative review process does not foreclose litigation. If the remedy is insufficient or if litigation is also warranted, then it can take place after or concurrent with the administrative process.

Internal Affairs Review

Internal affairs usually refers to a division or unit of a law enforcement agency that investigates incidents and complaints of possible or suspected lawbreaking or policy violations attributed to officers. Internal affairs is the traditional form of professional oversight within police departments and other law enforcement agencies in the United States. It may be called professional standards, internal investigations, internal review, or a similar name. The common factor, as the name implies, is that it is contained within and composed of personnel of the law enforcement entity.

The policies and rules governing the investigative procedures of a law enforcement agency vary not only from state to state but also from agency to agency. The factors that contribute to the internal affairs process involve state civil service or employment law, collective bargaining agreements, and local policies and procedures. There are, nevertheless, common attributes of internal affairs review units across the country.[2]

The investigators in internal affairs are usually sworn officers of the agency. They have the same law enforcement training as their fellow officers and may receive additional training in the requirements of employment law, collective bargaining procedures, and agency policies and procedures. The investigations are triggered by an incident or complaint. The incident does not necessarily need to have any indication or suspicion of wrongdoing. For example, an agency may have a policy of initiating an investigation for every shooting or use of force that results in injury.

The investigations in many ways parallel criminal investigations. Often there may be a preliminary investigation that gathers key statements and evidence with the goal of determining if the incident or complaint requires further investigation. The statements or facts may indicate that there is no merit to pursuing a full investigation. A straightforward example is when it is impossible for the misconduct to have occurred. A complaint may be received that alleges facts involving the supernatural or extraterrestrials. A mental health referral is more appropriate than a full investigation.

If a full investigation is warranted, then witness interviews and evidence will be gathered for the purpose of having all relevant information necessary to permit a determination to be made as to whether any misconduct occurred. The full investigation will be documented and organized. The investigation is usually composed of witness statements, either written or recorded, photographs and video (including the recent flood of "body-cam" footage), sketches, diagrams, physical evidence, forensic and laboratory testing reports, and, in serious matters, video reenactments of the incident. The completed investigation usually includes a determination as to whether a law, policy, or procedure was violated and a recommendation that discipline be considered for one or more officers involved in the incident. It may also include a recommendation for additional training for officers or a change to the law enforcement agency's policies and procedures. What is usually not included is a specific recommendation as to the discipline that should be meted out.

The completed investigation is then provided to the leadership of the law enforcement agency for a decision on further action. The traditional model of internal affairs review does not result in an adjudication over the conduct of the law enforcement officers. The review is an investigation and documentation of the incident at issue. A complete and full investigation should contain all the relevant information necessary for the supervising official, whether a police chief, sheriff, or other adjudicator, to make a determination as to whether the conduct violated law, policy, or procedure and the consequences that should result from that determination.[3]

It is worth noting that less than 10 percent of officers are ever the subject of an internal affairs investigation.[4] A recent review of internal affairs investigations found that most misconduct involved routine infractions.[5] Litigation is simply not a viable option for the conduct alleged in the majority of internal affairs investigations. The adjudication that occurs after the investigation is concluded is often the only remedy available to a complainant. This emphasizes that an administrative review process is both necessary and worthy of examination for its effectiveness.[6]

The criticism associated with internal affairs investigations begins with the lack of independence. Officers are "policing" their fellow officers. There is a case to be made for having trained investigators involved who have the same background and training as the individuals being investigated. However, those same circumstances point to a lack of distance between the investigators and the subjects. There is also the culture and peer pressures of being perceived as betraying the trust of their fellow officers. Often, investigators cycle in and out of internal affairs over the course of their careers. One day they are the investigator, the next day a partner or even a subordinate to officers that have been the subject of an investigation. And while an internal affairs investigation can lead to criminal charges filed against law enforcement officers, this is exceedingly rare.[7]

Also significant is that not every law enforcement agency is large enough to have a group of investigators assigned full time to an internal affairs unit. Approximately three-quarters of police departments employ 25 or fewer officers.[8] The investigation in a small police department may be conducted by a supervisor or by another law enforcement agency. There is also a wide disparity between law enforcement agencies in the level of resources that are dedicated to internal affairs reviews. A small or medium-sized police department will not be able to come close to matching a large municipal police department in the time, money, and infrastructure resources devoted to internal investigations.[9]

Then there is the perception that internal affairs investigations operate in the shadows. Transparency may be limited by state privacy laws or collective bargaining agreements.[10] The records of the investigation may be closed to public view and may be subject to destruction after a period of time. There are states that have enacted law enforcement "bills of rights" that operate to limit or shield access to investigations and resulting discipline.

It is also common that internal affairs investigations are often delayed or deferred in deference to any criminal investigation associated with the incident. There are practical reasons for this, including that the viability of a prosecution may be compromised by compelling administrative statements from police officers. Officers involved in a criminal investigation have Fifth Amendment protections from self-incrimination, and compelled statements may taint other evidence and jeopardize a prosecution.[11]

Another common occurrence is that officers are placed on paid administrative leave during the pendency of the investigation. While this is often the subject of media attention and unpopular with the public, there are also practical, legal issues that dictate the result. The practical concern is to achieve the removal of the officers from law enforcement duties, particularly after a fatal or serious incident. The legal issue is that the case law attaches due process rights to employment. Paid status is seen as dramatically different than unpaid leave when courts apply a balancing test of the effect on the officer against the government's interest.[12]

All of these factors act together to foster a lack of understanding of the function and operations of the law enforcement agency. That does not necessarily mean that the internal affairs administration is failing at its core function of investigating the conduct of law enforcement officers. However, if the purpose of the review is to serve two communities, the law enforcement community and the public, then it is underserving one of those communities when it fails in the categories of transparency and trust.

Independent Agency Review

Independent agency review exists in many forms in communities across the country. In essence, it is an entity that is considered external to the law enforcement agency. Its creation is often the result of reform efforts in response to perceived abuses of power. Models that include external oversight or require the involvement of individuals from outside a law enforcement agency ideally offer to deliver a sense of objectivity and transparency that fosters trust. Implementing any one of the external review models, therefore, promises to improve the public's faith in the fairness of the complaint process and review. There are at least three notable models of independent agency review for law enforcement that have developed: monitor, audit, and oversight/investigation.

Monitor Model

Examples of the monitor model are the Los Angeles Police Department (LAPD) Office of Inspector General created in 1995 in Los Angeles, California; the Office of Independent Monitor created in 2004 in Denver, Colorado; and the Independent Police Monitor created in 2008 in New Orleans, Louisiana. This model represents 25 percent of the independent agency review models.[13]

The monitor does not investigate individual complaints but reviews investigations of police misconduct with the goal of improving procedures and policies of the law enforcement agency. It is possible that a single reported incident or investigation may reveal the need for a change in the organization. More often, an independent monitor may review hundreds or thousands of internal affairs complaints and investigations before drawing any conclusions or making a recommendation. Internal affairs investigations are reviewed to identify deficiencies in policies, procedures, and training. This type of independent agency review may compile data and statistics, seeking to identify gaps in policies or areas needing policy review and revision. Discipline may be researched for consistency, disparate treatment, and sufficiency. The same tools may be applied to encounters with citizens. Disparities in the treatment of different populations can be revealed through the monitor data compilation and review.

Policies and training to address the revealed disparities may be drafted and recommended. There is also the opportunity to compare the best practices found in other law enforcement agencies.

The monitor model is well suited for identifying the need for and the creation of systemic change in a law enforcement agency. Patterns and practices of abuse may be linked to gaps in policies or the disregard for existing policies. The weakness in this model is the lack of direct interaction with the community. It may report out its findings, but it is not primarily a vehicle for community outreach. By focusing on the big picture, it is not seen as effective for or responsive to the individual complaint of misconduct. The monitor function does not directly build confidence in the fairness of the complaint process, as it focuses on identifying patterns over time and not in any single complaint.

Audit Model

Examples of the audit model are the Police Review & Advisory Board created in 1984 in Cambridge, Massachusetts; the Citizen's Police Complaint Office created in 1989 in Indianapolis, Indiana; and the Police Advisory Commission created in 1993 in Philadelphia, Pennsylvania. This model represents 40 percent of the independent agency review models and is the most common.[14]

The audit model focuses on the quality of the finalized complaint investigation. It seeks to ensure that the investigation was fair, timely, and accurate. It usually exists in the form of a volunteer citizen board that may hear appeals, hold public meetings, and make recommendations regarding the investigations. This model usually has the most direct interaction with the community.

The audit model more directly performs an oversight function of the law enforcement agency than the other administrative review models. It usually has access to internal affairs records and looks for patterns and trends in complaints. It may also provide a separate complaint intake process that provides an alternative to complainants that are uncomfortable with contacting a law enforcement agency.

Oversight/Investigation Model

Examples of the oversight/investigation model are the Office of Police Complaints created in Washington, D.C., in 1998; the Civilian Investigative Panel created in Miami, Florida, in 2001; and the Atlanta Citizen Review Board created in 2007. This model represents 35 percent of the independent agency review models.[15]

An independent investigation entity, whether a board or individual, exists outside of the police department and has the ability to oversee and direct the investigation of individual citizen complaints. This model permits the gathering of evidence and interviewing of witnesses. The independent investigation does not rely on investigators within the law enforcement agency to conduct and complete the investigation, although there may be access to the internal affairs investigation. The independent investigation may share its finding and the material it has gathered with internal affairs investigators for further action. It may also make recommendations directly to the controlling authority for the law enforcement agency. The effectiveness of the independent investigation is reliant upon the ability to issue subpoenas and compel production of documents.

Challenges in the Independent Review Models

The independent agency review models face several challenges in fulfilling their purposes. The review process often suffers from a lack of resources, a lack of authority, a lack of understanding of its function, a lack of community engagement, and the dynamic of institutional resistance.

A review process may be created with a broad mandate to oversee a law enforcement agency and effect change, but it will accomplish little if it does not have the resources to carry out its function. Whether it is staffing, supplies, software, or any other budgetary item, the support necessary to perform the functions it was assigned is essential. Inadequate funding can diminish the efficiency of any organization.

The process will also be weakened if it does not have the ability to reach the information that is necessary to perform any of the tasks that have been assigned. If there are not investigative tools assigned that correspond with the expected scope of the review, then false expectations are built into the results. The access that a review has to investigatory tools will directly impact the effectiveness of the review. If it is an audit or monitor model, then at a minimum it must have the authority to access internal affairs investigations, as well as the governing policies, procedures, and training materials of the law enforcement agency. As can be expected, the thoroughness of the review is dependent upon whether the entire investigation is available and whether the board can supplement the record through its own inquiry. If it is charged with conducting investigations, then the issue is whether it can gather evidence for the investigation through subpoenas and compelled production of documents.

Another aspect of the authority has to do with how much weight the recommendation of the independent review is afforded. There should be an established process for recommendations to be considered and either accepted or rejected by the law enforcement agency. The authority of the review may be seen as merely symbolic if the investigation and review have no effect. An effective review process that results in findings and recommendations achieves little if there is not an equally effective process for a review, discussion, and public decision-making strategy for its work product.

The independent agency review also suffers when there is a lack of understanding of its function. If the community has an unrealistic expectation of what the review is expected to achieve, then disappointment will surely follow. This will erode the trust of the community and lead to the increased ineffectiveness of the review process. If the review process will have no impact on the discipline decision in individual complaints, that fact should be made clear to the public at the commencement of the review. Overpromising has the same outcome as underdelivering. Calibrating expectations to correspond to the design of the independent agency review serves two purposes: it builds trust with the community and with stakeholders, and it reveals where the review model may be strengthened and improved.

Likewise, if the law enforcement community does not understand the entity or has the perception that it lacks substance, then it will neither fully cooperate nor respect its findings and recommendations. The same effort that is spent on educating the community regarding the purpose, scope, and expectations of the independent agency review must be directed toward the law enforcement agency and its officers. The authority of the review and the expected level of cooperation should be incorporated into the policies, procedures, and training of the agency. If the command structure of the agency reflects an affirmative understanding and expectation of the independent agency review, then that will permeate the organization. If the command structure is dismissive or undercuts the authority of the review, then the officers will do the same.

Similarly, a lack of community engagement or support for the independent review process will diminish the ability of the entity to function effectively. The review process most often comes into being as a result of community demands for its creation. Without that ongoing support and engagement, it will find it difficult to resist the pressure to reduce its resources and diminish its authority. One of the goals of the independent review process is to build a bridge between the community and law enforcement. That goal is also necessary to both the success and survival of its mission.

Finally, inertia or the resistance to change is a formidable obstacle to the success of any of the models of independent agency review. The organizational cultures of law enforcement agencies are notoriously slow to accept change. Even when there is a willingness to review policies, procedures, and training, there are collective bargaining agreements and employment laws that must be navigated.

The Successful Model

The recipe for success in implementing a model for administrative review of law enforcement conduct may require elements from all the models of review. When the functions of the various models are combined and operate together, the strengths of each one will counteract or offset the identified weaknesses.[16] While there are jurisdictions that have combined elements of civilian oversight and internal affairs, as noted below, this discussion is a hypothetical (and aspirational) recipe for success of administrative review.

The internal affairs investigation model is well established and has the advantage of the buy-in of the law enforcement community. Officers believe that only a fellow law enforcement officer has the skill and experience necessary to assess actions in response to the unique situations encountered. In contrast, the community trusts a process that is transparent and that is independently reviewed. Independent agency review does not require for its success the elimination of internal affairs investigations. Internal affairs reviews may achieve greater effectiveness through a partnership with an equally effective independent agency review process.

As for choosing between the three models of independent agency review, it is already common for aspects of these models to be combined into a single entity. The city of Chicago has a Bureau of Internal Affairs (BIA), Chicago Police Board, and the Civilian Office of Police Accountability, The BIA investigates, documents, and reviews allegations of misconduct by members of the Chicago Police Department.[17] The Chicago Police Board is a nine-member agency that decides disciplinary cases involving discharge or suspensions for more than 30 days for a police officer.[18] The board also resolves disciplinary cases when there is a dispute between the Chief Administrator of the Civilian Office of Police Accountability and the Superintendent of Police.[19] The Civilian Office of Police Accountability is an independent city agency that investigates allegations of police officer misconduct. It is empowered only to make recommendations on discipline action and policy.[20] Additional examples are Charlotte, North Carolina (Internal Affairs and Citizens Review Board[21]); New York City (Internal Affairs and Civilian Complaint Review Board[22]); and Washington, D.C. (Internal Affairs and Office of Police Complaints[23]). The hybrid models may combine audit with investigation or monitoring with audit. It is also not uncommon for these models to coexist as separate entities that perform their review functions apart from each other and yet at the same time. It matters that the functional review is effective and ongoing; it does not matter as much which ultimate form or combination of forms it assumes.

The three models of independent agency review are dependent on several essential features to be successful. They must be independent; have adequate resources, the necessary authority and scope of review, and community and stakeholder support; and be transparent. If the review model does not have these basic attributes, then it will struggle to achieve the expected outcomes.

The most important factor in the success and effectiveness of the independent agency review process is that it is both perceived as and is in reality independent. If that element is not incorporated at the outset, then all its other attributes are weakened and undermined. Independence is key to its standing in the community and its ability to receive community support and advance community outreach. That independence fosters an objective approach to the review process that supports the goal of a full, fair, and complete review. The review process is created to be separate and apart from the law enforcement agency.

The adequacy of the resources assigned to the independent review process is another important factor in the success and effectiveness of the entity. The best plans will not produce acceptable results if insufficient resources are available. A fully functional review that is charged with oversight, analysis, and problem-solving requires the necessary people, facilities, and budget to function.

Community engagement and stakeholder support strengthen and sustain the effectiveness of independent review. The independent review process often owes its existence to public pressure for change. Resistance to efforts at systemic change does not evaporate once the review body is created. Ongoing support is necessary to overcome those headwinds. An active community outreach is vital to fostering and maintaining that support. The lines of communication developed in the outreach may then be utilized to create and maintain a dialog between the community and the law enforcement agency. Public participation and engagement enhance the quality of decision-making within the law enforcement agency. Information and communication flowing back to the community serve transparency.

The necessary authority and scope of review include the full cooperation of the law enforcement agency that is the subject of review. The ideal design is that access is granted to all levels of the organization, ranging from the internal affairs investigators to the command and policy makers. Records in the internal affairs investigations should be readily accessible and reviewable. The policies, procedures, and training materials should also be made available, along with the history of their development and amendments in the past. Investigatory powers, including enforceable subpoena powers over persons and documents, should be included in the review process design. These are necessary tools to foster fair and complete inquiries into incidents and conduct.

Transparency means more than simply reporting findings and investigations. It begins with a complaint process that is accessible and easily understood. Then it is an investigation that is reviewable and understandable. The final step is that there is a review process that the community trusts to test the fairness and completeness of the internal investigation. Transparency promotes accountability of not only the investigatory process but also the underlying policies, procedures, and training.

Conclusion

As noted in the introduction, the administrative review process is not a replacement or substitute for litigation. However, it both is available when litigation is impractical and also can provide remedies concurrent with the litigation remedies. In its ideal form, it may offer transparency, foster reform, address misconduct, and provide closure to the complainant. It is also not an insignificant matter that it may show that a law enforcement officer acted lawfully and properly. The best result, after all, is not just fact-finding but truth-finding.

It is not being suggested that the ideal has been achieved. A variety of models are being utilized to review police misconduct allegations. No model has yet shown itself to be a guarantee of fair review. Law enforcement investigation methods with thorough and complete civilian review are still necessary in reviewing the conduct of law enforcement officers. Individual incidents can open a window into the deeper issues, flaws, and insufficiencies that are embodied in a law enforcement agency's policies, procedures, and training. Reviewing incidents and investigations over time, even when no misconduct is found, can inform and improve the policy-making function. Law enforcement agencies may be better equipped to anticipate and guide officers through difficult and challenging encounters, protecting both the citizen and the officer.

Endnotes

1. Samuel Walker, Police Accountability: Role of Citizen Oversight 32–33 (2001).

2. *See generally* Beau Thurnauer, Best Practices Guide for Internal Affairs, A Strategy for Small Departments, https://www.theiacp.org/sites/default/files/2018-08/BP-InternalAffairs.pdf and U.S. Department of Justice, Office of Community Oriented Policing Services, Standard and Guidelines for Internal Affairs: Recommendations from a Community Practice 59 (2012).

3. U.S. Department of Justice, *supra* note 2.

4. John Kelly & Mark Nichols, *We found 85,000 cops who've been investigated for misconduct. Now you can read their records,* USA Today (June 11, 2020), https://www.usatoday.com/in-depth/news/investigations/2019/04/24/usa-today-revealing-misconduct-records-police-cops/3223984002/.

5. *Id.*

6. *Id.*

7. Stephen Clarke, *Arrested Oversight: A Comparative Analysis and Case Study of How Civilian Oversight of the Police Should Function and How It Fails,* 43 Colum. J.L. & Soc. Probs. 1, 4 (2009).

8. U.S. Department of Justice, Office of Justice Programs, Bureau of Justice Statistics, National Sources of Law Enforcement Employment Data, revised Oct. 4, 2016.

9. Joseph De Angelis et. al., National Association for Civilian Oversight of Law Enforcement, Civilian Oversight of Law Enforcement (2016).

10. Law enforcement officer bills of rights and the impact of collective bargaining agreements are discussed further in Chapter 3.

11. Garrity v. New Jersey, 385 U.S. 493, 87 S. Ct. 616 (1967).

12. Mathews v. Eldridge, 424 U.S. 319, 335, 96 S. Ct. 893 (1976); Gilbert v. Homar, 520 U.S. 924, 931–32, 117 S. Ct. 1807 (1997).

13. *Id.*

14. *Id.*

15. *Id.*

16. Chapter 5 in this volume includes an informative discussions of a few independent review agency/board case studies.

17. *Bureau of Internal Affairs Reports*, Chicago Police Department, https://home.chicagopolice.org/inside-cpd/reports/.

18. Municipal Code of Chicago, ch. 2-84, including amendments passed on July 21, 2021.

19. Chicago Police Board, *The Process for Considering a Disagreement Between the Chief Administrative of COPA and the Superintendent of Police Over the Discipline of a Police Officer*, Apr. 1, 2021, https://www.chicago .gov/content/dam/city/depts/cpb/PoliceDiscipline/SummaryDisagree ments20210401.pdf.

20. Municipal Code of Chicago, ch. 2-78, including amendments passed on Oct 5, 2016.

21. Municipal Code Charlotte, §§ 16-56 through 64, including amendments passed on June 26, 2017.

22. NYC Civilian Complaint Review Board, 2020 Annual Report, https://www1.nyc.gov/assets/ccrb/downloads/pdf/policy_pdf/annual _bi-annual/2020_Annual.pdf.

23. Government of the District of Columbia, Police Complaints Board, Office of Police Complaints, G FY22 Mid-Year Report, https:// policecomplaints.dc.gov/sites/default/files/dc/sites/office%20of%20 police%20complaints/publication/attachments/Mid%20Year%202022.pdf.

Chapter 3

Accountability of Police as Public Employees

James Hanks

Introduction

Readers who seek a change in policing need to understand and appreciate the legal rights of employees and the challenges presented when those rights are impacted by any change. The rights of public employees are rooted in the Constitution, state and federal statutes, local laws, and collective bargaining agreements. A thoughtful consideration of these rights should precede or accompany a reassessment of policing practices with a clear recognition that employees may exercise these rights in any or all phases of the process: debate and formulation, enactment, and implementation. To be helpful to the process, the consideration of employee rights must be organized and comprehensive, and not an afterthought.

The purpose of this chapter is to provide a basic framework for the necessary consideration of employee rights. This is a skeleton to guide the reader's thinking. The bones are the Constitution and federal statutes that apply on a nationwide basis, but the flesh comes from state laws and local contracts that are beyond the scope of this work. No change is likely to be successful without an understanding of both.

Protected Interests as Public Employees

Liberty Interests That Are Constitutionally Protected

Freedom of Speech

As public employees, police officers have the right to engage in free speech related to their employment and to criticize their employer, provided they do not make statements that are knowingly or recklessly false.[1] For example, employees have the right to oppose any change in policing techniques, to conduct a vote of "no confidence" in the police chief or the city council, to advocate for the Blue Lives Matter movement, and to campaign for legislation that is protective of their interests. This employee right to free speech is balanced against the employer's right to provide efficient public services. That balance is tipped in favor of the employer "when a public employee speaks not as a citizen on matters of public concern, but instead as an employee upon matters only of personal interest."[2] Finally, the Supreme Court has ruled that "when public employees make statements pursuant to their official duties, the employees are not speaking as citizens for First Amendment purposes, and the Constitution does not insulate their communications from employer discipline."[3]

Freedom of Association

Under the Constitution, public employees have a right to "enter into and maintain certain intimate human relationships" and "a right to associate for the purpose of engaging in those activities protected by the First Amendment." The two forms of freedom of association are commonly referred to as the freedom of intimate association and the freedom of expressive association.[4]

The freedom of association that all citizens enjoy includes the right to affiliate with a political party (traditional or otherwise) or labor union and the right to shield information regarding that association from a public employer.[5]

Although mere membership in an organization without specific advocacy of any illegal conduct of the organization is constitutionally protected,[6] employees of law enforcement agencies are subject to greater First Amendment restraints than other citizens. Thus, the freedom of association that employees of law enforcement agencies enjoy does not extend to membership in the Ku Klux Klan.[7] But the question of whether an officer may belong to other anti-government groups or racist organizations or be required to reveal his or her membership in or association with such entities is as yet unsettled.

Freedom from Unreasonable Search and Seizure

The Fourth Amendment to the U.S. Constitution provides that all citizens shall be free from unreasonable search and seizure. In the context of public employment, the Supreme Court has held that "public employer intrusions on the constitutionally protected property interests of government employees for non-investigatory, work-related purposes, as well as investigations of work-related misconduct, should be judged by a standard of reasonableness under all the circumstances."[8] The Court noted that the expectation of privacy may be reduced by "actual office practices and procedures, or by legitimate regulation."[9]

When a public employer adopts a policy or follows a practice concerning searches in the workplace, the employee's expectation of privacy is diminished and a search consistent with the policy or practice is generally upheld. This was the result in cases involving searches of a desk and computer, credenza, personal locker, briefcase, and vehicle as well as cases of covert surveillance of common areas of a police station and a locker room.[10]

The interception and the inspection or searching of electronic communications are controlled or regulated by several federal laws, and, in the case of public employees, by the Fourth Amendment as well. In most states, there is also some state statute that protects the privacy of oral communications.

The applicable federal laws are the Omnibus Crime Control and Safe Streets Act of 1968, 18 U.S.C. §§ 2510–25 (the Wiretap Act), the Stored Wire Communications Act, 18 U.S.C. § 2710, *et seq.*, the Electronic Communications Privacy Act of 1986, 18 U.S.C. §§ 2510–3126, and the Communications Decency Act, 47 U.S.C.

§ 201, *et seq.* Title III of the Wiretap Act prohibits the interception of covered wire and oral communications, but interception is subject to a prior consent exemption.

The U.S. Supreme Court has addressed privacy issues pertaining to public employees and electronic communications in two cases. In *City of Ontario v. Quon*, the Court found that the police officers had a reasonable expectation of privacy in their text messages, that the audit of those messages was a search, and that the search itself was subject to the same principles that govern other workplace searches involving public employees.[11] And in *Riley v. California*, the Court held that the scope of a search incident to the arrest of an individual did not include a search of the digital contents of a cell phone.[12]

In 25 states, laws have been enacted to protect an employee's right of privacy on social media.[13] Most commonly, these laws prohibit an employer from requiring employees or applicants to disclose their usernames or passwords for social media accounts. In many of these states, if an employer is conducting an investigation into employee misconduct or violation of the law, the employer may require the employees to disclose content from their social media pages that is relevant to the investigation.[14] In the absence of a state statute, an employee's only protection with regard to social media passwords is the common law of privacy, and the author is not aware of any cases that have tested the scope of this protection.

Personal Interests That Are Constitutionally Protected

The Fifth and Fourteenth Amendments to the U.S. Constitution guarantee that individuals will be afforded due process before any property right or liberty interest is taken from them by the government.

Property rights in employment may be created by (1) a statutory provision protecting employment from arbitrary termination; (2) a collective bargaining agreement protecting employment from arbitrary termination, such as a "just cause" provision; (3) an employee handbook or personnel policy that protects employees from arbitrary discharge or that extends to employees some right to continued employment; (4) civil service rules or ordinances that protect employees from arbitrary discharge; (5) an internal manual, such as a standard operating procedures manual, which protects employees with regard to disciplinary action; (6) an individual contract of employment; and (7) oral promises or representations made by an employer with regard to disciplinary action or to the status of employment.

Before public employees are deprived of a property interest in their employment, they must first be afforded due process. Pre-deprivation due process requires (1) notice of the charges against the employee, (2) an explanation of the evidence in support of the charges, and (3) an opportunity to respond to the charges.[15] This minimal dues process is sufficient if the employee also has the right to a post-deprivation hearing that is more extensive in nature.

A liberty interest arises from a public employee's right to be free to pursue other employment and to be free from employer actions that might tend to stigmatize the employee or impair the employee's ability to seek other employment.

The Supreme Court has held that "[w]here a person's good name, reputation, honor or integrity is at stake because of what the government is doing to him, notice and an opportunity to be heard are essential."[16] Even when a public employee has no protected interest in employment, the employee is entitled to due process in the form of what is called a "name-clearing hearing." A public employee is entitled to a name-clearing hearing if the employee shows a stigma to his or her reputation plus deprivation of some additional right or interest.[17] Defamation in the course of a discharge satisfies this "stigma-plus" test.[18]

Procedural Rights Arising from State or Local Law, Departmental Policy, or Collective Bargaining Agreement, Commonly Referred to as a Bill of Rights

In order to protect the procedural rights of law enforcement officers involved in internal investigations, a number of states have adopted statutes that are generally referred to as a "bill of rights" for law enforcement or public safety employees. A review of the data indicates that there are 18 states with some version of a law enforcement officer bill of rights (LEOBOR).[19] In 1974, Maryland became the first state to adopt a LEOBOR. Reflecting the winds of change, Maryland in 2021 became the first state to repeal its LEOBOR (Police Reform and Accountability Act of 2021, House Bill 670).

A LEOBOR may also be enacted by local ordinance or may be created as a provision in a collective bargaining agreement between the governmental body and the labor organization representing its employees.

The rights afforded to law enforcement officers under a LEOBOR are more detailed and more extensive than the procedural rights mandated by the Constitution for all public employees. Provisions of a LEOBOR may include a "cooling-off" period prior to the commencement of an investigation (a period of time during which the officer may not be called in for questioning), notice of the nature of the investigation prior to any interrogation, the right to representation by a lawyer or by a union or other representative, the right to have the interview recorded, the right to have the interrogation conducted while on duty or on paid status, the right to have the interview conducted at a facility of the employer, the right to have the interrogation limited to a reasonable duration and to be permitted reasonable periods of time for rest and personal necessities, the right to be advised that any information provided by the officer in the course of the investigation will not be used in any subsequent criminal proceeding, the right to have an investigation completed in a reasonable period of time, the right to receive prompt or immediate notification of the results of the investigation when it is completed, the right to sue the employer for money damages for a violation of the provisions of a LEOBOR, and limitations on the rights of a civilian review board to impose discipline for officer misconduct.

Protection against Disclosure of Disciplinary Action Arising from State Law

Every state has some form of a public records law or freedom of information act. In general, all documents of or belonging to a governmental body are considered to be public records, regardless of the medium in which they are stored or preserved. This means that written reports, computer data, photographs, video recordings, audio recordings, email messages, text messages, body-camera footage, and information relating to the government in any other form are deemed to be public records.

Personnel records relating to state and local government employees are public records. However, employee disciplinary records are deemed to be confidential in many states. A study of public records laws by radio station WNYC in New York reveals that 23 states treat a police officer's disciplinary records as confidential, that 15 states make disciplinary records available to the public in some situations, and that 12 states provide public access to disciplinary records of public employees.[20]

In those states that permit partial disclosure of disciplinary records, the records that are subject to disclosure may be limited to ones that pertain to a suspension or termination[21] or only records that pertain to a dismissal.[22] When states provide more open access to disciplinary records, it is common for the release of records to be conditioned upon the completion of internal investigations or appeals.[23]

Weingarten *Rights*

Police officers who work in a department that is covered by a collective bargaining agreement generally have the right to union representation during an investigatory interview, even if there is no LEOBOR in effect in the state in which they work. This right to representation was first recognized by the U.S. Supreme Court in *NLRB v. Weingarten*.[24] In that case, the Court held that employee insistence upon union representation at an investigatory interview that the employee reasonably believes might result in the imposition of disciplinary action was concerted protected activity under the National Labor Relations Act.

The *Weingarten* case arose in the private sector and was an interpretation of federal law. But the principle on which it is based (the right of employees to engage in concerted protected activity) is one that is incorporated in most state collective bargaining laws.

This right to union representation is subject to the following conditions: (1) the employee must request representation, (2) the employee must reasonably believe that the investigation will result in disciplinary action, (3) the exercise of the right must not interfere with "legitimate employer prerogatives," (4) the employer may carry on the investigation without interviewing the employee and thus give the employee "the choice between having an interview unaccompanied by his representative, or having no interview and foregoing any benefit that might be derived from having one," and (5) the employer has no duty to bargain with any union representative who may be permitted to attend the interview.[25]

If an employee invokes his or her *Weingarten* rights, there will frequently be some delay in any interview of the employee because the union representative may not be immediately available. Once the union representative is present, the Supreme Court stated that the employee has the right to consult with the representative prior to the interview. The Court also indicated that the representative has the right to information regarding the charges before the interview. During the course of the interview, the union representative is entitled to participate in the interview process and may, for example, ask clarifying questions. In addition, the employee has the right to consult with the representative during the course of the interview.

The Garrity *Warning*

In a series of cases, the U.S. Supreme Court has ruled that (1) public employees may not be required to give statements that may be used against them in a prosecution and to waive their privilege against self-incrimination; (2) employees may not be discharged for refusing to waive their Fifth Amendment privileges; (3) employees may be compelled to answer questions specifically, directly, and narrowly tailored to the performance of their official duties and may be discharged for refusing to do so, if they are not required to waive their Fifth Amendment privileges in any criminal proceeding; and (4) answers given by employees may be used against them in administrative proceedings.[26]

The principles articulated in these decisions are now incorporated in the LEOBOR of many states.

When conducting an internal affairs investigation, the employer must consider the fact that the information obtained in the interview may not be used by a prosecutor in a criminal proceeding and assess the following: (1) whether the information may be obtained from another source, (2) whether the information will lead to the investigation of other employees or reveal other acts of misconduct, (3) whether a prompt disciplinary decision is preferable to a protracted criminal proceeding, and (4) whether the need to protect the confidentiality of the information will impair the employer's ability to be transparent in its decision-making.

Police as Union Members

Duty of Fair Representation

Unions Have a Duty to Fairly Represent All Employees in the Bargaining Unit for Which They Are the Exclusive Bargaining Agent

Where state or local law permits collective bargaining for police officers, that law generally includes, or has been interpreted to include, a duty on the part of the labor organization to fairly represent all employees in the bargaining unit. This duty was first recognized in the private sector in *Vaca v. Sipes*,[27] where the Court held that a union breaches its duty of fair representation "only when its conduct toward a member of the bargaining unit is arbitrary, discriminatory, or in bad faith," but does not breach its duty when it merely settles a grievance short of arbitration.[28]

In the context of employee misconduct, the duty of fair representation most frequently comes into play when the collective bargaining agreement contains provisions regarding procedures for discipline, standards for discipline, or both. The most common relevant contract provision is a "just cause" clause that states, very simply, that employees may only be disciplined for just cause. Where the contractual standard for discipline is "just cause" and an officer is disciplined, the officer can then file a grievance challenging the action. The final step of almost all grievance procedures is arbitration by a neutral third party, and access to that step of the process is controlled by the union. If the union does not appeal an employer's decision to arbitration, the employer's decision becomes final.

The duty of fair representation applies to matters arising out of the collective bargaining agreement. The duty does not require a union to represent an employee who is subject to disciplinary action when that action involves an internal disciplinary proceeding prior to the filing of a grievance, a civil service appeal, a civil rights complaint, a civil lawsuit, or a criminal prosecution.

A Union's Failure or Refusal to Represent an Employee Is Subject to Legal Challenge

When an officer files a grievance concerning disciplinary action, the union must first decide whether to represent the employee. To avoid a claim of breach of the duty of fair representation, unions almost always agree to provide representation to an employee who is filing a grievance, even if the employee is unpopular and even if the employee's actions are clearly inappropriate.

If a union fails or refuses to represent an employee when required to do so, the employee may sue the union for breach of the duty of fair representation and, if successful, may recover money damages. However, if an employee has been terminated, a successful suit against a union cannot restore the employee's job because the union is not the employer. Reinstatement can be achieved only through some legal action against the employer.

The cost to a union of arbitrating a grievance relating to the termination of a police officer is substantially less than the cost of defending a lawsuit for breach of the duty of fair representation. Moreover, a negative outcome in a grievance affects only the employee, not the union. Thus, practical considerations for a union weigh heavily in favor of choosing to represent a terminated employee through arbitration, even if a majority of union members believe that the officer deserved to be fired.

Contract Terms That May Affect Accountability

Collective bargaining is the process of negotiating an agreement between an employer and a group of employees. In the public sector, this topic is one that is controlled exclusively by state law. If a state law or state constitution does not authorize public employees to collectively bargain with their employer, they may not compel their employer to do so.

Currently, law enforcement employees in five states (Georgia, North Carolina, South Carolina, Tennessee, and West Virginia) do not have the right to require their employers to negotiate with them collectively.[29] In four other states (Alabama, Colorado, Mississippi, and Wyoming), there is no statute or case law addressing the right of police to negotiate with their employer.[30] In the 41 states that do permit collective bargaining by law enforcement employees, there are two basic models for negotiation: meet and confer, and binding arbitration.[31] Simply put, the difference between the two models lies in who has the final say regarding the terms of the contract. Under the meet and confer model, the employer has the final say; under the binding arbitration model, a neutral third party has the final say.

In states that permit public employee collective bargaining, the scope of the topics that may be included in an agreement varies. States that follow the approach of the National Labor Relations Act provide that negotiations may be required on "wages, hours, and other conditions of employment."[32] The quoted phrase contemplates bargaining on a broad range of topics, including discipline and discharge of employees. This means that unions may negotiate terms into a contract that directly affect disciplinary procedures or that affect the nature or extent of disciplinary action that the employer may take against an officer. However, there are some states (for example, Iowa) that permit law enforcement officers to negotiate collectively but exclude discipline and discharge from the list of mandatory subjects of bargaining for public employees.[33]

In states in which discipline is a mandatory subject of bargaining, the union may seek contractual provisions that replicate procedures found in a LEOBOR. Part of the reason for doing so is to provide the officer and the union with a cost-effective and expedient means to contest an employer's compliance with those procedures. The union may also try to expand upon the protections of a LEOBOR. Where there is no cooling-off period in the

LEOBOR (as is the case in the majority of such statutes), the union may negotiate time limitations or other restrictions on the questioning of employees following an incident involving the use of deadly force. Or the union may seek notice to the union itself, not just the employee, whenever an employee is summoned for an investigatory interview.

One of the most contentious topics for bargaining is a contractual provision concerning the removal of disciplinary action from an employee's personnel file. Where the removal of disciplinary documents is a permissible topic of bargaining, the union may seek contract terms that include what types of disciplinary actions are subject to removal (some contracts only permit the removal of lower-level discipline such as warnings or counselings), whether the disciplinary action is automatically removed after the passage of time or whether the officer must initiate an action to seek removal, the period of time that must elapse before an officer may seek removal (generally, not less than six months or more than five years), the conditions, if any, that must be met in order to be entitled to removal (the clean record clause), the procedure for seeking removal, the standard for determining whether the request for removal will be granted, and the identity of the decision-maker(s).

Inclusion of Immediate Supervisors in the Same Bargaining Unit as Officers May Affect Evaluations and Disciplinary Investigations

When the collective bargaining process is initiated for the very first time, one of the required steps is the determination of the composition of the bargaining unit (i.e., who will be covered by the terms of the contract to be negotiated). Most collective bargaining statutes exclude supervisors at some level from coverage under the law. So, for example, the chief of police or the sheriff are normally not eligible to be included in a bargaining unit. But most law enforcement agencies are composed of multiple ranks of officers, and very often sergeants, lieutenants, and captains are included as part of the department. So, a critical question is whether lower-level members of the command staff, most notably sergeants, may be included in the same bargaining unit as the employees they supervise.

The inclusion of first line supervisors in the same bargaining unit as the employees they supervise creates real challenges for the employer. First line supervisors are almost always involved to a greater or lesser degree in evaluating the performance of employees and are also frequently involved in determining lesser forms of discipline (such as a warning) even if the final decision on issuing such discipline is made by someone else in the command structure.

Officers May Be Entitled to Paid Leave Pending Completion of an Investigation

When an agency receives a report or complaint regarding an incident of alleged misconduct, the normal practice is to begin an investigation as soon as possible. In jurisdictions where a LEOBOR is in effect, prompt investigation is a statutory requirement.[34] However, the author has not identified any LEOBOR statutes that require that an employee under investigation be placed on a leave of absence or require that a leave of absence, if mandated, be on a paid rather than unpaid basis.

In the absence of statutory directives regarding the status of an officer who is under investigation and when considering whether to place an officer on a leave of absence, law enforcement agencies consider the terms of a collective bargaining agreement (if there is one in effect), constitutional requirements related to due process, and practical challenges related to the conduct of the investigation and maintaining public confidence.

In states where collective bargaining is permitted, it is common for "leaves of absence" to be a subject of bargaining. This topic of bargaining may include a leave of absence for any reason and a provision regarding the pay status of the employee while on leave. Thus, a union may propose that the collective bargaining agreement include a paid leave of absence for any employee who is under investigation. The fact that a union may make such a proposal does not mean that the proposal will be agreed upon by the employer or that it must be included in the bargaining agreement.

Even if no collective bargaining is in effect or if an agreement is in effect but is silent on the question of whether an employee is entitled to a paid leave of absence while under investigation, every public employer is bound by the provisions of the U.S. Constitution relating to due process. As noted earlier in this chapter, where public employees possess a property interest in their employment, they are entitled to due process before they are deprived of that property interest. This principle of due process applies to a suspension without pay and to an involuntary leave of absence without pay.[35] If the employer places an employee who possesses a property interest on an unpaid leave of absence without first providing due process to the employee, the employer may later be found to have violated the employee's constitutional rights and be required to compensate the employee for lost wages and for attorney fees. Thus, most law enforcement agencies err on the side of caution and place an employee who is under investigation on a paid leave of absence pending completion of the investigation.

In addition to contractual and constitutional obligations, employers must think about how to most effectively conduct and complete an investigation in a timely manner. If an employee under investigation is placed on a paid leave of absence, the employee is normally subject to questioning during the employee's regular working hours, the employee is not interacting with co-workers during those regular working hours, the employee is not interacting with members of the public in any official capacity, and the employee is not suffering any reduction in income that might affect his or her mental or emotional state. For practical reasons if none other, the employer will use a paid leave to expedite an investigation.

Officers May Be Provided Financial Support for Defense

One of the benefits employees derive from being a union member is access to some financial resources that are not required by law to be provided by the union to all members of the bargaining unit. Other than to comply with its duty of fair representation, a union is not required to provide or pay for an attorney to assist an employee who is under investigation. However, a union may create a legal defense fund for its members and may establish the terms and conditions under which union members obtain funds for their legal defense.

Grievability of Disciplinary Action

Collective bargaining agreements almost always contain a grievance procedure for resolving disputes between the parties regarding the meaning or application of the terms of the contract. Where a contract contains a grievance procedure, it is the norm that a dispute concerning any provision of the contract is subject to the grievance procedure and that the final step of the procedure is binding arbitration.

Wherever discipline is a mandatory subject of bargaining as a matter of state law, the union has the right to negotiate a provision into the contract regarding discipline. A typical discipline and discharge clause states as follows: "No employee shall be subject to discipline or discharge except for just cause." Thus, if a contract contains a just cause provision, an employee who is disciplined has the right to contest that action.

The final stage of the grievance procedure is arbitration. Arbitration provides a review of the employer's decision by a neutral third party. It is an almost universal rule that the union, not the employee, decides whether a grievance will proceed to arbitration. That is because the agreement to be construed by the arbitrator is an agreement between the employer and the union, not the employer and the employee. As noted above, the union has a duty of fair representation that obligates it to review the merits of the grievance and determine whether it should proceed to arbitration.

The standard most frequently used in arbitration proceedings involving discipline is just cause. The phrase "just cause" has been interpreted to mean that the employer diligently investigated a matter and then took action that was appropriate given the nature of the offense, the record of the employee, the disciplinary action it had taken in other similar cases, and any extenuating circumstances. There may also be an expectation of progressive discipline, meaning that an employee should ordinarily be disciplined along a continuum beginning with the lowest level (counseling or warning) and progressing thereafter to reprimand, suspension, and finally discharge.

It is well established that the employer has the burden of proof in sustaining disciplinary action. This means that the employer must proceed first and must persuade the arbitrator that the discipline was justified and appropriate. There is no presumption that the employer's action was correct.

Unlike a criminal trial, it is the almost universal practice that an arbitration proceeding is not open to the public. Thus, unless the arbitration decision itself is made public by the parties or is considered to be a public record not exempt from disclosure, the general public will never know why certain disciplinary action was sustained, modified, or reversed.

If the issue before the arbitrator is whether there is just cause for the termination of an employee, the arbitrator may be influenced by the notion that a termination is considered by some to be "economic capital punishment."[36] The description of the discharge of an employee as the "supreme industrial penalty" is reflective of the view of many arbitrators. It also helps to explain why arbitrators are reluctant to fully uphold an employer's decision to terminate an employee.

In 2015, attorney and author Will Aitchison complied a lengthy table of arbitration and court cases involving disciplinary action of any type taken against police officers. The earliest of the decisions was one issued in 1968, and the most recent was one issued in 2014. Aitchison made no claim to have comprehensively identified all relevant decisions in this time period, but the study is the most thorough one reviewed by this author. There were a total of 473 decisions included in Aitchison's study. The employer's disciplinary action was upheld completely in 45 percent of the cases, was reversed completely in 30.7 percent of the cases, and was modified in some form in 24.3 percent of the cases. Of the 473 decisions, 109 were arbitration cases pertaining to the termination of a law enforcement officer. In 38 of those 109 cases (34.9%), the arbitrator sustained the termination, and in the remaining 71 cases (65.1%), the termination was either modified or reversed.[37]

The study just cited and all others reviewed by the author reveal a consistent pattern when the issue is the likelihood that disciplinary action taken by an employer will be sustained by an arbitrator. Whether the employer is in the public sector or private sector, arbitrators sustain the full disciplinary penalty imposed by the employer roughly one-half of the time.

One of the grounds used in the defense of employees in deadly force cases is the assertion that the employee was simply acting in a manner consistent with department training, for example, when and how to employ a chokehold. If the department has provided training that is applicable to the employee's actions, this defense can be effective even if the training itself is inconsistent with prevailing norms. In such instances, the proper focus is on the administrators who selected the training and how their decisions were made. For city police departments, the chief of police and the training officer decide whether there will be training and what type of training will be provided. They can be held accountable, and their decisions may be overturned by legislative (city council) or executive (mayoral or managerial) action. However, where the chief executive of the agency is an independently elected official (such as a county sheriff), that official makes the training decisions and the only recourse is public scrutiny and pressure or political action (petition for recall or replacement in an election).

After an arbitration decision is received, the parties may consider challenging it in court. But a series of decisions issued in 1960 by the U.S. Supreme Court has severely limited the likelihood of any judicial relief: courts are required to uphold the decision of an arbitrator provided the decision "draws its essence from the collective bargaining agreement," even if the decision contains factual or legal errors.[38] An exception to this judicial standard of review does exist where enforcement of the award would violate some public policy that is explicit, well defined, and dominant.[39]

The knowledge that disciplinary action is sustained roughly one-half of the time and that an arbitrator's decision is, for all practical purposes, final and binding and not subject to appeal serves to moderate the decision of the employer. In less serious cases and in cases involving lesser discipline, the employer may choose certainty and settle for a reduced level of discipline. Even in cases involving termination, the employer may ultimately agree instead to a suspension without pay because it assures the employer that there will be serious disciplinary action in the employee's personnel file, that the action was accepted as appropriate by the employee, and that there will be a deterrent to future misconduct or a strong basis for termination.

Collective Bargaining Considerations

Collective Bargaining Occurs between Employer and Union, Mostly in a Private Setting, and the Public Has Little Access to Information or to the Process

Collective bargaining is a process that involves representatives of the employer and the employees meeting together to address and resolve issues pertaining to compensation, benefits, and the working conditions of the employees. The Office of Justice Programs of the U.S. Department of Justice prepared a study in 2013 of all local police departments.[40] The study found that, in a majority of cities with a population of 10,000 or more, the employers were engaged in collective bargaining with local police unions or associations.[41] While this is a high percentage, it is important to remember that there are eight states that do not expressly permit police employees to collectively bargain with their employer. And in a number of the other states that do permit law enforcement employee bargaining, the process is ultimately in the control of the employer and is sometimes referred to by employees as "collective begging."

The subjects that may be addressed in negotiations are statutorily defined in what is known as the scope of bargaining. If a matter is not included in the scope of negotiations, then neither party may insist that it be a topic of bargaining. The only items that may not be negotiated are illegal or excluded subjects of bargaining, such as, in some states, pension benefits.

The process of collective bargaining typically begins when the employee organization makes a request for negotiations.

Most often, the union presents its proposals to the employer, and then, at some later date, the employer responds and presents its proposals. Proposals may also be simultaneously exchanged. The public has the right to access these proposals only if the applicable state statute provides that the presentation of proposals must be made in an open meeting[42] or if the documents are considered to be non-confidential public records.

After the parties present their initial proposals, the bargaining begins. Unless the parties agree otherwise, bargaining is closed to the public.[43] Bargaining continues until the parties reach either an agreement or an impasse. If the parties reach an agreement, the agreement must be approved by the union and the employer. If the parties fail to reach an agreement, then impasse procedures are implemented. Impasse procedures typically include mediation and some other means of impasse resolution, such as fact-finding, non-binding arbitration, or binding arbitration. Mediation is typically not open to the public.[44] Depending on state statute, other impasse hearings may be open to the public.

Before a collective bargaining agreement is approved by the employer, it is generally made public[45] and is then voted upon in public. This last step of the process is most likely the first opportunity for citizens to learn what the agreement will contain.

The Bargaining Process Involves Give and Take, and Both Parties Are Reluctant to Give

Where a collective bargaining agreement has been in effect for even a small number of years, both parties are generally reluctant to change the non-economic provisions of the contract unless they receive a concession from the other party that is sufficient in value to warrant the change. The simple explanation for this is that all of the provisions of the contract are the product of good faith bargaining, concessions were made to obtain the inclusion of the language in question, and changes should not be made unless there has been a dramatic change in the conditions under which the provision was first negotiated. Newton's first law of motion applies to negotiations: a body at rest tends to stay at rest. As a result, contract provisions tend to remain unchanged in the agreement for a substantial period of time.

This tendency to maintain the status quo means that the party seeking a change must either persuade the other party that the change is in its best interest or offer a concession on some other provision of the contract. Thus, if the terms of an agreement include a provision permitting removal of disciplinary documents from an employee's personnel file, the employer may propose altering or deleting the provision, but the union would have little incentive for agreeing to a change that would be opposed by most of its members. Where the provision has great value to a party, the provision will be changed only if the other party makes a substantial concession or the change is ordered to be made by a third-party neutral.

The circumstances are a bit different if a proposal touches on a topic that is new to both parties, such as the wearing of body cameras. In such cases, the outcome of negotiations on the topic will be influenced heavily by the impasse procedures in effect in the state.

Since Statutory Impasse Procedure Generally Tend to Maintain the Status Quo with Regard to Non-Economic Issues, Any Change Needed in a Such Issues Must Normally Be Bargained by the Parties

Every state that permits collective bargaining also provides some reference to the resolution of bargaining disputes in its authorizing statute. The dispute resolution processes are called impasse procedures. There is quite a bit of variation among the impasse procedures in state law. Some states provide different impasse procedures for different classes of employees.[46] As a rule, in states such as these, police and firefighters tend to be treated more favorably.

There is also significant variation among the states with regard to the impasse procedures themselves. These are some of the variations that are applicable to police employee bargaining units: mediation and final and binding arbitration;[47] mediation and binding arbitration on economic issues;[48] mediation and binding arbitration with certain excluded subjects;[49] and mediation, fact-finding, and arbitration.[50]

Among the states that provide for arbitration for police officers, there is also variation with regard to the type of arbitration that is authorized. In Maine, the arbitration is advisory as to economic issues but binding as to all other issues. Arbitration may be structured to be issue by issue,[51] total package,[52] or conventional.[53]

In states that provide for arbitration, the statutory scheme normally includes a list or reference to standards that are to be used by the arbitrator or arbitration panel. Items that are typically included in the standards are the ability of the employer to pay; the cost of living; comparison of the wages, hours, and conditions of employment of the employees of the unit involved in the dispute with those provided to comparable employees by other public employers; the collective bargaining history of the parties; and the interests and welfare of the public.[54]

Regardless of the standards used in a statute, the end result is shaped in large part by the concept of comparability. Arbitration offers that are closely tied to comparable provisions in the collective bargaining agreements of similar employers are more likely to prevail than offers that are different than the pattern among comparable employers.

Perhaps even more important is the position of the parties relative to the status quo. The power of the status quo cannot be overstated because the status quo almost always represents what the parties themselves voluntarily agreed was an appropriate resolution of an issue. It may not represent what is perfect, but the status quo does represent what was mutually acceptable to the parties at the time the provision became part of the contract. Thus, there is a heavy burden on the party seeking to alter the status quo. And when the evidence in favor of a change in the status quo is not overwhelming, most arbitrators will choose to maintain the status quo.

Where parties understand how arbitration functions and appreciate the difficulty of obtaining a change in the status quo through arbitration, they will, by necessity, focus their attention on attempting to achieve a desired change through bargaining.

Arbitration Decisions Are Generally Not Subject to Substantive Judicial Review

With a few exceptions, the statutes that provide for collective bargaining and that include arbitration as a step in the impasse procedure also provide that the arbitration is "binding" or "final and binding."[55] In those rare instances where a party has challenged an arbitration award, the usual outcome is that the award is upheld.[56]

The use of the phrase "final and binding" is intended by the legislature to indicate that the bargaining and impasse processes end with arbitration and that there is no judicial review of the substance of an arbitrator's decision. This closure is critical to the operation of a bargaining statute and to the parties who are negotiating. It is one more force driving the parties back to the table to work out their differences voluntarily.

Civil Rights Protections

Disciplinary Action Is Subject to Federal and/or State Court Review if the Officer Claims the Action Was Discriminatorily Motivated or Procedurally Defective

Disciplinary decisions of public employers are subject to review in state and federal court with regard to both the substance of the decisions and the procedures that were followed in making them. The most notable federal laws affecting disciplinary actions of public employers are Title VII of the Civil Rights Act of 1964 (prohibiting discrimination based on race, color, religion, sex, or national origin), the Age Discrimination in Employment Act (prohibiting discrimination based on age), and the Americans with Disabilities Act (prohibiting discrimination based on disability). There are other federal statutory protections for employees that are applicable to public employees: Title VII of the Pregnancy Discrimination Act of 1978, Title II of the Genetic Information Nondiscrimination Act of 2008, the Fair Credit Reporting Act, the Employee Polygraph Protection Act of 1988, and the Uniformed Services Employment and Reemployment Act.

In addition to the federal statutes regulating employment, there are also constitutional provisions that affect employment decisions in terms of both substance (principally the First Amendment) and procedure (the Fourth, Fifth, and Fourteenth

Amendments). These constitutional provisions were discussed in the first part of this chapter.

Every state also has both statutes and constitutional provisions that apply to disciplinary decisions of public employers. In a number of states, there are statutory regulations that do not have a counterpart in federal law. Among the most common of these regulations are prohibitions against discrimination on the basis of sexual orientation and gender identity.[57] Many states also provide additional protection to military veterans[58] and to public employees who are union members or who exercise their rights under the applicable state collective bargaining law.[59] All states have some form of occupational health and safety law that protects employees. And a significant number of states have also enacted drug testing laws that apply to public employees.[60]

There are two basic ways these statutory and constitutional provisions can become applicable to a disciplinary decision. The first is called disparate treatment: the employee being disciplined alleges that the action being taken was improperly motivated—for example, the employee was disciplined or disciplined more severely than other employees because of the employee's race or gender. The second is called retaliation: the employee being disciplined alleges that, prior to the conduct that prompted the disciplinary action, the employee either engaged in some protected activity (such as posting some criticism of the chief of police on Facebook or filing a civil rights complaint, union grievance, or unfair labor practice complaint) or participated in some protected process (such as testifying as part of the investigation of a civil rights complaint).

Whether the employee alleges disparate treatment or retaliation, the employee will normally do so either internally using the employer's complaint procedure or externally using the procedure of the appropriate state or federal agency. There is usually little or no expense involved in filing a complaint, the filing can be accomplished without legal assistance or with free legal assistance provided by an advocacy organization, and the filing can be completed in a single day or a very brief period of time. So, although employees who file a civil rights or other type of complaint do not enjoy any special immunity from disciplinary action by virtue of their filing of the complaint, they may insulate themselves to some degree by filing a complaint, even if the complaint is groundless. As a practical matter, employers exercise caution in investigating and disciplining employees who have filed a complaint alleging discrimination or retaliation.

When an employee alleges disparate treatment, federal courts follow what has become known as the McDonnell Douglas burden-shifting framework to decide the case. In the case of *McDonnell Douglas Corp. v. Green*,[61] the U.S. Supreme Court interpreted Title VII of the Civil Rights Act of 1964 and adopted a procedure for analyzing cases under this law. The framework consists of three steps: (1) the employee must establish a prima facie case of discrimination, (2) if the employee does so, the employer must "articulate some legitimate, nondiscriminatory" reason for its actions, and (3) if the employer does so, the employee must then be given a fair opportunity to show that employer's stated reason for its action was in fact a pretext.

As a matter of practical application, this three-part test is not particularly burdensome for an employer, but it does require the employer to provide real proof of a proper reason for its actions, and it does permit the employee to pierce the veil of secrecy that may shroud the employer's true intentions.

A Judicial Challenge Can Proceed Regardless of the Outcome of Arbitration

Employees who are subjected to disciplinary action and who are covered by a collective bargaining agreement may file both a grievance under the bargaining agreement and a civil rights or other complaint under an applicable law. The two types of filings involve different procedures that act independently of one another. So, an employee may file and lose a grievance alleging that some disciplinary action violated the terms of the collective bargaining agreement and still pursue a separate complaint alleging that the same disciplinary action violated the provisions of a civil rights law.[62]

Insurance Companies May Settle a Legal Challenge to Disciplinary Action in Order to Avoid the Expense and Uncertainty of Litigation

Although some municipalities may be completely self-insured, it is most often the case that local governments procure some type of insurance that is applicable to employment-related litigation, including, but not limited to, civil rights complaints. If the litigation invokes insurance coverage that places the insurer at risk for the payment of monetary damages as well as for the payment of attorney fees for the employee's attorney and the cost of defense for the employer's attorney, the insurer will play a role in handling the litigation.

Insurers approach the defense of a matter in litigation as a transaction. There are costs associated with the transaction, and the goal of the insurer is to spend as little of its money as possible to bring the transaction to a conclusion. The insurer makes calculations regarding the probability of an unfavorable outcome, the range of a negative verdict, and the cost of defense in reaching that verdict. These calculations do not include an assessment of the popularity of the settlement in the local community or the impact of the settlement on the integrity of the disciplinary process or the standing of the actor or the victim in the community.

If the settlement of a matter in litigation concerning disciplinary action can be accomplished only by the elimination of or a reduction in a penalty that was imposed by the employer, the insurer may pressure the employer to accept those terms in order to avoid the financial risk of going forward.

Civil Service Protections

Civil Service Laws Were Enacted to Protect Employees from Arbitrary and Politically Motivated Decisions

Prior to the enactment of civil service laws, the hiring, promotion, and firing of public employees were left to the predominant political forces that were operative in the community (city, county, or state), and public employees served at the will or pleasure of those forces. Today, civil service laws and systems exist in most larger metropolitan communities, and they have been in existence for many decades.[63]

The typical civil service law includes provisions relating to screening and testing applicants for employment, testing and interviewing employees for promotions, and a process for reviewing and deciding disputes relating to the disciplining of employees. If these provisions are designed and implemented correctly, the result should be that personnel decisions are made on the basis of merit and fact, not favoritism, politics, or personal animosity.

Civil Service Laws Typically Provide for the Review of the Most Serious Forms of Discipline

The typical grievance and appeals process provides the opportunity for employees to challenge disciplinary action that has been taken against them.[64] The range of possible discipline varies by jurisdiction, but it may include the following: oral counseling, written counseling, oral warning, written warning, oral reprimand, written reprimand, suspension, demotion, and discharge.

Not every level of discipline is subject to appeal. The scope of the appeals process is defined in the authorizing legislation for the civil service system, and it likewise varies by jurisdiction. From a brief review of civil service commission rules, it appears that appeals processes usually limit the scope of review to suspensions, demotions, and discharges.[65]

Civil Service Commissions Are Most Often Locally Appointed, and the Appointing Authority Is Subject to the Usual Political Pressures

Members of a civil service commission are not usually required to possess any special qualifications or expertise in personnel matters, and they are locally appointed or locally elected. As a consequence, the commission itself is subject to the normal political pressures involved in any government enterprise. That pressure may manifest itself when the decision to be made is an unpopular one or when the employee whose discipline is subject to review is a popular or highly respected person.

Civil Service Disciplinary Hearings May Be Open to the Public or May Be Closed

The degree of public access to an employee's disciplinary hearing is determined by the legislation creating the civil service system and authorizing a commission to hear appeals of disciplinary action. Legislators have weighed the interests of the public in learning all it can about an employee's conduct and the interest of employees in protecting their privacy and reputation and have produced at least four different models for the conduct of civil service disciplinary hearings: (1) the hearing is closed to the public,[66] (2) the hearing is open to the public,[67] (3) the hearing is open to the public, but it may be closed upon a showing of good cause by either party or upon the motion of the hearing officer,[68] and (4) if the employee affected by the hearing makes a determination that the hearing should be held in a closed session, the hearing will be closed to the public.[69]

If a disciplinary hearing is open to the public, the decision of the civil service commission is a public record. The amount and degree of specificity of information contained in the decision will then determine how much or little the public learns about the employee's alleged misconduct, the investigation into that misconduct, the employer's disciplinary decision, and the reasons for that decision.

Where Employees Are Covered Both by a Collective Bargaining Agreement and by a Civil Service System, They May Have a Choice of Forum for the Appeal of Disciplinary Decisions

Statutes that create civil service systems and collective bargaining rights do not always address the question of which forum an employee may or must use to resolve a grievance. Some states expressly give employees the choice of using either grievance arbitration or a civil service appeal: Iowa, Minnesota, New York, Pennsylvania, and Wisconsin. However, in other states, such as Massachusetts, the applicable statute provides that, if an employee is covered by a collective bargaining agreement providing for binding arbitration of disputes pertaining to suspension, dismissal, removal, or termination, then grievance resolution is the exclusive means for resolving the grievance. The State Employees Labor Relations Act in Maine is to the same effect.

Civil Service Commissions Generally Have the Right to Modify the Disciplinary Action

The legislation that creates civil service commissions normally contains a provision regarding the power of the commission to affirm or reverse disciplinary action that is subject to appeal. A commission may also be authorized to modify a disciplinary decision. Although the issue appears to have been litigated only a limited number of times, at least two courts have held that, in addition to reducing a disciplinary penalty, a civil service commission that is empowered to "modify" a sanction may do so by increasing the penalty.

Decisions Are Subject to Judicial Review

Based upon the author's research, it appears that in every state where a civil service commission is authorized by law to review disciplinary decisions pertaining to law enforcement officers, the decisions of the civil service commission are subject to appeal to the courts.

Conclusion

The successful implementation of a law enforcement reform initiative depends upon the cooperation, or at least assent, of the affected employees. The likelihood of obtaining their cooperation is tied directly to the degree to which decision-makers both understand and appreciate the legal rights and interests of employees. This chapter is intended to assist the reader in understanding the legal rights of employees. A sincere appreciation of those rights requires a recognition that the employees are not the enemy and an emotional investment that cannot be supplied by any book.

Endnotes

1. Pickering v. Board of Education, 391 U.S. 563, 574 (1968).
2. Connick v. Meyers, 461 U.S. 138, 147 (1983).
3. Garcetti v. Ceballos, 547 U.S. 410, 419 (2006).
4. Roberts v. United States Jaycees, 468 U.S. 609 (1984).
5. Kusper v. Pontikes, 414 U.S. 51, 57 (1973); Smith v. Arkansas State Highway Employees, 441 U.S. 463 (1979); Shelton v. Tucker, 364 U.S. 479 (1960); Fraternal Order of Police, Lodge #5 v. City of Philadelphia, 812 F.2d 105, 119–20 (3d Cir. 1987).
6. United States v. Robel, 389 U.S. 258 (1967).
7. McMullen v. Carson, 754 F.2d 936 (11th Cir. 1985); State of Nebraska v. Henderson, 762 N.W.2d 1 (Neb. 2009).
8. O'Connor v. Ortega, 480 U.S. 709, 725–26 (1987).
9. *Id.* at 717.
10. Williams v. Philadelphia Housing Authority, 826 F. Supp. 952 (E.D. 1993); Schowengerdt v. U.S., 944 F.2d 483 (9th Cir. 1991); American Postal Workers Union v. U.S. Postal Service, 871 F.2d 556 (6th Cir. 1989); Finkelstein v. State Personnel Board, 218 Cal. App. 3d 264 (1990); McDonnell v. Hunter, 809 F.2d 1302 (8th Cir. 1987); Thompson v. Johnson County Community College, 930 F. Supp. 501 (D. Kan. 1996); Rosario v. U.S., 538 F. Supp. 2d 480 (P.R. 2008).
11. 560 U.S. 746 (2010).
12. 573 U.S. 373 (2014).
13. *7 Ways Employee Privacy Laws Impact Social Media in the Workplace,* Prime Group, LLC, https://allpryme.com/employee-privacy-laws/ (accessed Jan. 16, 2022).
14. Sachi Berreiro, *State Laws on Social Media Password Requests by Employers,* Nolo, https://www.nolo.com/legal-encyclopedia/state-laws-on-social-media-password-requests-by-employers.html (accessed Jan. 11, 2022).
15. Cleveland Board of Education v. Loudermill, 470 U.S. 532 (1985).
16. Wisconsin v. Constantine, 400 U.S. 433, 437 (1971).
17. Paul v. Davis, 424 U.S. 693, 701 (1976).
18. Hill v. Borough of Kutztown, 455 F.3d 225 (3d Cir. 2006).
19. Wayne W. Schmidt, *Peace Officers Bill of Rights Guarantees: Responding to Union Demands with a Management Sanctioned Version,* Law Enforcement Executive Forum (Mar. 2005), https://www.aele.org/pobr-iacp.pdf (accessed Jan. 11, 2022).
20. *Is Police Misconduct a Secret in Your State?,* WNYC, https://project.wnyc.org/disciplinary-records/#:~:text=Police%20disciplinary%20records%20are%20confidential%20under%20New%20York%20Civil%20Rights,employee%20personnel%20records%20are%20public (accessed Jan. 11, 2022).
21. Arkansas Code § 25-19-105(c)(1).
22. Hawaii Rev. Stat. § 92F-14, Uniform Information Practices Act.
23. Arizona Rev. Stat. §§ 39-121 through 39-128 and § 39-1109; Maine Rev. Stat. 30-A, § 503(1)(b)(5).
24. 420 U.S. 251 (1975).
25. *Id.*

26. Garrity v. State of New Jersey, 385 U.S. 493 (1967); Gardner v. Broderick, 392 U.S. 273 (1968); Uniformed Sanitation Men Association v. Commissioner of Sanitation, 392 U.S. 280 (1968); Lefkowitz v. Turley, 414 U.S. 70 (1973); Lefkowitz v. Cunningham, 431 U.S. 801 (1977).

27. 386 U.S. 171 (1967).

28. *Id.* at 190–93.

29. Milla Sanes & John Schmitt, *Regulation of Public Collective Bargaining in the States*, CENTER FOR ECONOMIC AND POLICY RESEARCH (Mar. 10, 2014), https://cepr.net/report/regulation-of-public-sector-collective-bargaining-in-the-states/ (accessed Jan. 15, 2022). The data in the preceding article is modified by the enactment of a law in Virginia in 2020 that permits public employees to collectively bargain with their employees effective May 1, 2021, and by the enactment of a law in West Virginia that prohibits collective bargaining by public employees. Union Station. *Public-sector collective bargaining legal in Virginia as of May 1*, BALLOTPEDIA (Apr. 30, 2021), https://news .ballotpedia.org/2021/04/30/union-station-public-sector-collective-bargaining-legal-in-virginia-as-of-may-1/#:~:text=The%20Virginia%20General%20 Assembly%20approved,an%20authorizing%20ordinance%20or%20resolu tion. (accessed Jan. 15, 2022). Lise Gelernter, *West Virginia Legislature Codifies Illegality of Public Employee Strikes*, ARBITRATION INFO (Apr. 18, 2021), https:// law.missouri.edu/arbitrationinfo/2021/04/18/west-virginia-legislature -codifies-illegality-of-public-employee-strikes/ (accessed Jan. 15, 2022).

30. Sanes & Schmitt, *supra* note 29. Collective bargaining with police in Colorado is neither expressly prohibited nor permitted. However, the author did identify 13 cities that have entered into collective bargaining agreements with their police officers: Denver, Aurora, Fort Collins, Lakewood, Thornton, Pueblo, Greeley, Boulder, Longmont, Castle Rock, Commerce City, Littleton, and Englewood.

31. Examples of the meet and confer model of collective bargaining with no provision for binding arbitration are Arizona (ARIZ. REV. STAT. ch. 8, art. 6, § 23-1411), Arkansas (ARK. CODE ANN. § 11-3-301), Florida (FL. STAT. §§ 447.309 and 447.403), and Kentucky (KY. REV. STAT. §§ 67A.6902 and 67A.6908). Examples of the binding arbitration model of collective bargaining are Iowa (IOWA CODE § 20.22), Michigan (MICH. COMPLIED LAWS §§ 423.215–40), and New York (CONSOLIDATED LAWS OF NEW YORK, Civil Service Law, art.14).

32. *E.g.*, CONN. GEN. STAT. tit. 5, § 5-271.

33. For an excellent review of the status of topics of bargaining in law enforcement officer contracts, *see* WILL AITCHISON, THE RIGHTS OF LAW ENFORCEMENT OFFICERS 20–68 (7th ed. 2015).

34. *E.g.*, IOWA CODE § 80F.1(3).

35. Schmidt v. Creedon, 639 F.3d 587 (3d Cir. 2011).

36. *See* Roland P. Wilder Jr., *Discharge in the "Law" of Arbitration*, 20 VANDERBILT LAW REV. 81 (1966).

37. Aitchison, *supra* note 33, at 102–75.

38. United Steelworkers v. American Manufacturing Co., 363 U.S. 564 (1960); United Steelworkers v. Enterprise Wheel & Car Corp., 363 U.S. 593

(1960); United Steelworkers v. Warrior & Gulf Navigation Co., 363 U.S. 574 (1960).

39. W.R. Grace & Co. v. Local 759 International Union of the United Rubber, Cork Linoleum & Plastic Workers of America, 461 U.S. 757, 766 (1983).

40. BRIAN A. REAVES, LOCAL POLICE DEPARTMENTS, 2013: PERSONNEL, POLICIES, AND PRACTICES (2015), https://bjs.ojp.gov/content/pub/pdf/lpd13ppp.pdf (accessed Jan. 11, 2022).

41. *Id.* at Appendix Table 3.

42. IOWA CODE § 20.17(3), sentence 4.

43. *E.g., see id.* at sentence 1.

44. *Id.*

45. *Id.* § 20.17(4).

46. Delaware, Illinois, Iowa, Michigan, Minnesota, and Nevada.

47. Alaska, Delaware, Iowa, Michigan, New Jersey, New York, and Washington.

48. California.

49. Illinois: the criterion pursuant to which deadly force may be used is a subject excluded from arbitration.

50. Ohio.

51. Iowa and Ohio.

52. Delaware, Nevada, Oklahoma, and Oregon.

53. New Jersey.

54. *See, e.g.,* IOWA CODE § 20.22(7) and MICH. COMP. LAWS § 423.239(9).

55. *See, e.g.,* DELAWARE LAWS, tit. 19, ch. 16, § 1615 and IOWA CODE § 20.22(12).

56. AFSCME/Iowa Council 61 v. State of Iowa, 484 N.W.2d 390 (1992).

57. IOWA CODE § 216.6(1)(a).

58. *Id.* § 35C.6.

59. *Id.* §§ 20.8 and 20.10(2).

60. Alaska, Alabama, Florida, Hawaii, Idaho, Louisiana, Maryland, Mississippi, Montana, Nebraska, North Carolina, Ohio, Oklahoma, Oregon, Rhode Island, South Carolina, Utah, and Vermont.

61. 411 U.S. 792 (1973).

62. Alexander v. Gardner-Denver Co., 415 U.S. 36, 51–52 (1974).

63. GEORGE W. GREISINGER, JEFFREY S. SLOVAK & JOSEPH J. MOLKUP, CIVIL SERVICE SYSTEMS: THEIR IMPACT ON POLICE ADMINISTRATION (U.S. Department of Justice 1979), pp. 36 and 41, *available at* https://www.ncjrs.gov/pdf files1/Digitization/58954NCJRS.pdf (accessed Jan. 11, 2022).

64. *Id.* at p. 29 (Table 1) and p. 47 (Table 4).

65. See the civil service commission rules for Des Moines, Iowa; Douglas County, Nebraska; St. Louis, Missouri; Denver, Colorado; Miami, Florida; Philadelphia, Pennsylvania; and Houston, Texas.

66. City of St. Louis, Missouri.

67. City of Philadelphia, Pennsylvania; City of Dallas, Texas, and State of Iowa.

68. City of Denver, Colorado.

69. City of Portland, Oregon.

Chapter 4

What Is Constitutional Policing?

Royce Russell

Constitutional policing is policing in which humanity is at the forefront for law enforcement personnel as they perform their duties to "protect and serve." "At its most fundamental, Constitutional Policing is legal policing—that is, policing that operates within the parameters set by the U.S. Constitution, States Constitution, the body of Court decisions, that have interpreted and spelled out in greater detail what the text of Constitutional means in terms of the everyday practices of policing."[1]

Several years have passed since the defining of constitutional policing and what the definition actually means in terms of everyday policing. And I assert that the average police officer is not knowledgeable on the "body of court decisions" that assist in interpreting what constitutional policing means legally.[2] Rather, police officers confront constitutional policing when accused of excessive use of force; unlawful stops, searches, and arrests; and racial bias, implicit or otherwise.

Moreover, when police officers encounter a civilian, in particular, a Black or Brown person, articulating his or her constitutional rights ranging from freedom of speech to Fourth and Fourteenth Amendment violations concerning illegal stops, searches, and arrests, the encounter escalates violently and aggressively.

Constitutional policing is often used in limited contexts, such as examining whether a policy, practice, or police officers' actions adhere with the U.S. Constitution or state constitutions.[3] It is the foundation for community policing and is aspirational in its implementation. Constitutional policing resembles community policing, which is a strategy of policing whereby police are assigned to particular neighborhoods and become part of the community. The police become engaged with the residents of the community, in particular the youths and young adults. The police take interest in the residents and develop a relationship that is about mentoring and assisting in the development of the residents they police. Constitutional policing includes community. It includes treating Black and Brown people with humanity and respect. It is policing where law enforcement is not offended by the fact that the community knows their rights and has expectations of the police and how they police. Constitutional policing optimizes communication between the police and detained civilians as a tool for better policing. Communication is vital in any civilian detention. Constitutional policing is not a fixed concept but is flexible to societal needs in conjunction with our rights according to the Constitution.

I contend that constitutional policing matters because it is one gateway to build trust between Black and Brown communities and law enforcement/police officers. Constitutional policing empowers and protects citizens, whereas presently police misconduct occurs too frequently and police accountability occurs infrequently.

Freedom of speech is the first constitutional right that empowers and protects all citizens. The use of the First Amendment allows the Black and Brown community an avenue to voice their concerns and ensure police are held accountable for misconduct. Also, use of freedom of speech protects against police misconduct as the misconduct is occurring by verbalizing to the offending officer that you are aware of your rights as a citizen and the offending officer will be held accountable.

In this chapter I discuss how the First Amendment and freedom of speech are married to constitutional policing. In all relationships, personal or professional, communication is the most vital component. Communication is freedom of speech. Therefore, it is fitting that when you address constitutional policing, you address the right to speak freely. Freedom of speech in this context is analogous to the right to freely communicate, and communication between Black and Brown communities and police is critical to constitutional policing. This chapter discusses obstacles to achieving constitutional policing such as quota-based policies and polling as well as prejudice and racial bias—implicit or otherwise—within policing. Also reviewed is the lack of humanity within policing and leadership actions that communities can employ to ensure constitutional policing is utilized in their community.

The above is highlighted by way of two civil rights case studies alleging false arrest, excessive use force, and illegal stop, search, and seizure.

Constitutional Policing and Freedom of Speech

Freedom of speech is the first right in the Bill of Rights, and it is this right that should be held in high esteem and utilized when describing constitutional policing. Freedom of speech should be exercised and not viewed as a challenge of authority when the detained civilian asks why he or she is being stopped. For example, when police detain a person, the arrested person should feel empowered to ask, "Why am I being stopped" without the threat of negative repercussions. This question should not translate to the detaining officer that his or her authority is being challenged. Rather, the detained civilian warrants an informative communication. Officers should be respectful in their contact regardless of the detained person's display of intolerance. The police must understand the experiences of the community they serve to be effective under constitutional policing.

The community has the responsibility of using freedom of speech in a manner that is respectful. Hostile communication can lead to hostile physical interaction. Respectful communication, however, should be acknowledged and reciprocated. I understand that when people are detained, fear, anxiety, frustration, and anger can reveal themselves in the tone of the communication with police. I also acknowledge that fear and anxiety (justified or not) can be revealed in the tone communicated by the police to the detained. But the police are the professionals, and it is their responsibility to endeavor to understand any and all communication that is the exercising of the constitutional right of free speech, which is not a crime.

The community's responsibility is to be tolerant toward the police and their duty to keep our communities safe because Black and Brown communities want their communities to be safe.

The abuses, deaths, rallies, and protests witnessed nationwide are not criminals hiding behind the Constitution but hardworking, law-abiding people, for the most part, trying to live their best life. Still, when confronted by the police, the encounters may turn tragic.

Police accountability is the best solution to ensure police are not violating citizens' constitutional rights such as freedom of speech.

The New York Civilian Complaint Review Board (CCRB) was established in 1993 by the then first African-American mayor, David Dinkins. The CCRB's mission is to review complaints of police misconduct and make recommendations as to disciplinary actions. The CCRB is the oversight agency of the New York City Police Department (NYPD) and is tasked with the investigation, mediation, and prosecution of complaints of misconduct on the part of the NYPD and its police officers.[4] The CCRB consists of civilians who are defined as non-police employees but often include retired police officers or law enforcement members.[5]

The CCRB, although not perfect, is a proven approach to ensure some level of police accountability not governed by the police itself such as the Internal Affairs Bureau. CCRB disciplinary hearings are public, which displays some transparency to the Black and Brown communities. Some cases are mediated or resolved by way of negotiated admission.

For communities and jurisdictions that do not have an independent oversight agency, you should engage your local and national politicians to create an oversight agency or provide access to the police department leadership to secure police accountability.

Quota Policing and Its Conflicts with Constitutional Policing

We need to recognize that one of the motivations for unlawful police detentions is quotas. Quota policing encourages police officers to detain those in the community in hopes of issuing a summons or effectuating arrests to meet a certain number of arrests for the year to advance an officer's career within the police department. The eradication of actual and de facto quotas within the institution of policing is a necessary step toward reform and constitutional policing.

Quotas used within policing serve to prod police officers to increase their activity while on patrol as opposed to good policing to decrease violence and/or major crimes. Increased activity such as detentions and issuance of summons, regarding quality of life offenses, does not decrease major crimes or crimes of violence or make the community patrolled feel safer. Rather, quotas serve to annoy the patrolled community because the detentions and issuance of summons are not viewed as good police work and raise the question of the utilization of tax dollars that pay the salaries of the police.[6]

A review of the Department of Justice Ferguson Report (a report examining policing in Ferguson, Missouri) revealed that quotas in policing exist mostly to support the economy by way of fines and court fees. The Illinois police Labor Counsel recognized that quotas in policing create an unnecessary tension between the public and law enforcement.[7]

New York, Illinois, and Texas have denounced quota-based policing. However, the denouncing of its existence does little to eradicate quota-based policing because quotas are often disguised as activity goals within the police department. These activity goals can force police to manufacture an arrest to meet that activity goal. An example of an activity goal was New York City's "stop and frisk" policy. The intent was to reduce the illegal possession of weapons and as a result reduce violent crimes. The implementation was quota based and encouraged racial profiling.

The implementation was grounded on how many people an officer could stop to create stop and frisk reports and/or arrest for minor crimes or no crime at all because the people detained did not possess illegal weapons.[8]

Quota-based policing is in violation of constitutional policing because it violates a citizen's Fourth Amendment right against illegal search and seizure of one's person and property.[9]

One solution to limit quota-based policing is to consistently review the implementation of activity goals within the police department from the lens of intent verses impact/implementation. The question that must always be asked is, is the implementation of this policy/goal driven by numbers? If the answer is yes, the policy is number driven, then the policy is quota based and violates constitutional policing.

Law Enforcement Trends That Are Obstacles to Constitutional Policing

I have often described three other tendencies of law enforcement officers that police departments nationwide should eliminate if the goal is to obtain constitutional policing. The broad brush categories are classism, prejudice, and power.

The classist officer's conduct is grounded in classism/economics. Simply put, when policing poor communities compared to affluent neighborhoods, the policing style changes. Abuse of the voiceless in poor communities is far more likely to occur than abuse/misconduct in wealthy neighborhoods. Constitutional policing does not shift based on the detained civilian's social-economic class. Police departments need to study how classism affects the decision-making of patrolling officers. By recognizing the effects of classism on the decision-making of police officers, police academies can speak to this bias and implement training concerning the same.

Class and race are interwoven in America, so you must address them together when defining constitutional policing. As stated, the eradication of classism is necessary to achieve constitutional policing, and that also means the eradication of racism as it relates to policing. The reality is that the lower you are on the economic scale, the higher the probability that you are a person of color.[10] Therefore, if we accept the this as a fact, and we should, then we can achieve constitutional policing by examining how police professionalism changes based on social-economic status. We can examine how hostile, violent, and sometimes deadly force is used in underserved/poor communities related to Black and Brown civilians.

We must admit that police misconduct happens primarily to Black and Brown people and within Black and Brown communities.[11] Thus, racism must be eradicated within policing, and consistent examining and reexamining of law enforcement officers and candidates for the police academy are necessary.

We must admit that not everyone who applies to become a police officer should be a police officer. There are some people who just cannot manage power appropriately. Hence, you have the abuse of power within policing. The admission that many are called but only a few are chosen should be the motto used regarding the selection of those chosen to serve as the guardians of our communities. I contend that psychological evaluations would be useful in determining who is fit to handle the power bestowed on police officers. Continuing evaluations are necessary to ensure the police do not become jaded because of their profession and become abusive to the community they are to protect and serve.

Abuse of authority is the violation label by the NYPD CCRB when a police officer has abused his or her power. The misuse of power by the police in Black and Brown communities has created resentment and mistrust. Resentment is created as a result of the offending officer's abuse of power because people of color are certain that if they were white, they would not be mistreated, disrespected, or verbally/physically abused.[12]

The abuse of power is usually dehumanizing, such as an unwarranted search and seizure, use of handcuffs, excessive force, or verbal abuse such as being ordered to be quiet, sarcasm, or unwanted comments about parenting or style of dress.

Abuse of power has no place in constitutional policing. Constitutional policing looks to quash dehumanizing behavior that results from abuse of power.

There are all too many real-life examples that show how classism, prejudice, and power inhibit constitutional policing and lead to violations of civilians' constitutional and civil rights, often with severe consequences for those civilians.

D.J. and J.J. v. The City of New York, cited below, is a case I litigated and where I managed all phases. I secured the dismissal of all the criminal matters and settled the civil rights, false arrest, and police brutality lawsuits. This case highlights classism and abuse of power within policing.

Case Study: Classism and Abuse of Power in Policing

A review of the police's conduct in the case of D.J. and J.J. v. The City of New York revealed that when the police are misinformed about civilian rights, misconduct will undoubtedly occur. This case highlighted the involved officers' lack of knowledge of the law, lack of humanity, and abusive conduct—"the use of excessive force." The abuse/use of excessive force, lack of humanity, and false arrest of D.J. and J.J. directly result from the involved officers' ignorance of civilian rights or total disregard for those rights.

In this case, plaintiff J.J. observed the arrest of a neighbor. During this arrest, J.J. began recording the officers' conduct toward the neighbor who was being detained. J.J. was ordered to stop recording; he stated he knew his rights and had the right to record. The officers responded by turning on their flashlights and shinning them directly into J.J.'s cell phone, which he was using to record. J.J. was also ordered to stand back. J.J. was approximately 20 feet or more from the detention. He was ordered several times to stand back, and each time he complied. J.J. complied with the officers' orders until his back was pressed against the gate of his building and he had nowhere to retreat. The detention was being performed in the middle of the street, which consisted of four lanes of traffic. J.J. was not preventing or obstructing the officers' ability to perform their duties. Given J.J.'s conduct of merely recording, there was no reason for the present officers to feel unsafe.

Contemporaneously, D.J., J.J.'s elderly mother, who was legally blind in one eye and walking with the aid of a walker,

Nationally, we can reflect on the wrongful death of George Floyd and how he died at the hands of the police. Once again, race, class, and abuse of power are the foundation for mistreatment.

The police failed to adhere to their protocols and displayed the inability to investigate, de-escalate, and act with humanity appropriately in the above cases. In both cases, the involved officers failed to call the Emergency Service Unit (ESU) to assist in their investigation. Had they requested the assistance of the ESU, I submit that neither Kawaski nor Ramarley would have died. The police failed to isolate and contain them, given they alleged Kawaski and Ramarley possessed deadly weapons. Police protocol dictates that officers are to isolate and stop the assailant from injuring others and then proceed to de-escalate. The involved officers in both cases failed to follow their police protocol; instead, they illegally entered both apartments, placing themselves in danger. As a result of their negligence, two people are dead.

If the above is acknowledged and/or accepted by law enforcement agencies, then we can find our way back to community policing/humanity policing.

The above case studies underscore that police misconduct most often occurs with no disciplinary actions against the offending officers. Therefore, the misconduct is revisited again and again. In New York, police officers are guided by the NYPD Patrol Guide. The Patrol Guide should serve to prevent misconduct, yet it rarely does. For example, section 208-03 of the guide states that civilians have the right to film police as they perform their duties. Nonetheless, police officers routinely violate this guideline or create alternatives to it to effectuate a false arrest. This is demonstrated by the officer in the D.J. and J.J. v. The City of New York lawsuit where the officer insisted that plaintiff J.J. stand back, although J.J. was sufficiently distant from the offending officer. The more vigorously the Internal Affairs Bureau within the NYPD prosecutes/punishes offending officers as to minor infractions, the less likely the officers will be to commit misconduct that results in death.

I assert that the reason why misconduct/abuse of power reoccurs is because there is a lack of accountability. Without accountability/consequences, the Patrol Guide is useless and meaningless.

Positive Steps toward Constitutional Policing

Other factors can assist in achieving constitutional policing, such as proper accountability for officers found liable for misconduct. Genuine accountability means financial accountability where a percentage of any settlement or trial (1–2 percent of the settlement/award) is directly paid by the liable officer.

If the NYPD itself will not hold offending officers accountable, then the responsibility falls on the community to push local and state officials to legislate other ways to hold offending police officers accountable such as personal financial liability. The chilling effect of personal financial liability would certainly quash police misconduct. No consequences, no change.

Another factor that can bring about constitutional policing in the context of community policing is residency requirements—fostering an environment where law enforcement is part of the community they serve. An environment where patrolling police reside in the community affords police the opportunity to engage and know the community they protect and serve in a humanistic way. This personal connection will prevent crime by mere presence and facilitate the free flow of information that could potentially prevent crime.

Community Engagement

Over the years, I have seen the rise of civic and community engagement. Community engagement is necessary to establish constitutional policing. Communication is paramount in achieving constitutional policing. Communication serves to build trust and tolerance while reducing tragedy within a community,[19] trust by launching a new norm, meaning police and civilians talk while the officer is patrolling. The conversation should not be police related, such as, "How are you doing?" or "Did you see the game last night?" It sounds corny or elementary, but that is where we need to start. By way of communication, the community at large will grow to be tolerant of the police and the duties of policing. By way of communication, trust and the understanding of perspectives are established.

Communication should not only exist when grievances need to be filed at police or a district community meeting or when the community is grieving because of police misconduct. Communication has to be at the forefront of everyone's mind to establish the parameters for constitutional policing. A successful relationship is built on communication. Constitutional policing requires communication to achieve safe communities.

All communities want to be safe and enjoy a police presence. The question presented is what does safe mean, and what does a police presence looks like. Safe means more community control within the community and more community involvement in policing themselves. A police presence is flexible depending on the community's needs. It is the total investment of all parties involved, not policing by occupying presence or exercise of force when called upon for protection. Some police departments have recognized the complete community investment approach by working with organizations to decrease gun violence within specific communities. Police departments are now availing themselves to having social workers assist in policing when managing a person with mental and emotional challenges. I submit, presently, policing is more focused on what police can do legally, not what police should do professionally and morally.

A Commitment to Equal Justice under Law

Constitutional policing understands the law related to litigating cases concerning false arrest, police brutality, and wrongful death.

The aim of constitutional policing is not to see how far the law allows officers to go in achieving a particular law enforcement goal. Constitutional policing understands the law, protects peoples' constitutional rights, and seeks true social justice. How the law and more significant societal concerns over the legitimacy of police action should inform constitutional policing is exemplified in recent court rulings on law enforcement use of force and recent incidents involving officer use of force across the country. The aggressive policing of people of color has led to incidents such as the deaths of Breonna Taylor, George Floyd, and Daunte Wright and spurred mass protests. The size of the demonstrations has highlighted a national outcry to change policing and aggressive police tactics, and a call for greater accountability of law enforcement. Additionally, further galvanizing the protest movement were the police responses to mass protests in cities such as Washington, D.C., New York, Los Angeles, and Minneapolis, where police engaged in mass arrests and used aggressive policing to control crowds. For many protestors, the police brutality incidents they had been protesting became all too real, as they too became the targets of aggressive policing.

As mentioned above, law enforcement must understand the law to ensure constitutional policing in the first instance. This is essential in police use of force cases, as the law will dictate when, how, and what officers can do in given situations. This is exemplified in the Supreme Court's recent decision in *Torres v. Madrid*.[20] In the case in New Mexico, officers, while executing a search warrant, approached Roxanne Torres as she was standing by her car. Although the officers wanted to ascertain Ms. Torres's identity, she was not the subject of the warrant. The officers attempted to speak to Ms. Torres as she got into the driver's seat. Ms. Torres thought the officers were carjackers, so she tried to drive off. The officers shot at the car to stop its escape and hit Ms. Torres twice in the back. Ms. Torres drove from the scene and went to the hospital. She was eventually arrested for crimes related to the event. Ms. Torres then later filed a lawsuit against the officers alleging excessive force and claiming that the officers violated her Fourth Amendment right against unreasonable seizures. Among the issues the Court considered was when a person is "seized" within the Fourth Amendment's meaning. The Court held that "application of physical force to the body of a person with the intent to restrain is a seizure" within the meaning of the Fourth Amendment, "even if the force does not succeed in subduing the person." Notably, the Court found that when there is police action similar to what occurred in *Torres*, police action qualifies as a seizure and will be subject to the Fourth Amendment's limits on the use of force. Thus, using police use of force cases as an example, constitutional policing will require that law enforcement agencies understand whenever they use force with the intent to seize a suspect, they must be conscientious in their exercise of force as it may violate an individual's rights.

Awareness of Social Justice

However, constitutional policing is not simply policing with an awareness of the law but also policing that seeks to achieve social justice. This circumstance is perhaps best illustrated in the mass arrests and aggressive use of force by the police in the protests that occurred in Washington, D.C., after the George Floyd incident and the lawsuit brought by protesters in the U.S. District Court for the District of Columbia in *B.L.M. v. Trump*.[21] In that lawsuit, the plaintiff protestors, among other things, alleged that excessive force was used against them when, following an order to clear Lafayette Square from Attorney General Barr, military, local, and federal police forces used tear gas, pepper spray capsules, rubber bullets, and flash bombs to disperse them to clear the path for President Trump to walk to nearby St. John's Church. Of relevance here, defendant the District of Columbia's Metropolitan Police Department argued that their use of force did not violate the Fourth Amendment as the officers had not seized protestors when they fired tear gas at them. There was no clearly established law governing their conduct. The court agreed that there was no clearly established right concerning whether tear gas to move members of a crowd can constitute a seizure and dismissed the excessive force claim against the municipal defendants.

Using this case as an example, constitutional policing that only considers the law would ignore the public outcry over the aggressive police tactics that characterized the events. And importantly, law enforcement would lose its legitimacy, the trust of the people, and concomitantly its perceived authority. Indeed, constitutional policing in this circumstance would require law enforcement to reexamine its actions in the context of more significant societal concerns over aggressive policing and seek to develop different police tactics that will gain the acceptance of the community as a whole.

Importantly, constitutional policing abides by the law and recognizes that to increase the legitimacy of police departments in our communities, police practices that engender continuing controversy or that impact segments of society differently should be discussed. Law enforcement must be open to changing techniques that are no longer perceived as legitimate in Black and Brown communities.

Conclusion

As stated previously, quotas, racial profiling, implicit bias, classism, prejudice, abuse of power, and lack of accountability and humanity all prevent constitutional policing from becoming a reality. A concerted effort is needed to eradicate classism, quotas, racial profiling, implicit bias, and prejudice within policing. Accountability, responsibility, and meaningful deterrence will be necessary to stop police misconduct. Community policing was and is an effective strategy because it creates trust by way of positive presence and communication among the police and the community. If we can extract the positive communication and community relations and interweave them with constitutional policing where the constitutional rights of the community are not only acknowledged but also respected, society would be better served.

I submit that to achieve constitutional policing, as a society, we have to realize we are not suggesting police reform; rather, we are advancing a revolution to policing as it exists. I use the term "revolution" because it embodies the prefixed "re," which reflects and stands for the word "reform," and the term "volution" because it represents the word "evolution." This is warranted to establish constitutional policing: the reform of policing as it now exists, and the evolution of policing to what society demands, thus a "REVOLUTION" of policing as it now exists.

observed the exchange and interaction between J.J. and the police. As she watched the interaction, she eventually called to J.J. The police then slapped J.J.'s cell phone out of his hands and threw him to the ground. They placed their knees in his back as he was tightly handcuffed. J.J. was maced/pepper-sprayed in his eyes and arrested.

D.J. observed the police abuse her son and yelled for them to stop. D.J. was then thrown to the ground, maced/pepper-sprayed, tightly handcuffed, and arrested.

J.J. was criminally charged with assault, disorderly conduct, obstruction of governmental administration, and resisting arrest. D.J. was arrested and criminally charged with disorderly conduct and obstruction of governmental administration.

The criminal charges faced by the plaintiffs are relevant because they were the start of the false narrative used by the police to cover up their misconduct. The conduct they conspired to cover up is the abuse of power, false arrest, and use of force on D.J. and J.J. All of the officers present failed to intervene when confronted with this misconduct and abuse of power.

Assault is defined as the intent to cause physical injury to another person. A person causes such injury to such person or a third person, or he or she recklessly causes physical injury to another person. Based on the presented facts, that did not occur.[13]

Disorderly conduct is defined as conduct with intent to cause public inconvenience, annoyance, or alarm or recklessly creating a risk thereof. Examples include the following:

1. A person engages in fighting or violent, tumultuous, or threatening behavior.
2. A person makes unreasonable noise.
3. In a public place, a person uses abusive or obscene language or makes an obscene gesture.
4. Without lawful authority, a person disturbs any lawful assembly or meeting of persons.
5. A person obstructs vehicular or pedestrian traffic.
6. A person congregates with other persons in a public place and refuses to comply with a lawful order of the police to disperse.

7. A person creates a hazardous or physically offensive condition by any act that serves no legitimate purpose.[14]

Based on the presented facts, that did not occur.

Obstruction of governmental administration is defined as intentionally obstructing, impairing, or preventing the administration of the law or other governmental function or preventing or attempting to prevent a public servant from performing an official function by means of intimidation, physical force, or interference by means of an independent unlawful act. Based on the presented facts, that did not occur.[15]

Resisting arrest is defined as someone intentionally preventing or attempting to prevent a police officer or peace officer from effecting an authorized arrest of him or herself or another person. Based on the presented facts, that did not occur.[16]

After one court appearance, D.J.'s criminal case was dismissed. After eight to ten months of appearing in court, J.J.'s criminal case was dismissed.

Due to the numerous court appearances, J.J. was terminated from his employment.

I will not discuss the overwhelming collateral damage and the mental and emotional damage derived from this miscarriage of justice, but I will state that it is sad, unnecessary, forever lasting, and not constitutional policing.

Under constitutional policing, these officers would have recognized J.J.'s right to record them performing their duties. The First Amendment protects civilians' right to observe and record government officials engaged in public duties. Recordings have been characterized as a form of speech that furthers the First Amendment's interest in protecting and promoting the "Free discussion of governmental affairs."[17]

The Supreme Court has not confronted the issue of whether there is a right to film or record police activity; however, every circuit has ruled such a right exists and is only subjected to reasonable time, place, and manner restrictions. The court in *Turner v. Driver*, 848 F.3d 678, 690 (5th Cir. 2017), stated, "We agree with every circuit that has ruled on this question . . . the First Amendment protects the rights to record the police . . . the filming of governmental officials engaged in their duties in a public place, *including police officers performing their responsibilities, fits comfortably within the basic First Amendment principles."* In *Charles v. City of New York*, 12-CV-6180 (S.L.T.) (S.M.G.), 2017 U.S. Dist. Lexis 17943, at 64–65 (E.D.N.Y. Feb. 8, 2017), the court recognized a First Amendment right to film police.

Recording a detention/arrest is not a criminal offense or violation of any administrative code. Instead, the prevention of such is actually in violation of the New York Police Patrol Guide. Section 208-03 of the guide reads in pertinent part:

> None of the following constitute probable cause for arrest or detention of an onlooker unless the safety of officers or other persons is directly endangered, or the officer reasonably believes they are endangered, or the law is violated:
>
> 1. Speech alone, even though crude and vulgar;
> 2. Requesting and making notes of shields numbers or names of members of the Service;
> 3. Taking photographs, videotapes, or tape recording;
> 4. Remaining in the vicinity of the stop or arrest.

Constitutional policing embodies the police knowing, acknowledging, and adhering to the law and the rights of civilians and their own administrative rules and procedures within their Patrol Guide.

In the instant case, neither D.J. nor J.J. violated the section 208-03. No police officers were endangered; thus, no fear for safety was present. D.J. and J.J. did not commit a crime and only exercised their First Amendment rights. According to their Patrol Guide, the officers committed violations, including falsely arresting D.J. and J.J. Their misconduct was grounded on not knowing the law or a blatant disregard for the law.

Police knowing the law is one of the first and most essential factors in establishing constitutional policing. Police must recognize and respect when civilians exercise the law, specifically Black and Brown people, and not feel threatened. Being threatened by the use of the First Amendment, such as recording police in the D.J. and J.J. matter, resulted in their abuse of power, false arrest, use of excessive force, and inhumane treatment.

As stated previously, the police attempted to prevent J.J. from recording, and he was physically battered and assaulted. D.J. was also physically battered and attacked because she demanded the police stop mistreating her son.

The physical abuse suffered by D.J. and J.J. has no place in constitution policing. Both civilians were maced/pepper-sprayed, thrown to the ground, and tightly handcuffed. This exercise of excessive force directly results from the officers feeling threatened by Black and Brown civilians exercising their rights afforded and protected by the Constitution.

The use of excessive force by police when unpunished is what occurred to J.J. and D.J. This will continue until police are held accountable for their actions. Excessive force in Black and Brown communities is grounded on race, class, and power.

It has been my experience that most victims of police abuse are people of color and lower-income to poor people. Although the people within these communities have mouths, they are voiceless or their voices are being ignored. The lack of accountability created the tragedy endured by D.J. and J.J. The abuse of power, false arrest, and excessive force by the police will always occur if left unpunished.

This incident of excessive force illustrates the lack of humanity that occurs within communities of color daily. Constitutional policing requires humanity. When the police confronted J.J. and D.J., they did not see their brother, friend, or mother because if they did, the treatment toward them and the outcome would have been different.

Humanity affords you the ability to de-escalate and still be effective at policing. Humanity and policing are not in conflict, according to constitutional policing. Humanity may not be taught; however, training and re-training can be used to detect implicit bias and cultural insensitivities.

Constitutional policing does require a mental health component to ensure that abusive people are not employed and/ or trusted to perform the lofty duty to protect and serve. A mandatory mental health evaluation will assist in preventing abuse of power within policing that is perpetrated on civilians in specific communities.

A case study regarding the use of excessive force, detention, and arrest of Z.H. illustrates the impact of classism and prejudice/racial bias (whether implicit or not) within policing that must be recognized and abolished.

Z.H.'s detention was captured on video, and his experience, I submit, reflects incidents of police misconduct suffered by many other Black and Brown people. Z.H. was in a New Jersey mall with alleged friends and classmates. The video depicts him as the only person of color in the group of students with school knapsacks gathered together. You see Z.H. exchange words with a bigger, taller white student during this assembly. Finger-pointing occurs, and Z.H. is pushed. As a result of being pushed, Z.H.'s cell phone drops out of his hand. The two boys begin to fight, at which point the white boy is the aggressor. The video does not show whether the involved officers were present to see the entire altercation or just arrived after the fight commenced.

The involved officers consisted of what appears to be a white female officer and a white male officer. The video shows the two officers running to the scuffle and Z.H. on his back with the bigger, taller white boy on top of him and hitting him. When the officers intervened, the female officer pulled the aggressor off Z.H. and seated him on the couch. She then held his chest as if to see if he was okay. Immediately after that, she assisted her partner, who had his knees on Z.H.'s back and placed him in handcuffs. Z.H. was not depicted resisting the officers. The aggressive white teenager was left unattended and was standing over the officers while saying something to Z.H.

The other kids scattered, but you can hear one kid clearly state that the police are only doing this because Z.H. is black; that's racial profiling.

Constitutional policing recognizes that ill-treatment by police occurs because "the victims of such ill-treatment are BLACK." This concept is not foreign, as expressed by the white high school teenager in the video. Police every day have the opportunity to prove the teenager's statement wrong. Still, I submit the police fail miserably because, as an institution, police departments will not accept the reality that racial profiling, racial biases (implicit or conscious), and prejudice exist within police departments and police.[18]

Z.H.'s negative police encounter occurred because of racial profiling, conscious or implicit bias, and prejudice. Constitutional policing looks to eliminate prejudice police. I submit that psychological examinations accomplish this before a candidate is invited to the police academy and during the tenure of being a police officer. Prejudiced police are police offers who make decisions and arrest based exclusively on race, ethnic, and cultural bases. Psychological testing should be administered to confront racial bias, cultural tendencies and prejudice within policing.

Suppose discrimination or racial bias is not revealed and eliminated. In that case, you will continue to have negative and hostile police encounters and excessive use of force experiences with Black and Brown civilians. Z.H.'s incident occurred in suburban America.

The negative stigma of mental/emotional health evaluations within policing must be abolished to effectuate constitutional policing. We all have biases and prejudices. Police are people too, so how would it be possible that they are immune from racial discrimination and prejudice? How do their actions based on bias/prejudice make them immune from accountability?

Had the police acted with de-escalation and humanity in mind, they would have just separated the two teens and questioned them about the cause of the altercation. The police would have discovered that Z.H. was intervening on behalf of a younger student being bullied by the taller, bigger, and more aggressive white student. I contend that with this information, the involved officers would have conducted themselves differently.

If these officers saw Z.H. as their child or just a child, they would have acted like referees in a basketball game looking to de-escalate at the very least and as parents trying to mend a relationship between the two teenage boys. Instead, I assert they saw only race, and their racial bias led to the tragic negative encounter.

Once again, constitutional policing requires humanity.

The Z.H. incident and the D.J. and J.J. matter are examples of hostile police encounters that occur daily within Black and Brown communities, resulting in Black and Brown people's disengagement with the legal system. These negative encounters do not support the ambition for people of color to become police officers; instead, they create disdain for the profession.

Under the Constitution, all people should invoke their role and rights in society. No race, gender, or culture should be systematically disengaged with the legal system because of the negative encounters they endured related to police. There cannot exist a jury of your peers if certain groups of people are not wholly participating or exercising their rights within the legal system.

I chose to highlight these two real-life instances because they reflect most of the misconduct in Black and Brown communities. The extremes related to police misconduct are the wrongful death cases that present many issues stemming from racial profiling, classism, abuse of power, and lawlessness with no accountability.

The Z.H. incident speaks to the abuse of power that results in dehumanizing behavior. The dehumanizing behavior in this instance was the excessive force used on a kid, a teenager who was defending someone else from being bullied. The dehumanization of Z.H. started with how the abusive officers viewed him. The officers viewed Z.H. as a villain or enemy, not as their kid, relative, or teenager in a minor scuffle.

The Wrongful Deaths of Kawaski Trawick and Ramarley Graham: The Impact of Racial Bias, Classism, and the Lack of Humanity within Policing

In the case of the wrongful death of Kawaski Trawick for which I am counsel, prejudice, classism, racial bias, lack of accountability, and lack of humanity are front and center.

It should be noted that the involved NYPD officers have not been held accountable by way of an internal police investigation, and the NYPD position is that the officers involved were justified in their actions.

Kawaski was asserting his First Amendment right, freedom of speech, when repeatedly asking why the police were in his apartment at the time of his death. And at the time of his death, he was asserting his Fourth Amendment right to be secure in his person and house, to be secure against unreasonable search and seizure.

In the wrongful death case of Kawaski Trawick, the police officers' conduct was lawless and egregious. In this case, police illegally entered Kawaski's apartment while he was cooking and yelled and ordered him to put down the knife he was using to cook. Confused and in response to the yelling, Kawaski yelled back for the police to get out of his apartment. He also asked why they were in his apartment. The officers never responded to his question. This encounter resulted in Kawaski's death despite one officer ordering the other officer not to use force, that being a taser. This order was ignored, and Kawaski was shot dead.

It should be noted the experienced officer is Black, and he ordered his less experienced officer, who is white, not to use force.

The police conduct was rooted in racial bias, classism, and lack of humanity. I assert you will never learn of police illegally entering a house in the suburbs where the white occupant is home alone cooking in his or her kitchen, resulting in death.

Constitutional policing recognizes this tragedy as a direct result of racial bias, classism, abuse of power, and lack of accountability. However, the police department has adopted the position that this tragedy was the result of a lack of communication while at the same time vilifying Kawaski.

In the Ramarley Graham wrongful death case, police once again entered illegally into an apartment. This illegal entry resulted in the shooting death of Ramarley in front of his grandmother and six-year-old brother. It was alleged that Ramarley reached for a weapon, but no gun was ever recovered. The police once again created a scenario for which they used deadly force. I submit that racism, classism, abuse of power, lack of accountability, and lack of humanity led to Ramarley's death.

Nationally, we can reflect on the wrongful death of George Floyd and how he died at the hands of the police. Once again, race, class, and abuse of power are the foundation for mistreatment.

The police failed to adhere to their protocols and displayed the inability to investigate, de-escalate, and act with humanity appropriately in the above cases. In both cases, the involved officers failed to call the Emergency Service Unit (ESU) to assist in their investigation. Had they requested the assistance of the ESU, I submit that neither Kawaski nor Ramarley would have died. The police failed to isolate and contain them, given they alleged Kawaski and Ramarley possessed deadly weapons. Police protocol dictates that officers are to isolate and stop the assailant from injuring others and then proceed to de-escalate. The involved officers in both cases failed to follow their police protocol; instead, they illegally entered both apartments, placing themselves in danger. As a result of their negligence, two people are dead.

If the above is acknowledged and/or accepted by law enforcement agencies, then we can find our way back to community policing/humanity policing.

The above case studies underscore that police misconduct most often occurs with no disciplinary actions against the offending officers. Therefore, the misconduct is revisited again and again. In New York, police officers are guided by the NYPD Patrol Guide. The Patrol Guide should serve to prevent misconduct, yet it rarely does. For example, section 208-03 of the guide states that civilians have the right to film police as they perform their duties. Nonetheless, police officers routinely violate this guideline or create alternatives to it to effectuate a false arrest. This is demonstrated by the officer in the D.J. and J.J. v. The City of New York lawsuit where the officer insisted that plaintiff J.J. stand back, although J.J. was sufficiently distant from the offending officer. The more vigorously the Internal Affairs Bureau within the NYPD prosecutes/punishes offending officers as to minor infractions, the less likely the officers will be to commit misconduct that results in death.

I assert that the reason why misconduct/abuse of power reoccurs is because there is a lack of accountability. Without accountability/consequences, the Patrol Guide is useless and meaningless.

Positive Steps toward Constitutional Policing

Other factors can assist in achieving constitutional policing, such as proper accountability for officers found liable for misconduct. Genuine accountability means financial accountability where a percentage of any settlement or trial (1–2 percent of the settlement/award) is directly paid by the liable officer.

If the NYPD itself will not hold offending officers accountable, then the responsibility falls on the community to push local and state officials to legislate other ways to hold offending police officers accountable such as personal financial liability. The chilling effect of personal financial liability would certainly quash police misconduct. No consequences, no change.

Another factor that can bring about constitutional policing in the context of community policing is residency requirements—fostering an environment where law enforcement is part of the community they serve. An environment where patrolling police reside in the community affords police the opportunity to engage and know the community they protect and serve in a humanistic way. This personal connection will prevent crime by mere presence and facilitate the free flow of information that could potentially prevent crime.

Community Engagement

Over the years, I have seen the rise of civic and community engagement. Community engagement is necessary to establish constitutional policing. Communication is paramount in achieving constitutional policing. Communication serves to build trust and tolerance while reducing tragedy within a community,[19] trust by launching a new norm, meaning police and civilians talk while the officer is patrolling. The conversation should not be police related, such as, "How are you doing?" or "Did you see the game last night?" It sounds corny or elementary, but that is where we need to start. By way of communication, the community at large will grow to be tolerant of the police and the duties of policing. By way of communication, trust and the understanding of perspectives are established.

Communication should not only exist when grievances need to be filed at police or a district community meeting or when the community is grieving because of police misconduct. Communication has to be at the forefront of everyone's mind to establish the parameters for constitutional policing. A successful relationship is built on communication. Constitutional policing requires communication to achieve safe communities.

All communities want to be safe and enjoy a police presence. The question presented is what does safe mean, and what does a police presence looks like. Safe means more community control within the community and more community involvement in policing themselves. A police presence is flexible depending on the community's needs. It is the total investment of all parties involved, not policing by occupying presence or exercise of force when called upon for protection. Some police departments have recognized the complete community investment approach by working with organizations to decrease gun violence within specific communities. Police departments are now availing themselves to having social workers assist in policing when managing a person with mental and emotional challenges. I submit, presently, policing is more focused on what police can do legally, not what police should do professionally and morally.

A Commitment to Equal Justice under Law

Constitutional policing understands the law related to litigating cases concerning false arrest, police brutality, and wrongful death.

The aim of constitutional policing is not to see how far the law allows officers to go in achieving a particular law enforcement goal. Constitutional policing understands the law, protects peoples' constitutional rights, and seeks true social justice. How the law and more significant societal concerns over the legitimacy of police action should inform constitutional policing is exemplified in recent court rulings on law enforcement use of force and recent incidents involving officer use of force across the country. The aggressive policing of people of color has led to incidents such as the deaths of Breonna Taylor, George Floyd, and Daunte Wright and spurred mass protests. The size of the demonstrations has highlighted a national outcry to change policing and aggressive police tactics, and a call for greater accountability of law enforcement. Additionally, further galvanizing the protest movement were the police responses to mass protests in cities such as Washington, D.C., New York, Los Angeles, and Minneapolis, where police engaged in mass arrests and used aggressive policing to control crowds. For many protestors, the police brutality incidents they had been protesting became all too real, as they too became the targets of aggressive policing.

As mentioned above, law enforcement must understand the law to ensure constitutional policing in the first instance. This is essential in police use of force cases, as the law will dictate when, how, and what officers can do in given situations. This is exemplified in the Supreme Court's recent decision in *Torres v. Madrid*.[20] In the case in New Mexico, officers, while executing a search warrant, approached Roxanne Torres as she was standing by her car. Although the officers wanted to ascertain Ms. Torres's identity, she was not the subject of the warrant. The officers attempted to speak to Ms. Torres as she got into the driver's seat. Ms. Torres thought the officers were carjackers, so she tried to drive off. The officers shot at the car to stop its escape and hit Ms. Torres twice in the back. Ms. Torres drove from the scene and went to the hospital. She was eventually arrested for crimes related to the event. Ms. Torres then later filed a lawsuit against the officers alleging excessive force and claiming that the officers violated her Fourth Amendment right against unreasonable seizures. Among the issues the Court considered was when a person is "seized" within the Fourth Amendment's meaning. The Court held that "application of physical force to the body of a person with the intent to restrain is a seizure" within the meaning of the Fourth Amendment, "even if the force does not succeed in subduing the person." Notably, the Court found that when there is police action similar to what occurred in *Torres*, police action qualifies as a seizure and will be subject to the Fourth Amendment's limits on the use of force. Thus, using police use of force cases as an example, constitutional policing will require that law enforcement agencies understand whenever they use force with the intent to seize a suspect, they must be conscientious in their exercise of force as it may violate an individual's rights.

Awareness of Social Justice

However, constitutional policing is not simply policing with an awareness of the law but also policing that seeks to achieve social justice. This circumstance is perhaps best illustrated in the mass arrests and aggressive use of force by the police in the protests that occurred in Washington, D.C., after the George Floyd incident and the lawsuit brought by protesters in the U.S. District Court for the District of Columbia in *B.L.M. v. Trump*.[21] In that lawsuit, the plaintiff protestors, among other things, alleged that excessive force was used against them when, following an order to clear Lafayette Square from Attorney General Barr, military, local, and federal police forces used tear gas, pepper spray capsules, rubber bullets, and flash bombs to disperse them to clear the path for President Trump to walk to nearby St. John's Church. Of relevance here, defendant the District of Columbia's Metropolitan Police Department argued that their use of force did not violate the Fourth Amendment as the officers had not seized protestors when they fired tear gas at them. There was no clearly established law governing their conduct. The court agreed that there was no clearly established right concerning whether tear gas to move members of a crowd can constitute a seizure and dismissed the excessive force claim against the municipal defendants.

Using this case as an example, constitutional policing that only considers the law would ignore the public outcry over the aggressive police tactics that characterized the events. And importantly, law enforcement would lose its legitimacy, the trust of the people, and concomitantly its perceived authority. Indeed, constitutional policing in this circumstance would require law enforcement to reexamine its actions in the context of more significant societal concerns over aggressive policing and seek to develop different police tactics that will gain the acceptance of the community as a whole.

Importantly, constitutional policing abides by the law and recognizes that to increase the legitimacy of police departments in our communities, police practices that engender continuing controversy or that impact segments of society differently should be discussed. Law enforcement must be open to changing techniques that are no longer perceived as legitimate in Black and Brown communities.

Conclusion

As stated previously, quotas, racial profiling, implicit bias, classism, prejudice, abuse of power, and lack of accountability and humanity all prevent constitutional policing from becoming a reality. A concerted effort is needed to eradicate classism, quotas, racial profiling, implicit bias, and prejudice within policing. Accountability, responsibility, and meaningful deterrence will be necessary to stop police misconduct. Community policing was and is an effective strategy because it creates trust by way of positive presence and communication among the police and the community. If we can extract the positive communication and community relations and interweave them with constitutional policing where the constitutional rights of the community are not only acknowledged but also respected, society would be better served.

I submit that to achieve constitutional policing, as a society, we have to realize we are not suggesting police reform; rather, we are advancing a revolution to policing as it exists. I use the term "revolution" because it embodies the prefixed "re," which reflects and stands for the word "reform," and the term "volution" because it represents the word "evolution." This is warranted to establish constitutional policing: the reform of policing as it now exists, and the evolution of policing to what society demands, thus a "REVOLUTION" of policing as it now exists.

Endnotes

1. *See* Police Executive Research Forum, Constitutional Policing as a Cornerstone of Community Policing: A Report by Police Executive Forum (2015), https://cops.usdoj.gov/ric/Publications/cops-p324-pub.pdf.

2. *See id.*

3. *See id.*

4. *See Civilian Complaint Review Board*, City of New York, https://www.nyc.gov/site/ccrb/index.page.

5. *See id.*

6. *See* Shaun Ossei-Owusu, *Race and Tragedy of Quota-Based Policing*, The American Prospect (Nov. 3, 2016), https://prospect.org/justice/race-tragedy-quota-based-policing/; Arthur G. Sharp, *Quota by Any Other Name*, 53(12) Law and Order 14 (2005).

7. Ossei-Owusu, *supra* note 6; Sharp, *supra* note 6.

8. *See* Floyd v. City of New York et al., 959 F. Supp. 2d 540 (S.D.N.Y. 2013). Ossei-Owusu, *supra* note 6; Sharp, *supra* note 6.

9. *Floyd*, 959 F. Supp. 2d 540; Gerwer v. Kelly 980 N.Y.S.2d 275 (Sup. Ct. 2013); John Marzulli, *We Fabricated Drug Charges against Innocent People to Meet Arrest Quotas, Former Detectives Testifies*, NY Daily News (Oct. 13, 2011)

10. Robert O. Motley, Jr. & Sean Joe, *Police Use of Force by Ethnicity, Sex, and Socioeconomic Class*, 9(1) J. Soc. Social Work and Res. 46 (2018), https://www.journals.uchicago.edu/doi/pdf/10.1086/696355.

11. *Id.*; Andre Haley & Kwan Lamar Blount-Hill, *Race and Police Misconduct Cases*, Oxford Research Encyclopedia of Criminology (2021), https://doi.org/10.1093/acrefore/9780190264079.013.703.

12. *See* Albor Ruiz, *A 'Crisis of police abuse' is dehumanizing' communities of color*, NY Daily News (May 4, 2015), https://www.nydailynews.com/new-york/police-abuse-dehumanizing-communities-color-article-1.2205540.

13. *See* N.Y. Consol. Laws, Penal Code § 120.11.

14. *See* N.Y. Consol. Laws, Penal Code.

15. *See id.* § 195.05.

16. *See id.* § 205.30.

17. Gilk v. Cunniffe, 685 F.3d 78, 82 (1st Cir. 2011) (quoting Mills v. Alabama, 384 U.S. 214 (1966)).

18. *See* Motley & Joe, *supra* note 10; *Department of Justice Launches Law Enforcement Knowledge Lab*, U.S. Department of Justice (Apr. 27, 2002), https://www.justice.gov/opa/pr/department-justice-launches-law-enforcement-knowledge-lab.

19. *Importance of Police-Community Relationships and Resources for Further Reading*, U.S. Department of Justice, https://www.justice.gov/file/1437336/download. See H. Oltman, *Police–Community Relations—The Problem and Response*, U.S. Department of Justice, https://www.ncjrs.gov/pdffiles1/Digitization/83306NCJRS.pdf.

20. Torres v. Madrid, 141 S. Ct. 989 (2021).

21. B.L.M. v. Trump, 2021 U.S. Dist. Lexis 114699.

PART II

Effecting Positive Changes toward a More Perfect Union

Chapter 5

Contemporary Civilian Oversight of Law Enforcement

Sharon R. Fairley

Prior to 2014, Ferguson, Missouri, was relatively unknown outside of the greater St. Louis metropolitan area. That all changed after a young Black man, Michael Brown, was shot and killed by police in what had previously been a relatively quiet suburban enclave with fewer than 25,000 residents. Brown's killing was not an isolated incident; rather, it was just one in a series of tragic events involving police violence. But it sparked indignation, forcing a conversation about policing on the national stage. For many Americans, the tragic, fatal encounter created a sense of urgency around the need for police reform. Activism behind police reform erupted in American cities, both large and small.

Eager to find a way to channel the activism into progressive action, in December 2014, then President Obama issued an executive order creating the President's Task Force on 21st Century Policing. The president assembled several of the country's foremost experts on law enforcement and criminal justice and charged them with identifying best practices and recommendations for fighting crime while also rebuilding public trust. But he gave them a mere 90 days in which to do it—a tall order, indeed. The 11-member panel quickly set about its work, convening seven times and holding listening sessions across the country. Having been given such a short runway for its work, the Task Force set off to define the critical issues undermining police-community relations by challenging whether many of the long-held assumptions about what makes for effective policing remain relevant and accurate. In May 2015, the Task Force issued its final report laying out 156 recommendations to guide the nation's more than 18,000 federal, state, and local law enforcement agencies.[1]

Some recommendations were quite specific, such as the need for specific types of training, making it easier to identify those recommendations that have since been accepted and implemented by law enforcement agencies. Others were more aspirational. For example, the Task Force recommended that "law enforcement culture should embrace a guardian mindset to build public trust and legitimacy," a cultural shift that is not easily measured.[2] These broader strategic and institutional reforms continue to represent a significant challenge for many law enforcement organizations as they push directly against long-standing norms, resource constraints, and bureaucratic hurdles.[3]

The president's Task Force organized its recommendations around six "pillars" or topic areas: building trust and legitimacy, policy and oversight, technology and social media, community policing and crime reduction, officer training and education, and officer safety and wellness. The Task Force report addressed the issue of civilian oversight of law enforcement under the second pillar, policy and oversight. More specifically, Task Force recommendation #2.8 states:

> Some form of civilian oversight of law enforcement is important in order to strengthen trust with the community. Every community should define the appropriate form and structure of civilian oversight to meet the needs of that community.[4]

The Task Force also directed the Department of Justice to add civilian oversight to its research agenda and to provide technical assistance for cities seeking to create or improve their civilian oversight structures.[5]

Reaction to the Task Force's recommendation—that every community should have civilian oversight in some form—among the law enforcement community was lukewarm at best. The Major Cities Chiefs Association published a report that complained of a lack of evidence supporting the value of civilian oversight. The report also highlighted anecdotes from across the country about problematic relationships between police chiefs and civilian oversight entities.[6] The report made clear that police chiefs continue to hold fast to their view that civilian oversight entities should not be positioned to undermine the decision-making authority police chiefs hold in disciplinary matters.[7]

The response among city leaders was similarly unenthusiastic. The National League of Cities, an advocacy group representing city officials across the United States, published a guide to policing in the 21st century for city officials.[8] That report's discussion of the president's Task Force recommendation regarding civilian oversight was limited to an expression of the view that the decision to establish a civilian oversight board "rests solely with elected or appointed officials."[9] In the years since that report was issued, it has become quite clear that city officials no longer wield such plenary power over the creation of civilian oversight. Community groups and activists in dozens of U.S. cities have proven capable of garnering public support for civilian oversight sufficient to overcome the objections of recalcitrant city leaders.

A Historical Perspective: The Growth of Civilian Oversight

The concept of using civilians to police the police is by no means a recent phenomenon. By 1911, the Chicago Police Department began using civilians to investigate allegations of police misconduct because the public had lost confidence in the department's ability to hold its own members accountable. Back then, the idea of making civilians responsible for handling complaints about the police was considered by some as quite radical or even dangerous.[10] Yet, by mid-century, the idea had gained sufficient traction to support the formation of the earliest civilian oversight entities in large, urban U.S. jurisdictions such as Washington, D.C., Philadelphia, and New York City.[11]

Early experience with civilian oversight boards was not without its fits and starts. Philadelphia established a review board in

1958 that lasted less than a decade, after which it was scuttled by criticism that it recommended discipline in too few cases.[12] The first incarnation of New York City's Citizen Complaint Board was created in 1966 but survived for only four months.[13]

Nonetheless, the civilian oversight movement took root in the late 1960s and early 1970s, developing in parallel with the civil rights movement.[14] Yet, by the 1980s, civilian oversight remained somewhat rare.[15] By then, most police organizations continued to achieve accountability by creating "internal affairs" divisions or departments to investigate misconduct.[16]

Through the 1980s and 1990s and into the 2000s, there was a slow but steady upward trend in the creation of civilian oversight entities among the larger U.S. cities.[17] The span of 2016 through 2020 proved to be a watershed era in the creation and evolution of civilian oversight across the country. A spate of controversial fatal police encounters from 2014 to 2016 created an inflection point in civilian agency startups. A powerful combination of activism and community engagement around policing issues brought attention to civilian oversight as an important and compelling police reform strategy. Between 2016 and 2020, 35 new civilian oversight entities were created based on research conducted among the largest 100 U.S. cities (by population).[18] In addition, during that same timeframe, changes were made to strengthen the power or structure of 30 of the 76 entities that existed prior to 2016 in the cities studied.[19] The mid-2020 killing of George Floyd sparked an even greater uptick in the creation of civilian oversight entities in 2020 and 2021. During the first half of 2021, an additional eight civilian oversight entities came online.

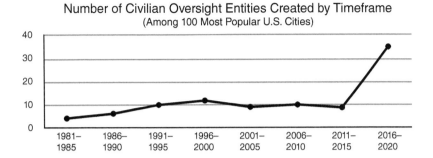

By mid-2021, the prevalence of civilian oversight had increased substantially. A survey identified at least 113 civilian oversight entities operating in 71 of the largest 100 U.S. cities.[20]

Why Has Civilian Oversight Flourished despite a Dearth of Supporting Empirical Evidence?

Civilian oversight has grown and evolved over a period of decades despite the fact that there remains limited evidence that it actually works. In fact, the president's Task Force advocated for civilian oversight while acknowledging the paucity of available empirical evidence proving that it actually improves policing, police accountability, or police-community relations. In fact, since the Task Force recommendation was made, numerous examples of the seeming failure of civilian oversight have emerged. In 2015, when 15-year-old Laquan McDonald was shot and killed by former Chicago police officer Jason Van Dyke, Chicago's civilian investigative agency, the Independent Police Review Authority, had been responsible for investigating officer-involved shooting incidents for over seven years. During that time, the agency had reviewed over 300 incidents, yet it had found only two in which the officers had violated use of force policy or law. In 2020, when George Floyd was killed at the hands of Minneapolis police officer Derek Chauvin, that city's Office of Police Conduct Review had been providing oversight of the Minneapolis Police Department for 30 years. Earlier that year, when Louisville police charged in and fatally shot Breonna Taylor in her own home, the Louisville Citizens Commission on Police Accountability had been reviewing fatal police encounters for almost 20 years.

So why are more and more cities looking to civilian oversight as a key police reform strategy even though it lacks a strong track record? Consider the three examples discussed above. None of the civilian oversight entities operating when these incidents occurred had sufficient power to have a substantive impact on the quality of the policing provided by the agencies they were charged with overseeing. At the time of the killing of Laquan McDonald, Chicago's Independent Police Review Authority was anything but independent. The agency was woefully under-resourced and remained tethered to the Chicago Police Department in important ways. When Breonna Taylor was killed, there was little the Louisville's Citizen's Commission on Police Accountability could do about it. It had no independent investigatory jurisdiction.[21] When George Floyd was killed, the Minneapolis Office of Police Conduct Review was widely viewed as a toothless watchdog. The *Washington Post* reported that, out of more than 3,100 complaints against Minneapolis police officers filed from October 2012 through June 2020, only 16 officers had been disciplined.[22] There is no question that civilian oversight is no panacea to police accountability. However, it would be a mistake to look to these and other historical failures and conclude that civilian oversight is ineffectual.

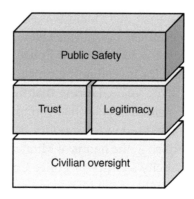

It is important to bear in mind that the goal of civilian oversight is to address some of the most foundational questions of public law such as the balancing of factional power, the prevention of interest group capture, and the promotion of responsive and accountable governance.[23] As authors Rahman and Siminson have noted, the establishment of civilian oversight is the kind of democraticizing reform that can "better enable countervailing interests and community groups to assert their views, to hold government and other actors to account, and to claim a share of governing power."[24] As many proponents of civilian oversight suggest, when citizens have a say in how they are policed they are more likely to see the police as legitimate, which is essential to public safety.[25]

What Do Civilian Oversight Entities Really Do?

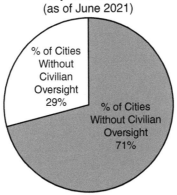

Prevalence of Civilian Oversight Within Top 100 Cities (as of June 2021)

% of Cities Without Civilian Oversight 29%

% of Cities Without Civilian Oversight 71%

Historically, the composition, duties, and powers of civilian oversight entities have varied across jurisdictions. No single approach has been broadly adopted, and most experts would agree that there is no single "right way" to structure a civilian oversight body.[26] Each jurisdiction tends to carve out the combination of duties and responsibilities that are appropriate or necessary given the characteristics of the law enforcement organization being overseen and the needs and desires of the community being served. Legal constraints that vary across local, county, and state lines also impact what oversight entities can and cannot do.

In general, civilian oversight entities are typically empowered with an array of duties and responsibilities related to law enforcement agency policies, procedures, operations, and disciplinary matters. Civilian oversight entities also provide community engagement and transparency regarding policing and police accountability issues.

Civilian Oversight Duties & Responsibilities

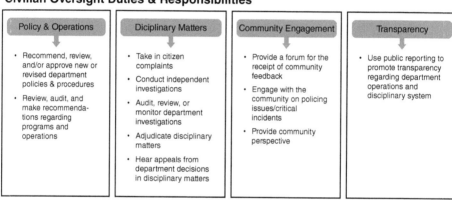

Creating New Civilian Oversight Entities Requires Patience and Perseverance

From its very inception, civilian oversight has typically been born out of intense, emotionally charged, and often politicized debate that has erupted in the wake of a highly publicized incident of police abuse or corruption.[27] Despite their increasing prevalence and longevity, the effectiveness of civilian oversight agencies continues to face pushback on a variety of fronts. Police unions and police leadership organizations almost always oppose the creation or enhancement of civilian oversight.[28] Indeed, in some jurisdictions, police unions have negotiated for provisions that bar or limit the role of civilian oversight in police disciplinary matters.[29]

The law enforcement community tends to focus on two key arguments regarding why placing groups of civilians in positions of power over law enforcement is a bad idea. First, they assume oversight by civilians will have an anti-law enforcement bias. Second, they believe civilians are incapable of fairly and accurately judging the conduct of sworn law enforcement professionals. Other arguments frequently invoked to counter civilian oversight proposals include that civilian oversight (1) undermines department management prerogatives and authority; (2) contributes to hostile police-community relations by focusing on isolated, bad acts by the police; (3) creates a focus on isolated police misconduct that detracts attention from more important policy issues; and (4) unnecessarily duplicates existing remedies for misconduct.[30]

Political leaders are similarly reluctant to embrace civilian oversight. Many public officials raise concerns similar to those voiced by the law enforcement community. In addition, city and county leaders may also be reluctant to share or cede any of their own power over policing policy and operations to an entity beyond their control. Some commentators suggest that the hesitancy around ceding control over policing (and other local government functions for that matter) to an independent body could be based on "an elite suspicion of, and hesitancy with, bottom-up democracy itself," a phenomenon Rahman and Simonson refer to as "demophobia."[31] The demophobe city or county leader may lack trust in the collective judgment of community-based strategic guidance for policing. Or perhaps the official merely views his or her own judgment as superior. It is also possible that political leaders are reluctant to accept civilian oversight because it would require tacit acknowledgment that policing under their leadership had failed in some way. Then there is also the issue of scapegoating. When things go wrong with policing, such as controversial police-citizen encounters or spikes in crime, the blame almost always falls squarely in the laps of political officials. So perhaps political leaders are unwilling to give up control at the risk of being blamed for bad outcomes resulting from strategies they did not own.

Because efforts to create new civilian oversight mechanisms have historically faced pushback from the law enforcement community and political leadership based on the reasoning and arguments above, activism behind the creation of new civilian oversight of law enforcement is not for the faint of heart. In most cases, the creation of civilian oversight requires legislation at the city or county level and may require revisions to city or county charters. Cobbling together a political coalition sufficient to get the required legislation enacted can be quite a challenge. Even when and where this hurdle has been surmounted, the legitimacy and authority of civilian oversight entities are often subject to legal challenge. The following are two recent examples where community groups and police reform activists successfully overcame legal and political obstacles in the creation of civilian oversight.

Civilian Complaint Review Board— Newark, New Jersey

The leaders and citizens of Newark, New Jersey, have demonstrated great perseverance in their decades-long pursuit of civilian oversight for the Newark Police Department. In 2015, Ras Baraka, who took over as mayor of Newark after Cory Booker was elected to the U.S. Senate, issued an executive order creating a new Civilian Complaint Review Board (CCRB), modeled closely on New York City's agency of the same name.[32] The new oversight entity would be the first civilian oversight agency in the state.[33] Just over a year later, the city council passed an ordinance that codified the establishment of the new agency to ensure it would survive Baraka's mayoral administration.[34] As originally envisioned, the CCRB would have significant oversight powers: the use of civilian investigators to conduct independent investigations, the issuance of subpoenas to compel testimony, and the power to make disciplinary recommendations that would be binding on the department barring clear error in findings of fact.[35] Newark's police union, the Fraternal Order of Police (FOP) of Newark Lodge No. 12, immediately challenged the legality of the new board, questioning its authority to influence the outcome of disciplinary matters.[36] The union launched what turned out to be a roller-coaster-like ride through the New Jersey courts as it sought to quash the fledgling agency. In the Superior Court of New Jersey, the union argued that the structure and powers of the CCRB ran afoul of New Jersey statutory and administrative law.[37] More specifically, the union alleged that the CCRB's subpoena power was in conflict with New Jersey law for several reasons, including that (1) the CCRB's ability to conduct independent investigations was inconsistent with the New Jersey Attorney General's guidelines on discipline of police officers, (2) the CCRB's powers deprived officers of due process in violation of statutory law and the New Jersey constitution, and (3) the CCRB's involvement in disciplinary matters infringed on the statutorily granted rights of police chiefs.[38]

The superior court handed the union an early win when it permanently enjoined the city from "implementing or enforcing" the ordinance "except to the extent" that the CCRB would be permitted to "serve strictly in an oversight capacity."[39] In particular, the court quashed the CCRB's subpoena power.[40] The practical effect of the order was to bring the CCRB's start-up operations to a screeching halt.[41]

However, the story does not end there. On appeal, the Appellate Division of the New Jersey Superior Court was much less sympathetic to the union's concerns. The appellate court found the ordinance valid on its face and rejected the trial court's conclusion that there was potential for "political mischief" in the CCRB's design because members would be chosen from organizations that had already taken strong positions on how the city's police disciplinary system needed to be changed.[42] In addition, the appellate court found that the city's delegation of subpoena authority to the CCRB was entirely proper.[43] Yet the appellate ruling did not leave the city's plans for the CCRB unscathed. The agency was precluded from making findings that would be binding on the department.[44] The court found such oversight power in conflict with New Jersey law that gives police chiefs "express authority . . . to avoid undue interference by a governing body into the operation of the police force."[45] The appellate court also ordered that the identity of complainants and police officers remain confidential.[46]

Not surprisingly, the Newark FOP then petitioned for certification before the New Jersey Supreme Court,[47] where the matter elicited numerous briefs from amici curiae.[48] The New Jersey Attorney General and the New Jersey State Association of Chiefs of Police filed briefs on behalf of the union.[49] The city's position was supported by briefs filed by the American Civil Liberties Union of New Jersey, the New Jersey Urban Mayors Association, Newark Communities for Accountable Policing, the Urban League of Essex County and Libertarians for Transparent Government, and Latino Leadership Alliance of New Jersey.[50]

In deciding the matter, the New Jersey Supreme Court identified the threshold issue as whether Newark "had the power to legislate, by ordinance, the creation of a citizen oversight board to have a role in the review of the handling of citizens' police misconduct complaints."[51] Given the long-established history and prevalence of civilian oversight elsewhere, this question might seem axiomatic. But New Jersey's approach to state oversight of local law enforcement is somewhat anomalous in that the New Jersey Attorney General has significant statutory and regulatory power governing the discipline of the law enforcement personnel employed throughout the state.[52] The foundation of the attorney general's power over law enforcement discipline dates back to 1991, when the attorney general issued a set of procedures related to disciplinary matters that the New Jersey legislature deemed binding on every law enforcement agency in the state.[53] Other New Jersey attorneys general have similarly leveraged this power to promulgate regulations on police accountability issues.[54] For example, in response to the 2020 killing of George Floyd in Minneapolis, the New Jersey Attorney General issued new directives calling for the public release of the names of law enforcement officers subject to "major discipline."[55]

The New Jersey Supreme Court acknowledged that Newark's CCRB ordinance pitted the city's statutory authority to maintain and regulate its police force directly against the attorney general's statutory oversight powers.[56] For Newark and other New Jersey municipalities considering civilian oversight, the court provided somewhat of a win, in that it validated Newark's authority to create an oversight board pursuant to its broad statutory police powers.[57] Yet, the win was perhaps more of a consolation prize because the court significantly dialed back the CCRB's investigatory powers.[58] The court held that the CCRB's investigatory power was in conflict with the internal affairs process outlined in the attorney general's regulations and, therefore, the CCRB is precluded from conducting investigations concurrently with the police department's internal affairs unit.[59] Dealing another blow, the court affirmed the trial court's conclusion that the city lacked authority to delegate its subpoena power to the CCRB.[60] The court did appear to offer some words of conciliation by reminding the city that the CCRB can function with its other investigatory powers such as creating a disciplinary matrix, conducting oversight reviews, and reporting periodically to the city administration and council.[61]

Presumably finding limited solace in that outcome, the city quickly filed a petition for certiorari to the U.S. Supreme Court.[62] As with the matter below, the certiorari petition generated briefs from numerous amici curiae. By the time of briefing on the certiorari petition, the leaders of Jersey City, New Jersey, were making plans for their own civilian oversight board.[63] Jersey City officials filed a brief in support of Newark's petition, while Jersey City's police union filed a brief in opposition to the petition.[64] Unfortunately for Newark and the CCRB, the extra support did not help them prevail, and the Court declined to hear the case.[65] The future of the Newark CCRB and the new civilian oversight entity Jersey City seeks to create may rest with New Jersey state legislators, one of whom has proposed a bill that would allow civilian oversight entities to wield subpoena power, conduct independent investigations, and recommend discipline.[66]

Where state law is similarly unfavorable toward civilian oversight, some cities are proactively seeking state law changes to accommodate the civilian oversight powers they seek. For example, the city of Greensboro, North Carolina, sought and obtained state legislation to override state law that prohibited the city's oversight agency from having access to disciplinary records.

Community Commission for Public Safety and Accountability—Chicago, Illinois

Chicago was among the early adopters of civilian oversight as the Chicago Police Board, now one of four civilian entities overseeing the Chicago Police Department, dates back to 1960. Chicago's civilian oversight infrastructure was born out of and has grown as a result of a series of highly publicized and political police misconduct scandals. The Chicago Police Board, which is responsible for adjudicating serious police misconduct matters, was created in the wake of the Summerdale scandal, the discovery that several officers, including some high-ranking department members, were complicit in a lucrative burglary ring operating in the city. The other three entities were proposed in the wake of the 2014 officer-involved shooting of Laquan McDonald at the hands of former Chicago police officer Jason Van Dyke, who now stands convicted of second-degree murder based on the fatal encounter. The incident was the catalyst behind the enhancement of Chicago's civilian oversight structure as well as a consent decree enforced by a federal monitor.

In the midst of significant political fallout from the McDonald incident, then Mayor Rahm Emanuel empaneled a task force on police accountability that advocated for a complete overhaul of the city's police accountability infrastructure. The task force plan included three key components: a redesigned civilian investigative agency, enhanced auditing powers for the inspector general, and a completely new oversight commission with sweeping strategic and supervisory powers over the Chicago Police Department.

The first two elements of the new design were implemented in 2016 via an ordinance that established the new Civilian Office of Police Accountability (COPA) and the Office of the Deputy Inspector General for Public Safety (PSIG). COPA was imbued with broader subject matter jurisdiction relative to its predecessor agency, the Independent Police Review Authority, including the power to conduct pattern and practice investigations. The PSIG was given authority to independently audit and monitor the police department and the civilian oversight entities, namely, COPA and the long-standing Chicago Police Board. While these reforms were put in place relatively quickly, the third element in the task force's design—the creation of a civilian oversight commission—was years in the making.

Two community groups, the Grassroots Alliance for Police Accountability (GAPA) and the Civilian Police Accountability Council (CPAC), spent the next few years working up and proposing conceptual designs for the structure and powers of the new oversight commission. However, neither Emanuel nor his successor, Mayor Lori Lightfoot, embraced the proposals put forth by either community group. Both GAPA and CPAC advocated for their respective visions for the new oversight board over a period of years, during which it became obvious that it would be extremely difficult if not impossible for either group to gain sufficient political support for the necessary city legislation.

However, in the summer of 2020, the killing of George Floyd thrust police reform back to the front and center of political discourse across the country. In early 2021, the two community groups were able to reconcile their competing visions for the new commission, and they came to the negotiating table with the mayor and city council as a united front. Together the activists were able to exert sufficient pressure on the mayor and the city council to get the job done. In July 2021, the city council passed an ordinance that created a complex, two-tiered commission to oversee policing policy and operations. Chicago will have a seven-member Community Commission for Public Safety that will be supported by a set of three-member community councils elected to represent each of the city's 22 police districts.

What Characteristics Are Important to Successful Civilian Oversight?

Most experts would agree that there is no one "right" way to do civilian oversight. There is tremendous variation across jurisdictions in terms of what the community wants or needs from law enforcement and the kinds of law enforcement policy and operational challenges that oversight is meant to address. However, there are some fundamental characteristics that are widely recognized as contributing to more successful civilian oversight.

Civilian Oversight: Key Success Factors

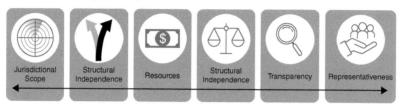

Jurisdictional Scope

The scope of a civilian oversight entity's jurisdiction must be both clearly defined and broad enough to generate real operational impact. The entity's subject matter jurisdiction should be broad enough to encompass the types of issues, complaints, matters, and policies of interest to the community. Where civilian oversight entities have subject matter jurisdiction related to disciplinary matters, it is typically focused on situations where police-citizen encounters have the potential to go awry. Typically, these entities are empowered to review, audit, or investigate certain types of complaints made against officers ("complaint-based jurisdiction"), certain types of incidents arising from police-citizen encounters ("incident-based jurisdiction"), or both. Civilian oversight entities are poised to have the most impact when their subject matter jurisdiction is both complaint based and incident based. Complaint-based jurisdiction for civilian entities usually encompasses allegations involving various forms of abuse of power that can occur in the context of police-citizen encounters. These may range from less serious allegations such as verbal abuse to the most serious including excessive force and sexual assault. However, because citizens may not always file a complaint following an instance of police misconduct, it is also important that civilian oversight entities be empowered to investigate critical incidents without a complaint having been lodged. This incident-based subject matter jurisdiction permits the entity to review or investigate critical incidents such as officer-involved shootings or deaths in custody. For example, by ordinance, Chicago's Civilian Office of Police Accountability, or COPA, has subject matter jurisdiction to conduct both complaint-based and incident-based independent investigations.[67] The agency's complaint-based subject matter jurisdiction includes allegations of excessive force, verbal abuse, coercion, domestic violence, and improper search and seizure.[68] But the agency also has jurisdiction to investigate officer-involved shootings, deaths in custody, and motor vehicle accidents resulting in the death of a citizen.[69]

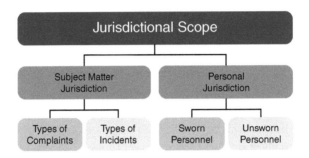

The scope of an oversight entity's personal jurisdiction is also an important consideration. An oversight entity's impact may be undermined where its personal jurisdiction, meaning the types of law enforcement personnel the entity oversees, is limited. For example, the subject matter jurisdiction of San Diego's Civilian Law Enforcement Review Board encompasses the power to conduct investigations and make policy recommendations related to the San Diego Sheriff's Department.[70] However, the board's personal jurisdiction is limited to sworn deputies. Thus, the board is prohibited from making findings or recommendations related to policies governing or misconduct committed by unsworn sheriff's department employees such as detention aides or medical personnel working within the department's jails.

Structural Independence

For civilian entities to be effective, they should have a formal role in the disciplinary and policy development processes that is independent from the law enforcement agency or the city administration, with sufficient organizational structures that foster this independence. The most critical aspects of structural independence include access to law enforcement records, subpoena power, the ability to conduct operations independently from the law enforcement agency, and access to independent legal advice.

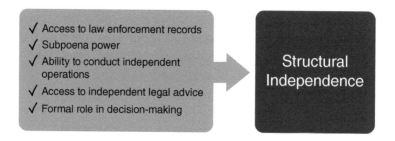

Historically, access to law enforcement records has been a challenge for many civilian oversight entities. Access to this information is essential to almost every aspect of an oversight entity's work. Review of critical incidents or investigation of complaints requires that oversight entities have access to the law enforcement agency's reports and documents related to the incidents or events that gave rise to the complaint. Access to law enforcement records is also necessary for an oversight entity to fulfill its policy review and transparency responsibilities. Ideally, an oversight entity should have direct access to the law enforcement agency's record systems and data. Where an entity must rely on a law enforcement agency to provide records or data on request, the timeliness and accuracy of the agency's work can be undermined because the entity may not receive the material in a timely manner and may not receive all the relevant material.

In some jurisdictions, access to records may be limited by state statutes governing the confidentiality of police disciplinary records. This is the case in North Carolina where, to overcome this issue, the city of Greensboro pursued state legislation that would afford Greensboro's Criminal Justice Advisory Commission and Police Community Review Board access to police disciplinary records.[71] This is also the case in California where, until recently, state law prohibited access to most police disciplinary records and still precludes civilian oversight entities from holding public hearings on police disciplinary matters within their jurisdiction.[72]

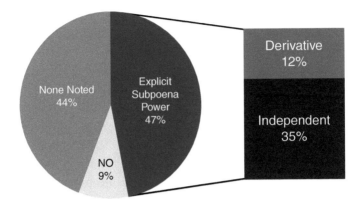

The ability to issue subpoenas to compel the appearance of witnesses and the production of records is considered essential to independent oversight. Whether a civilian oversight entity should wield subpoena power is often a source of substantial political debate when the powers of a new entity are being defined. For example, in Austin, Texas, the collective bargaining agreement between the city and the police union prohibits any civilian review board established by the city manager from having subpoena power.[73]

Among the civilian oversight entities operating in the largest 100 U.S. cities in 2021, just under one-half (approximately 46 percent) are explicitly authorized to issue subpoenas. Some, approximately 35 percent, of these entities have independent subpoena power. Others, approximately 11 percent, derive their subpoena power from another government entity such as the city council or the corporation counsel. Those entities must request the issuance of a subpoena from a government entity with the authority to issue subpoenas on their behalf. For example, the Columbus Civilian Police Review Board may issue subpoenas with the approval of the city attorney.[74] In some states there is either statutory law or case law on the books that precludes civilian oversight entities from issuing subpoenas independently. For example, in 2019, Tennessee lawmakers enacted a measure that precludes civilian oversight entities from issuing subpoenas.[75] Conversely, in 2020, California enacted a statute that explicitly authorized counties to bestow subpoena power on civilian entities that oversee sheriff's offices.[76]

Access to independent legal counsel is an important aspect of structural independence. The legal framework in which civilian oversight operates is a complex web of intersecting federal, state, and municipal law and an array of intersecting law enforcement agency policies. Many oversight entities are established as distinct units of city or county government for which a city or county has a statutorily designated legal representative such as a corporation counsel or city attorney. While representation by a city attorney may be appropriate for guiding the oversight entity in the fulfillment of ministerial duties, where an entity is exercising its substantive oversight powers such representation can be problematic. Most city and county legal departments defend the city or county and its police officers in civil litigation arising from police misconduct, and in most cases they take the position that misconduct did not occur. In some matters, the city or county's denial that an officer committed misconduct in the context of civil litigation may be at odds with an oversight entity's efforts to determine whether misconduct did in fact occur and its responsibility to pursue administrative remedies where appropriate. Some jurisdictions have recognized this conflict of interest and have explicitly given an oversight entity the power to retain outside legal counsel.[77]

Another important facet of structural independence is an entity's power to influence policing policies and procedures. Historically, civilian oversight entities have lacked direct control over how policing is done in their jurisdictions. Rather, the success of civilian oversight has stemmed from an entity's ability to influence policing policies and procedures by conducting audits, reviews, and investigations that lead to recommended reforms. An oversight entity's ability to influence appears greatest where law enforcement is required to respond to an oversight entity's recommendations and where both the oversight entity's recommendations and the law enforcement agency's responses are made public so that communities can assess the quality of the oversight entity's work as well as how, if at all, the law enforcement entity is responding to the feedback it receives. Entities that merely provide recommendations to which the law enforcement agency may or may not choose to respond have significantly less impact. Entities whose recommendations are not made publicly available may have even less impact because communities are limited in their ability to assess the oversight entity's work.

In the wake of George Floyd's killing in 2020, activists have increasingly pushed for civilian oversight entities to have more direct oversight with an actual say in decision-making regarding both policing policy and police discipline. Power over policing policy was a major source of debate between the mayor and advocates behind Chicago's Community Commission for Public Safety and Accountability. Now that the new oversight commission is seated, it shares policy-making responsibilities with the mayor and city council. Under the new regime, the commission can draft new policy for the Chicago Police Department.[78] The mayor will have veto power over the new policies, but the mayor's veto can be overridden by a vote of two-thirds of the city council.[79]

Resources

Historically, many oversight entities have failed because they were not given sufficient resources to fulfill their responsibilities in a quality and timely manner. Under-resourced agencies lose community trust because they struggle to manage the complaints they receive and end up with a backlog of cases. Complainants become disillusioned when their complaints are not resolved in a timely manner, if at all. Successful civilian oversight entities are those that have garnered sufficient financial, human, and technical resources. Agencies need sufficient funding to afford appropriate staffing levels, compensation, and training, as well as other operational needs. Agencies also need sufficient human resources in terms of the type and number of professionals and administrative support needed to manage the agency's work. Lastly, successful agencies also leverage technology to maximize the timeliness and quality of their work through effective information management and data analysis.

Neutrality and Professionalism

Neutrality is an essential organizational value for civilian oversight. A civilian oversight entity that is perceived to harbor a bias in favor of law enforcement risks losing the confidence of the community. Citizens will remain skeptical of the entity's output and question whether it can fulfill its primary reason for being, which is to ensure that policing reflects community values. However, perceived bias against law enforcement can be equally problematic. A civilian oversight entity that is perceived as biased against law enforcement will lose the confidence of the law enforcement community, which can undermine its ability to achieve the necessary influence with its law enforcement agency partners. Many members of the law enforcement community assume oversight entities harbor anti-law enforcement bias from the terms "civilian" or "citizen" in the entity's name. Many also share the concern that civilian oversight practitioners lack sufficient law enforcement knowledge and professionalism to do the job well. This is simply not the case. To be sure, many oversight entities exist in the form of volunteer boards populated by citizens that may or may not have any prior experience or expertise in public safety. Currently, however, most entities require oversight board members, even those that serve on a volunteer basis, to undergo substantive training on topics relevant to the work. For example, pursuant to the collective bargaining agreement between the city of Austin, Texas, and the police union, volunteer members of Austin's Community Police Review Commission are required to attend three to four days of training by the Austin Police Department and its Internal Affairs unit on topics such as special investigations, officer-involved shootings, response to resistance, crisis intervention, and firearms.[80] Entities that operate in the form of oversight agencies typically employ experienced professional auditors and investigators. Civilian oversight has become a profession in its own right, and there are numerous quite experienced practitioners engaged in the work nationwide. The National Association of Civilian Oversight of Law Enforcement, an organization formed in 1995 to serve as a resource for civilian oversight practitioners, counts more than 1,500 civilian oversight professionals from over 100 organizations among its membership.[81]

Transparency

Transparency is essential to maintaining community trust in every aspect of policing. Civilian oversight is no different. Successful civilian oversight entities should not only be transparent about their own work but also should promote the transparency of their law enforcement agency partners. Civilian oversight entities often play a critical role in promoting transparency related to critical incidents. For example, in 2016, following the police accountability crisis that erupted following the release of video footage of the Laquan McDonald killing, Chicago instituted a groundbreaking video release policy whereby the Civilian Office of Police Accountability publicly releases video material and key reports related to officer-involved shootings and other police encounters resulting in death or serious injury within 60 days of the incident.[82] Civilian oversight entities can also enhance law enforcement transparency by analyzing and reporting on important law enforcement data and information. For example, the Office of the Inspector General for the Los Angeles Police Department (LAPD) routinely analyzes and reports on use of force by LAPD members.[83]

Representativeness

Policing is hyper-localized, and it is widely recognized that certain communities and demographic groups are disproportionately affected by over-policing and unconstitutional policing. Civilian oversight can best fulfill its mission of providing community input to policing when the work of the civilian oversight body is driven by geographically and demographically diverse representation. This is particularly important in the context of civilian oversight boards, but diversity is also an important consideration in the staffing of civilian oversight agencies.

There are several ways that jurisdictions across the country pursue diverse representation for civilian oversight boards. Many, if not most, jurisdictions express a commitment to diversity in the establishing ordinance for the board. For example, the ordinance establishing the Buffalo Commission on Citizen Rights and Community Relations states that the eleven members of that board are "selected for diversity and demonstrated commitment to social justice."[84] Many cities and counties strive to achieve diversity by outlining specific criteria for board member selection in the establishing ordinance. For example, two of the fifteen members of the Atlanta Civilian Review Board are to be appointed from a "Youth-Serving Organization," and two spots on the board are reserved for persons between the ages of 18 and 30.[85] Some jurisdictions seek diversity by giving community groups a role in the nomination or appointment process. Some of the boards emerging from the George Floyd activism of 2020 and 2021 have chosen this approach. Boston revamped its oversight system in 2021 to include a new nine-member Civilian Review Board of which six members are appointed from "a pool of applicants recommended by civil rights advocacy groups, youth organizations, neighborhood associations and individuals with past experience and knowledge of law enforcement."[86] Louisville made significant changes to its civilian oversight infrastructure in 2020 in response to activism arising from the killing of Breonna Taylor. When the city created its new Civilian Review & Accountability Board, it set aside four of the eleven board seats for candidates nominated by a list of eight community groups including local chapters of the ACLU, NAACP, and Urban League.[87] Some jurisdictions work to ensure that prospective board members understand community wants and needs by seeking public input on board candidates including, for example, by holding public events at which candidates address questions from the public. Some civilian oversight practitioners strongly advocate for the practice of having board candidates appear before the public as part of the selection process because doing so serves as an important reminder to candidates that community representation is essential to the role.

The Future of Civilian Oversight: Emerging Trends in Structure and Power

Based on the structural design of new and improved civilian oversight structures put in place in recent years, there are some commonalities starting to emerge.

A Shift from Oversight Boards to Oversight Agencies

Historically, boards have been the most prevalent form of civilian oversight. Oversight in the form of a board offers the important benefit of democratic representation to ensure the board reflects the attitudes and opinions of the community it serves. In recent years there has been a shift in the type of oversight entities that cities are creating. Prior to 2016, a majority, approximately 70 percent, of civilian oversight entities were boards, meaning entities composed of a group of a specified number of individuals who were appointed or elected to serve.[88] Numerous oversight entities were established in the form of a governmental agency, meaning a unit of the municipal government composed of paid employees. Prior to 2016, approximately 22 percent of the oversight entities operating were agencies, while an additional 8 percent were entities that encompassed both a board and an agency.[89]

Between 2016 and 2021, the board form of oversight continued to account for over half (58 percent) of the entities created, but there was increase in favor of creating agencies that accounted for 37 percent of the entities created during the 2016 to 2020 time period.[90] One hypothesis for this shift is that cities have recognized some of the drawbacks of oversight in the form of a board of civilian volunteers. Boards composed of civilian volunteers that may or may not have expertise in law enforcement or police accountability are frequently subject to criticism regarding their lack of expertise or professionalism.

Moreover, because civilian oversight boards participate on a volunteer basis, it may be difficult for cities to manage the quality and timeliness of their work. In contrast, civilian entities in the form of government agencies typically employ professionals with relevant experience. As city and county employees, the individuals doing the work can be subject to formal performance management procedures. In addition, given that they tend to be populated with professionals, civilian oversight entities in the form of professional agencies may be somewhat less susceptible to criticism by the law enforcement community.

The larger U.S. jurisdictions are increasingly establishing multi-tiered oversight systems composed of multiple agencies that perform various forms of oversight. Often this includes establishing an agency that conducts investigations or audits that are submitted to a board that promulgates findings and recommendations. The mayor of Houston revamped that city's oversight structure in this way in 2021. Via an executive order, the mayor explicitly stated that the purpose of the new structure was "to create a hybrid model of civilian police oversight, which includes both a reformed and diverse civilian board and a full-time, paid administrative and investigative staff."[91] Similarly, in 2020, the city of Madison, Wisconsin, created a new civilian oversight structure combining an Office of the Independent Monitor with a 13-member Police Civilian Oversight Board.[92] The Office of the Independent Monitor will employ professional and administrative staff and be led by a full-time city employee who will serve as the independent monitor. The office will have primary responsibility for monitoring police department programs, activities, and use of force investigations. By ordinance, the monitor will be an experienced civilian oversight professional who will be recruited, hired, and supervised by the board.[93] In this way, the city benefits from having an experienced investigative professional doing the work that requires significant expertise, while also benefiting from having a diverse group of community representatives to provide community-based input and feedback.

Boston Civilian Oversight Structure
(as of January 2021)

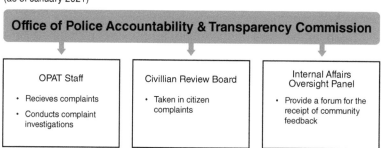

In 2021, the City Council passed an ordinance establishing a completely revamped infrastructure for civilian oversight for the Boston Police Department under the banner of the Office of Police Accountability and Transparency (OPAT).[94] At the top of the organizational structure is the mayor-appointed three-member OPAT Commission, which wields subpoena power.[95] The OPAT Commission oversees the work of three additional oversight entities: the OPAT staff, the Civilian Review Board (CRB), and the Internal Affairs Oversight Panel (IAOP).[96] The three members of the OPAT Commission are the individuals designated by the mayor to serve as the executive director of OPAT staff, the chair of the IAOP, and the chair of the CRB.[97] The OPAT staff takes in complaints and conducts investigations pursuant to the jurisdiction of the CRB and the IAOP.[98] The CRB has jurisdiction to review or, where appropriate, conduct investigations of critical incidents and certain types of complaint allegations such as unlawful seizures and perjury.[99] The IAOP provides external oversight of internal affairs investigations to ensure they are thorough and fair.[100]

Stepping Up from the Power to Influence to the Power to Control

The foundational purpose of civilian oversight of law enforcement over time has remained essentially the same—to transfer some important aspects of governance over policing from the police back to the community. Historically, civilian oversight has been designed to reflect community input by having the opportunity to *influence* policy making or the outcome of disciplinary matters. More recently there has been more urgency around civilian oversight's lack of power to *decide* policy and disciplinary matters. In many cities, activists are increasingly calling for the transference of at least some governance power to bodies composed of community representatives.[101] The policy-making power of Chicago's new Community Commission for Public Safety and Accountability is an example of this trend.

Changes to oversight in Atlanta are part of this trend as well. In 2020, Atlanta enhanced the authority of its Civilian Review Board to have greater impact on disciplinary findings and recommendations.[102] Under the new regime the police chief is required to respond to the board and identify which recommendations are being accepted, rejected, or held pending further investigation by the department.[103] The chief must outline the legal or factual justification or indicate a managerial prerogative in writing while describing the reasons for accepting, rejecting, or modifying board's recommendations.[104] The board may then request reconsideration upon a two-thirds vote of the full board.[105]

Enhanced Investigative Jurisdiction and Powers

Many cities have been working to broaden the investigative jurisdiction and powers of existing oversight entities. Houston's revamped oversight board has the discretion to review "any and all internal investigations" and is not just permitted but is required to review investigations of use of force, firearms discharge incidents, and incidents resulting in serious bodily injury or death.[106] The board also, in its discretion, may direct the investigative agency to conduct independent investigations in specific cases.[107]

In 2020, the Indianapolis city council passed an ordinance that enhanced the powers of the Citizens' Police Complaint Office, allowing that agency to conduct complaint investigations concurrently and in collaboration with the police department's internal affairs.[108] In 2020, the city of Nashville entered into an agreement with the police department that enables its Community Oversight Board to obtain confidential police records, visit crime scenes, and conduct independent interviews.[109]

Exerting Power over Policing by Influencing the Hiring and Firing of Police Chiefs

Another strategy that communities are employing to provide greater influence in policing policy is providing civilian oversight entities with a role in the hiring and firing of police chiefs. Some of the recently created or enhanced civilian oversight boards have been given either the opportunity to nominate candidates for the top job at a police agency whose philosophies and professional experiences are most consistent with the community's strategic vision for policing and public safety, or the power to get rid of a police agency head whose vision or performance is a mismatch with community needs, or both. Although only a handful of civilian oversight entities presently wield the power to fire the top police official, there is an upward trend in cities transferring some of the hiring and firing power away from mayors and city managers to oversight boards.

Historically, only the long-established police commissions, such as the Los Angeles Police Commission established back in the 1920s, held the power to *hire and fire* police leaders. These powers arose from a police commission's plenary supervisory power over police department operations. However, more recently, the power to influence the hiring and firing of chiefs has been bestowed upon a handful of new civilian oversight boards and commissions. In 2016, Oakland residents overwhelmingly approved a ballot measure that would require the mayor to select a new police chief from a list of candidates provided by a new police commission.[110] What is still somewhat unusual is that the commission has also been afforded the power to fire the police chief, with or without the mayor's concurrence.[111] Chicago's new Community Commission for Public Safety and Accountability has a role in the selection of candidates for the superintendent's job[112] and can instigate the ouster of the superintendent by adopting a two-thirds vote behind a "resolution of no confidence" in the superintendent's fitness for the job requiring the city council to consider the matter.[113]

Conclusion

Although the ambitious goal set by Obama's presidential task force—that there be some form of civilian oversight in every jurisdiction—has not yet been fully realized, there has been substantial progress in the intervening years. Police reform activism has translated into political action that has coalesced behind civilian oversight as an important police reform strategy and an integral component of police accountability systems nationwide. While not quite yet ubiquitous, civilian oversight can be found in most large American cities. The concept also continues to gain traction in smaller municipalities, as cities such as Morgantown, West Virginia, with fewer residents than there are sworn New York City police officers, look to civilian oversight to enhance community input to policing.[114] Yet the practice of civilian oversight continues to be constrained by a complex legal framework and political efforts by law enforcement and reluctant city leaders seeking to limit its scope. Despite this inhospitable environment, if the trends observed in 2020 and 2021 continue, civilian oversight is likely to continue to flourish in prevalence, complexity, and potential impact as police reform and accountability remain poignant national public concerns.

Endnotes

1. Office of Community-Oriented Policing Services, Department of Justice, Final Report of the President's Task Force on 21st Century Policing (May 2015) (hereineafter President's Task Force Report).

2. *Id*. at 11.

3. Brent Kendall, *Obama-Era Policing Proposals Find Some Success, but Ambitious Ideas Are Slow-Moving*, Wall Street Journal, June 15, 2020, 2:11 pm ET.

4. President's Task Force Report, *supra* note 1, at 26.

5. *Id*.

6. Major City Chiefs Association, *Discussions on the President's Task Force on 21st Century Policing: How Police Agencies Are Using the Report, How Police Agencies Are Implementing the Recommendations, Police Agencies' Reactions to the Recommendations, and the Value of Understanding Historical Context*, Police Executive Leadership Series (2016).

7. *Id*. at 22.

8. Yucel Ors & Nicole DuPuis, *City Officials Guide to Policing in the 21st Century*, National League of Cities (2016).

9. *Id*. at 7.

10. Samuel Walker, Police Accountability: The Role of Citizen Oversight, at 19 (2001).

11. *Id*.

12. A.I. Jolin & D.C. Gibbons, *Policing the Police: The Portland Experience*, 12 Journal of Police Science & Administration 315, 317.

13. *Id*..

14. *Id*.

15. *Id*. at 316.

16. *Id*.

17. Mark Iris, *Police Discipline in Chicago: Arbitration or Arbitrary?*, 89 Crim. L. & Criminology 215, 217 (1998).

18. The statistics that follow are based on a survey the author conducted of civilian oversight entities operating in the most populous 100 U.S. cities as of mid-2021 (hereinafter 2021 Civilian Oversight Survey).

19. *Id*.

20. *Id*.

21. City of Louisville, Kentucky Ordinance No. 10, Series 2003; *see also* Nicole Dungca & Jenn Abelson, *When Communities Try to Hold Police Accountable, Law Enforcement Fights Back*, WASH. POST, Apr. 27, 2021.

22. *Id.*

23. K. Sabeel Rahman & Jocelyn Simonson, *The Institutional Design of Community Control*, 108 CALIF. L. REV. 679, 683 (2020).

24. *Id.* at 690.

25. EXECUTIVE SUMMARY OF THE FINAL REPORT OF THE PRESIDENT'S TASK FORCE ON 21ST CENTURY POLICING at 26 (noting the commentary of a civilian oversight expert Brian Buchner who stated, "Civilian oversight alone is not sufficient to gain legitimacy; without it, however, it is difficult, if not impossible, for the police to maintain the public's trust.").

26. Iris, *supra* note 17, at 217.

27. *The Administration of Complaints by Civilians*, 77 HARV. L. REV. 499, 511 (1964).

28. *Id.*

29. For example, the 2018 collective bargaining agreement governing the Austin Police Department precludes Austin's Office of Police Oversight from independently gathering evidence, interviewing witnesses, or otherwise independently investigating a complaint. Agreement between the City of Austin and the Austin Police Association, Effective Nov. 15, 2018, Article 16. For additional discussion of the impact of police unions on police accountability, see Chapter 3.

30. Jolin & Gibbons, *supra* note 12, at 316.

31. Sabeel Rahman & Simonson, *supra* note 23, at 688.

32. *Civil Rights, Community Organizations Hail the Creation of a Strong and Permanent Vehicle for Police Accountability, See the Beginning of a New Day in Newark*, ACLU NEW JERSEY, Mar. 16, 2016, https://www.aclu-nj.org/news/2016/03/16/newark-makes-history-councils-passage-permanent-police-overs.

33. *Id.*

34. CITY OF NEWARK, ORDINANCE 6PSF-b031616 (Mar. 16, 2016), codified at CITY OF NEWARK MUNICIPAL CODE § 2:2-86.1 *et seq.*

35. *Id.*

36. Ryan Hutchins & Katherine Landergan, *Newark Council OKs Powerful Police Review Board*, POLITICO, Mar. 16, 2016, 08:28 PM EDT, https://www.politico.com/states/new-jersey/story/2016/03/newark-council-oks-powerful-police-review-board-032481.

37. Fraternal Ord. of Police, Newark Lodge No. 12 v. City of Newark, 212 A.3d 454, 482 (N.J. App. Div. 2019), *aff'd in part, rev'd in part*, 244 N.J. 75, 236 A.3d 965 (2020) (*FOP v. Newark I*).

38. *Id.* at 469.

39. *Id.* at 461.

40. *Id.*

41. *Id.*

42. *Id.*at 483.

43. *Id.*at 487.

44. *Id.* at 477.

45. *Id.* (citing a discussion of the purpose of N.J.S.A. 40A:14-118 in *Falcone v. De Furia*, 510 A.2d 1174, 1176 (N.J. 1986)).

46. *Id.* at 488.

47. Fraternal Ord. of Police, Newark Lodge No. 12 v. City of Newark, 236 A.3d 965 (N.J. 2020) (*FOP v. Newark II*).

48. *Id.*

49. *Id.*

50. *Id.*

51. *Id.* at 975.

52. New Jersey's Criminal Justice Act of 1970 states that it is "the public policy of this State to encourage cooperation among law enforcement officers and to provide for the general supervision of criminal justice by the Attorney General as chief law enforcement officer of the State." N.J.S.A. 52:17B-98. This statute has been liberally construed to imbue the attorney general with the power to establish standards and policies for disciplinary matters of local law enforcement agencies. *In re* Attorney General Law Enforcement Directive Nos. 2020-5 and 2020-6, 252 A.3d 135 (N.J. 2021).

53. N.J.S.A. 40A:14-181.

54. *See, e.g., In re* Attorney General Law Enforcement Directive Nos. 2020-5 and 2020-6, 252 A.3d 135 (N.J. 2021).

55. *Id.*

56. *FOP v. Newark II*, 236 A.3d at 976.

57. *Id.* at 980.

58. *Id.* at 983.

59. *Id.*

60. *Id.* at 985.

61. *Id.* at 984.

62. City of Newark, New Jersey v. Fraternal Order of Police, Newark Lodge No. 12, U.S. Supreme Court, No. 20-989.

63. Shortly before the U.S. Supreme Court denied Newark's petition, the Jersey City Council passed a resolution supporting the creation of a civilian police review board, prompting litigation by that city's police union. John Heinis, *Jersey City Police Unions Suing City, Council over Resolution Supporting Creation of CCRB*, HUDSON COUNTY VIEW, Apr. 26, 2021.

64. City of Newark, New Jersey v. Fraternal Order of Police, Newark Lodge No. 12, U.S. Supreme Court, No. 20-989, Docket entries Feb. 25, 2021 and Mar. 29, 2021, respectively.

65. City of Newark, N.J. v. Fraternal Order of Police, Newark Lodge No. 12, U.S. Supreme Court, No. 20-989, petition denied May 3, 2021.

66. New Jersey Assembly Bill No. 4656, introduced Sept. 17, 2020.

67. CITY OF CHICAGO MUNICIPAL CODE § 2-78-120.

68. *Id.*

69. *Id.*

70. SAN DIEGO COUNTY CODE, art. XVIII, § 340 *et seq.*

71. North Carolina House Bill 1080, Session Law 2018-105.

72. Berkeley Police Assoc. v. City of Berkeley, 167 Cal. App. 4th 385 (Cal. Ct. App. 2008) (interpreting *Copley Press Inc. v. Superior Court*, 39 Cal. 4th 1272 (Cal. 2006) in holding that Berkeley's Police Review Commission was

subject to the confidentiality provisions of the California Public Safety Officers Procedural Bill of Rights Act and thus precluded from disclosing police disciplinary records in public hearings).

73. Agreement between the City of Austin and the Austin Police Association, Eff. Nov. 15, 2018, at 51 (nothing that any review panel would not have the power to subpoena witnesses and that there would be no administrative requirement for officers to appear before the panel).

74. COLUMBUS CITY CHARTER § 216 ("With the approval of the City Attorney or the City Attorney's designee, the Board shall have the authority to request that a subpoena issue to compel the attendance of a key witness or the production of any documents, photographs, audio recordings, electronic files or other tangible evidence relating to any matter under investigation, review, or evaluation by the Board in accordance with relevant provisions of the Charter, subject to the restrictions of applicable federal and state and, for city employee members of a bargaining unit, the terms of any collective bargaining agreement.").

75. TENNESSEE CODE § 38-8-312(b)(1) ("A community oversight board does not have the power to issue subpoenas for documents or to compel witness testimony.").

76. California Assembly Bill 1185 (2019–2020), codified at CALIFORNIA GOVT. CODE § 25303.7.

77. CITY OF CHICAGO MUNICIPAL CODE § 2-78-120(q).

78. *Id.* § 2-80-050(i) (noting the commission has the power to "draft, review and approve by majority vote any proposed new or amended Policy").

79. *Id.* § 2-80-110(c)(7).

80. Agreement Between the City of Austin and the Austin Police Association, Eff. Nov. 15, 2018, pp. 50–51.

81. According to Cameron McEllhiney, NACOLE, Director of Training, as of Apr. 26, 2022.

82. *Video Release Policy*, CITY OF CHICAGO, https://www.chicago.gov /city/en/depts/cpd/supp_info/video_release_policy.html.

83. *Use of Force Reports*, OFFICE OF THE INSPECTOR GENERAL LOS ANGELES POLICE COMMISSION, https://www.oig.lacity.org/use-of-force-reports.

84. BUFFALO CITY CODE § 18-21.

85. ATLANTA CITY CODE §§ 2-2203 and 2-2204.

86. BOSTON CODE OF ORDINANCES ch. XII, § 12-16.8.

87. LOUISVILLE METRO CODE OF ORDINANCES § 36.71.

88. 2021 Civilian Oversight Survey, *supra* note 18.

89. *Id.*

90. *Id.*

91. Houston Executive Order 1-5 Rev., Eff. May 21, 2021.

92. MADISON GENERAL ORDINANCES §§ 5.19 and 5.20.

93. *Id.* § 5.19.

94. CITY OF BOSTON CODE, ORDINANCES § 12-16 *et seq.*

95. *Id.* § 12-16.4.

96. *Id.* § 12-16 *et seq.*

97. *Id.* § 12-16.3.

98. *Id.* § 12-16.7

99. *Id.* § 12-16.10(a).

100. *Id.* § 12-16.13.

101. Sabeel Rahman & Simonson, *supra* note 23, at 681–82.

102. ATLANTA ORDINANCE 20-O-1445.

103. *Id.* § 2-2213(o).

104. *Id.*

105. *Id.*

106. City of Houston, Executive Order 1-5, revised May 25, 2021, § 5.1.1.1.

107. *Id.* § 5.1.1.4.

108. INDIANAPOLIS CODE OF ORDINANCES G.O. 35, 2020, § 202-806(a).

109. Memorandum of Understanding between the Community Oversight Board and the Metropolitan Nashville Police Department, filed with the Metro Clerk Dec. 14, 2020, *available at* https://www.nashville.gov/sites/default/files/2021-03/MOU-with-MNPD.pdf?ct=1616767674.

110. Measure LL, codified in OAKLAND CITY CHARTER § 2.45 *et seq.*

111. OAKLAND CITY CHARTER § 2.45.070(E).

112. CITY OF CHICAGO MUNICIPAL CODE § 2-80-080.

113. *Id.* § 2-80-090.

114. In 2021, Morgantown created a Civilian Police Review and Advisory Board to facilitate community input to police department policies, practices, and procedures and to review misconduct complaints. *Civilian Police Review and Advisory Board*, CITY OF MORGANTOWN, https://www.morgantownwv.gov/640/Civilian-Police-Review-and-Advisory-Board.

Chapter 6

Pattern or Practice Investigations and Consent Decrees

Michael A. Hardy[1]

In the areas of policing, police/civilian encounters, and policing oversight and accountability, there is no more powerful or effective check and balance than the U.S. Department of Justice (DOJ). For practitioners who litigate in the areas of criminal justice reform, juvenile justice matters, state and local government, civil rights, police misconduct, wrongful deaths, and police accountability, knowing how to navigate the DOJ's Civil Rights Division, which is tasked with enforcing the nation's civil rights laws and protections, is essential.[2]

While it is generally recognized that most police officers are doing their best to protect people and reduce crime, there are substantial situations when police disregard their own policing protocols in ways that violate the law and require investigations into the pattern or practices of those police officers and the police departments or bureaus in which they work.

A community that does not commit to oversight of its police departments or other law enforcements units under its jurisdiction, by prosecuting and disciplining officers and departments who break the law, sets dangerous precedents that can have devasting effects on those who are supposed to be protected and served. The result of unchecked and unconstitutional policing is communities, citizens, and the good police officers who are subsequently harmed in cruel and unusual manners.

The DOJ's primary tools for investigating systemic violations of state and local policing and enforcing the laws are pattern or practice investigations. This chapter examines not only how the DOJ determines when it will use its pattern or practice authority but also why good and constitutional policing matters. It examines the significance of community involvement, including the importance in some instances of the community working to lay the foundations for the DOJ's determination to commence a pattern or practice investigation. It also examines how "consent decrees" can facilitate the DOJ's ability to bring about resolutions that create better, stronger, and constitutionally protected communities.

Understanding Pattern or Practice Investigations

Pattern or practice investigations are just what the term indicates. They describe situations where the law allows for the DOJ's intervention when it is determined that a person or a group of persons is engaged in a "pattern or practice" of conduct in violation of rights, privileges, or immunities secured or protected by the Constitution or laws of the United States. The term "pattern or practice" has also been used in Title VII of the 1964 Civil Rights Act, which allowed the Equal Employment Opportunity Commission to bring a claim that "any person or group of persons is engaged in a pattern or practice" of illegal conduct in violation of the civil rights law.[3]

The legal basis for pattern or practice investigations is 42 U.S.C. § 14141 (recodified as 34 U.S.C. § 12601), which allows the DOJ to review and investigate state and local law enforcement agencies that may be acting in violation of the Constitution or federal law and systemically violating the protected rights of their citizens.

Section 14141 (34 U.S.C. § 12601) states:[4]

(a) Unlawful conduct
It shall be unlawful for any governmental authority, or any agent thereof, or any person acting on behalf of a governmental authority, to engage in a pattern or practice of conduct by law enforcement officers or by officials

or employees of any governmental agency with responsibility for the administration of juvenile justice or the incarceration of juveniles that deprives persons of rights, privileges, or immunities secured or protected by the Constitution or laws of the United States.

(b) Civil Action by Attorney General
Whenever the Attorney General has reasonable cause to believe that a violation of paragraph (1) has occurred, the Attorney General, for or in the name of the United States, may in a civil action obtain appropriate equitable and declaratory relief to eliminate the pattern or practice.

Section 12601 "serves as the primary federal law aiming to ensure that law enforcement agencies comply with the Constitution."[5] Specifically:

- Section 12601 authorizes the attorney general to sue local law enforcement agencies for "engag[ing] in a pattern or practice of conduct" that "deprives persons of rights, privileges, or immunities secured or protected by the Constitution or laws of the United States."
- Section 12601 does not allow for any private right of action, meaning individuals cannot sue to enforce it. Only the DOJ can sue to enforce this law. Individuals can, however, sue for civil penalties regarding actions and behaviors that are unconstitutional.
  - Pattern or practice investigation cases are initiated and "geared toward changing polices, practices, and culture across a law enforcement agency."
  - Pattern or practice is defined as a "more than an isolated, sporadic incident," and wrongdoing and bad behavior must be "repeated, routine, or of a generalized nature."
  - The most common type of section 12601 investigations stem from Fourth Amendment violations, specifically improper searches, seizures, detentions, and use of force.
  - Section 12601 cases are overseen by attorneys in the Special Litigation Section of the DOJ's Civil Rights Division.

The DOJ's pattern or practice investigations are not triggered by standalone "high-profile incidents—such as a shooting death, a use of excessive force, or a false arrest." While these types of high-profile situations may, in fact, be evidence of a pattern or practice, section 12601 exists "to identify, remedy and even prevent substantive violations."[6]

A Note about Private Right of Action

Individuals can pursue private rights of action against local, state, and federal policing authorities. Section 1983 and "Bivens" actions allow for these private rights of action.[7] They, too, can provide substantial checks and balances on the conduct of those policing agencies. It should not be misunderstood in discussing the value and effectiveness of the DOJ's pattern or practice investigative actions that individual private actions cannot result in some meaningful change in policing agencies. The DOJ's pattern or practice investigations do not take the place of private rights of action. In many cases it is the private actions that can bring relief to individuals and families that have sustained serious injuries and/or financial harm that cannot be addressed in the DOJ's pattern or practice investigations.

However, the strength of the DOJ's pattern or practice authority under section 12601 allows it to seek extensive use of its equitable and declaratory judgement relief, which is not as readily available to private litigants.[8]

Good Policing/Constitutional Policing Matters

From the moment America declared itself a new nation and held that we were endowed with certain unalienable rights of "life, liberty and the pursuit of happiness," policing in this nation would always be of paramount importance.[9] When we adopted our Bill of Rights to our ratified Constitution, those rights would have to be protected from unconstitutional government intrusion by the rule of law.[10] In our times, that rule of law falls within the domains of our courts and police departments in state and local communities across the country.

Good communities, safe communities, and healthy communities are all somewhat defined by police-community relations. When those policing relationships go bad, so do large portions of those communities. It is in those moments when the DOJ's powers to commence pattern or practice investigations become significant. It is also in those moments when private attorneys, community groups, civil rights organizations, and community members also become critical in how they too can participate and assist in ensuring that our communities are served and protected by police departments that respect the communities they serve and seek to uphold their constitutional duties to not violate the constitutional rights of the citizens they are sworn to protect and serve.

The DOJ's Community Relations Service (CRS)[11] published a toolkit for policing. It included the following five points to enhance police-community relationship building:

1. Acknowledge and discuss with your communities the challenges you are facing.
   - Controversial uses of force and other incidents can damage relationships between police and their communities . . . not just locally but nationwide attention can reduce trust of the police generally.
   - Police should acknowledge the history of racial minorities and others who have faced injustice at the hands of the police.
2. Be transparent and accountable.
   - When a critical incident occurs, agencies should try to release as much information about it as possible . . . so the community will not feel that information is being purposefully withheld from them.
   - Police leaders should let the news media and public know that early information may not be correct and should correct any misinformation quickly.
   - Police departments should post information on their websites detailing policies on use of force, community member complaints, and other issues.

3. Take steps to reduce bias and improve cultural competency.
   - Many civil rights leaders and police executives also recommend that officers at all levels receive training on diversity, implicit bias, and cultural competency.
   - Research shows that individuals who are made aware of their implicit biases are motivated to implement unbiased behaviors.
4. Maintain focus on the importance of collaboration and be visible in the community.
   - It is important for the police to be visible in their communities and know their residents.
   - Personal interactions between police officers and community members build mutual trust, which is essential to addressing neighborhood problems and reducing crime.
5. Promote internal diversity and ensure professional growth opportunities.
   - Police agencies need to present policing as a profession.
   - Internal processes of a department regarding recruiting, promotions, and other matters should be transparent and fair.
   - When an agency creates an environment that promotes internal fairness and respect, officers are more likely to demonstrate these qualities in their daily interactions with the community.

The CRS's report also indicated that many of its findings were reviewed in the final report by President Barack Obama's Task Force on 21st Century Policing in 2015.[12]

Likewise, a report conducted through the *Proceedings of the National Academy of Sciences of the United States of America (PNAS)*[13] found that "positive contact with police—delivered via brief door-to-door non-enforcement community policing visits—substantially improved residents' attitudes toward police, including legitimacy and willingness to cooperate." The report also noted that the effects were largest among non-white respondents. Many jurisdictions throughout the United States are experimenting with or utilizing community policing models.[14] Generally, community policing is defined as follows:[15]

A law enforcement philosophy that allows officers to continuously operate in the same area in order to create a stronger bond with the citizens living and working in that area. This allows public safety officers to engage with local residents and prevent crime from happening instead of responding to incidents after they occur.

Nevertheless, notwithstanding many of the reform efforts that followed, in notorious incidents such as in Staten Island, New York, in 2014 resulting in the death of Eric Garner from a police chokehold or the uprisings that occurred in Ferguson, Missouri, after the shooting death of Michael Brown, when policing goes bad and unconstitutional violations occur, serious damage happens to the order, respect, and relationships between the communities and the police who are protecting and serving those very communities.

In *Floyd v. City of New York*,[16] Judge Shira A. Scheindlin, writing for the court in a non-DOJ case involving the controversial "stop and frisk" policies of the New York City Police Department (NYPD), wrote about the impact that unconstitutional policing has on the entire community where such violations occur:

The Supreme Court has recognized that "the degree of community resentment aroused by particular practices is clearly relevant to an assessment of the quality of the intrusion upon reasonable expectations of personal security."

In light of the very active and public debate on the issues addressed in this Opinion—and the passionate positions taken by both sides—it is important to recognize the human toll of unconstitutional stops. While it is true that any one stop is a limited intrusion in duration and deprivation of liberty, each stop is also a demeaning and humiliating experience. No one should live in fear of being stopped whenever he leaves his home to go about the activities of daily life. Those who are routinely subjected to stops are overwhelmingly people of color, and they are justifiably troubled to be singled out when many of them have done nothing to attract the unwarranted attention. Some plaintiffs testified that stops make them feel unwelcome in some parts of the city, and distrustful of the police. This alienation cannot be good for the police, the community, or its leaders. Fostering trust and confidence between the police and the community would be an improvement for everyone.

Similarly, in announcing the findings of a 2015 DOJ pattern or practice investigation commenced after the shooting death of Michael Brown in Ferguson, Missouri, then Attorney General Eric Holder spoke to the pains and wounds communities suffer when police routinely violate the constitutional protections of the citizens they are supposed to serve and protect. Holder stated,[17]

> Our investigation showed that Ferguson police officers routinely violate the Fourth Amendment in stopping people without reasonable suspicion, arresting them without probable cause, and using unreasonable force against them. . . . And today- now that our investigation has reached its conclusion, it is time for Ferguson's leaders to take immediate, wholesale and structural corrective action. . . . The report we have issued and the steps we have taken are only the beginning of a necessarily resource intensive and inclusive process to promote reconciliation, to reduce and eliminate bias, and to bridge gaps and build understanding.

To be sure, since the incidents in Ferguson, Missouri; Louisville, Kentucky; and other policing situations that ended badly for both the communities and the individuals involved, there has been a nationwide focus on how to significantly improve community/police relations and ensure constitutional policing. No situation grabbed the nation's attention more than the death of George Floyd. Floyd was killed by a police officer who restrained Floyd for over nine minutes by kneeling on his neck and asphyxiating him. There were demonstrations throughout the nation and calls for the officers involved to be prosecuted (which they were and convicted) and for Congress to pass federal policing legislation in the name of George Floyd.

In that background, the DOJ did, in fact, on April 21, 2021, commence a pattern or practice investigation of the Minneapolis, Minnesota, police department. Attorney General Merrick B. Garland stated,[18]

> Most of our nation's law enforcement officers do their difficult jobs honorably and lawfully.
>
> I strongly believe that good officers do not want to work in systems that allow bad practices. Good officers' welcome accountability because accountability is an essential part of building trust with the community, and public safety requires public trust. I have been involved in the legal system, in one way or another, for most of my adult life. I know that justice is sometimes slow, sometimes elusive, and sometimes never comes. The Department of Justice will be unwavering in its pursuit of equal justice under law.
>
> The challenges we face are deeply woven in our history—they did not arise today or last year. Building trust between the community and law enforcement will take time and effort by all of us, but we undertake this task with determination and urgency, knowing that change cannot wait.

If anything is clear, it is that good policing and constitutional policing matter. Bad policing is not only dangerous to the citizens subject to its jurisdiction but also a poor use of their resources. Bad policing is costly on both the human resource and financial concerns of those jurisdictions. State and local governments must be active in using their resources to learn from jurisdictions that have successfully passed through DOJ pattern and practice investigations or have had experiences that have led them to seek the best practices advice to ensure that their police/community relations are a benefit to their jurisdictions, are respectful of their residents, and constitutionally protect and serve their public.

The National League of Cities has created recommendations for best practices in how state and local governments can "reimagine policing" to develop safer communities.[19] The DOJ's Office of Community Oriented Policing Services (COPS) recently published a manual: *Law Enforcement Best Practices—Lessons Learned from the Field.*[20]

Terrence M. Cunningham, a former police chief and currently the chief operating officer for the International Association of Chiefs of Police (IACP), penned an article for the American Bar Association's *Human Rights* magazine titled "How Police and Communities Can Move Forward Together." In the article he outlines seven points that "law enforcement agencies, community leaders, and elected officials should be in engaged in":

- Adoption of National Consensus Use of Force Policy
- Mandatory Participation in the National Use of Force Database
- Development of National Standards for Discipline and Termination of Officers
- Participation in the Police Officer Decertification Database
- Enhancement of Police Leadership and Culture
- Implementation of Improved Recruitment, Hiring and Promotion Practices, and
- Enhanced Ability of Police Agencies to Implement Effective Discipline

He concludes that "[t]hese changes would impact both the culture of policing and the laws and regulations that govern police operations."[21]

The Role of Community and Litigators in Constitutional Policing

The build up to situations where the DOJ steps in to conduct pattern or practice investigations is not generally a mystery. Those who live and work in communities where the federal justice department steps in are often too well aware of the tensions, misunderstandings, abuses, and fear that both the police and those they are sworn to protect and serve feel toward each other. It is imperative in this 21st century, local communities and the professional support apparatus that may exist in those communities (attorneys, bar associations, civil rights organizations, and so on) become familiar and comfortable in exercising their unique position and insight into the problems and challenges that may confront the localities where they live, work, and raise their families.

It should never be the case that communities are waiting for the match that will ignite the flames that will destroy the fabric of their community. Tools exist for communities across America to learn the signs and seek out the data that will help move governmental oversight institutions into action. That is not, of course, to excuse or remove government from being even more proactive and responsible for intervening and holding accountable their employees, agencies, and policing authorities from also exercising the proper oversight and accountability of their law enforcement agencies and departments.

Too often, community action or governmental intervention follow both the incident that ignites and the demonstrations that burn. Civil rights organizations, those groups or attorneys that are involved in police/civilian litigations, those representing police and police unions, or those representing victims of police or civil rights abuses should know the signs and data that will move the DOJ to act. This is the type of litigation that can truly save lives and restore respect, understanding, and order to the communities where we live and work. These are important tools on the road to a more perfect union.

Building the Foundation for DOJ Pattern or Practice Investigations

There is the biblical expression "seek, and ye shall find."[22] While it does take work and the investment of resources, communities and their local legal support organizations or attorneys can seek and find the data and information that can be brought forth to support the claims or concerns within a community to motivate official intervention. In the area of police/civilian interactions, that data sought will be information that will give a foundation to valid and urgent community concerns over improper patterns or practices of their state or city police agencies.

In many situations, the data is more than likely resting in plain sight. It will be data that covers patterns and practices such as

- Excessive force;
- Discriminatory harassment;
- False arrests;
- Coercive sexual conduct;
- Unlawful stops, searches, or arrests;
- Police shooting incidents;
- Violations of police policies; or
- Property theft by police, among other types of pattern or practice misconduct.

Community practitioners, attorneys, and organizations can use the federal Freedom of Information Act[23] and state and local open records laws to gather a wealth of supporting information that can be used as a foundation for appeals to the DOJ (or in certain situations state attorney general offices) to commence official pattern or practice investigations.

The DOJ recognizes the importance of community input. In the DOJ's Civil Rights Division report in 2017, it notes:[24]

Community input and engagement is a core part of every pattern-or-practice investigation . . . . The Division engages the community proactively from the very start of its pattern-or-practice investigations . . . . The Division almost always conducts a series of community or town hall meetings in different locations designed to create a forum for members of the community to speak to their experiences and insights. The Division also canvasses places communities gather—places of worship, street corners, Apartment complexes, parks, shopping malls, and local businesses . . . . The Division also gathers evidence from people who have experienced specific instances of police misconduct themselves or within their families.

There are several useful resources for where to start gathering data to provide such input. The American Civil Liberties

Union (ACLU) and its local affiliates have a manual, *Fighting Police Abuse: A Community Action Manual*, that is a tremendous report and guide to communities and their local support professionals and attorneys as to where and how to seek out critical data that can underpin approaches to the DOJ to commence pattern or practice investigations. The manual outlines "what you really need to know, and why" and "where to get the information and how."[25] The National Bar Association compiled a compelling report on the "top 25 States and Cities regarding the number of unarmed individuals who have been killed or injured while pursued or in police custody."[26]

It should be noted that communities that have suffered from systemic constitutional violations are impacted on many levels, and it is difficult to fully express the damage both physically and mentally that the citizens and non-offending officers may suffer. It is oftentimes dangerous for both citizens and non-offending officers to come forward and cooperate with these DOJ pattern or practice investigations. The importance of community is that they do come together, notwithstanding these dangers, to facilitate and welcome the DOJ's commencement of pattern or practice investigations.

Consent Decrees

Conducting DOJ pattern or practice investigations is clearly among the most effective and productive tools for bringing about police reform and securing communities where policing has breached the equal protection barriers the Constitution affords every person within its confines. Securing the findings of a DOJ pattern or practice investigation is equally important, as the result of any investigation must inure to the long-term constitutional protection of the citizens and institutions that were a part of the DOJ's investigative process, The tool that is most often used to accomplish and secure the product, results, and reforms of any pattern or practice investigation is the consent decree.

Consent decrees are voluntary agreements by parties to a litigation that are then adopted as a judgment of the court.[27] As indicated in *United States v. Armour & Co.,*[28]

Consent decrees are entered into by parties to a case after careful negotiation has produced agreement on their precise terms. The parties waive their right to litigate the issues involved in the case and thus save themselves the time, expense, and inevitable risk of litigation.

FRCP Rule 54 recognizes consent decrees as judgments. As stated in the rule, the term judgment "as used in these rules includes a decree and any order from which an appeal lies." Consent decrees are primarily used in federal courts and generally involve litigation in institutional settings. They have been commonly used in Title VII (Equal Employment & Opportunity), environmental litigation, telecommunications, trade and commerce, correctional and prison, and of course in policing and public safety matters.

As consent decrees are entered into and litigated by the parties, the parties are not limited to just resolving matters by consent decree. They can fully litigate the matter to trial and judgment or jury verdict, they can resolve it with a settlement agreement that can be enforced by the court, or they can resolve it outside of a court filing by a letter of agreement.

Consent decrees cannot be entered by the court as a judgment if any party to the decree objects or has not consented.[29] Consent decrees are subject to appeal[30] and to modifications.[31] However, as to modifications, the Supreme Court has noted that[32]

> A proposed modification should not strive to rewrite a consent decree so that it conforms to the constitutional floor. Once a court has determined that changed circumstances warrant a modification in a consent decree, the focus should be on whether the proposed modification is tailored to resolve the problems created by the change in circumstances. A court should do no more, for a consent decree is a final judgment that may be reopened only to the extent that equity requires.

Most importantly as it relates to the use of consent decrees, the court has noted a decree must generate from the four corners of the complaint that give rise to it:[33]

Accordingly, a consent decree must spring from and serve to resolve a dispute within the court's subject-matter jurisdiction. Furthermore, consistent with this requirement, the consent decree must "com[e] within the general scope of the case made by the pleadings"[34] and must further the objectives of the law upon which the complaint was based.[35]

It is largely for these reasons that consent decrees have so fittingly worked in the DOJ's pattern or practice litigation.

DOJ's Consent Decrees

"At the conclusion of an investigation, the division issues a public report detailing the findings. If the investigation finds no systemic violations of constitutional or federal statutory rights by the law enforcement agency, the DOJ will state that in the report and close the investigation. If, on the other hand, there are findings of patterns or practices of misconduct, the division will articulate precisely what those patterns or practices are and will identify any systemic deficiencies underlying those patterns."[36] Those findings are then generally recorded as part of the settlement agreement with the offending jurisdiction in a consent decree.

The DOJ's pattern or practice investigations have been described as giving the "federal government the chance to get under the hood of state and local police departments, and even to compel offending departments to clean up their acts."[37] Consent decrees have been very effective in bringing about compliance, change, community trust, and more effective policing. Over the last 30 years the DOJ has been actively using its pattern or practice investigations to bring about significant reforms in police agencies. Many of those agencies having experienced unresolved allegations of abuse of their policing authority and deteriorating police/community relations. Indeed, the "Justice Department considers consent decrees to be the 'most effective' in ensuring transparency and accountability for the implementation of institutional reforms."[38]

As policing in this nation is important, and as communities want to be safe from both the cops and the robbers, the DOJ's pattern or practice consent decrees have successfully brought enhanced confidence to communities about those police departments that are supposed to serve and protect them. Likewise, the DOJ's pattern and practice consent decrees have helped to reform the departments under the decrees and ensured adherence to the requirements of constitutional policing.

Recent DOJ Pattern or Practice Investigations and Consent Decrees

The City of Springfield, Massachusetts[39]

On April 12, 2022, the DOJ announced the first pattern or practice police investigation to be resolved through a settlement agreement (consent decree) under the administration of President Joseph R. Biden, Jr. and Attorney General Merrick B. Garland.

The Division's Civil Rights Bureau, which investigated the allegations against the Springfield Police Department's Narcotics Bureau, found that the bureau engaged in a "pattern or practice of excessive force that deprived individuals of their rights under the Fourth Amendment to the U.S. Constitution."

The decree will provide for an independent monitor who will be named as a compliance evaluator. It will also provide for the following:

- Improved polices and training related to officers' use of force.
- The training will be designed to ensure that officers avoid force whenever possible through the use of de-escalation tactics.
- Officers become familiar with and know when force can and cannot be used.
- Officers will be required to report all instances of where force is used.
- Will provide better supervision to officers and improve internal investigations of complaints of officer misconduct.
- When officers violate use of force policies, the Agreement will ensure that the Springfield Police Department holds the officers accountable.

In announcing the agreement, Kristen Clarke, Assistant Attorney General for the DOJ's Civil Rights Division, stated, "This consent decree will rebuild the public's trust by ensuring that Springfield officers who use excessive force in violation of the Fourth Amendment are held accountable."[40]

The Albuquerque Police Department, New Mexico[41]

The pattern or practice investigation and the resulting consent decree that were entered in the Albuquerque Police Department (APD) matter demonstrate how government, policing authorities, and community can come together to tackle community/policing issues.

The DOJ commenced its investigation of the APD in November of 2012; it completed its investigation in April 2014 and entered into a consent decree with the City of Albuquerque in November 2014. The court monitoring process of the APD continues, and reports have been filed as recently as May 2022.

Most particularly, the APD was accused of using a "significant amount of force . . . against persons with mental illness and in crisis." Also, its personnel had "too often used deadly force in an unconstitutional manner in their use of firearms" and had, in fact, shot and killed a homeless individual, James Matthew Boyd, in a controversial deadly use of force during the course of the DOJ's investigation. Indeed, the DOJ concluded that the "use of excessive force by APD officers is not isolated or sporadic. The pattern or practice of excessive force stems from systemic deficiencies in oversight, training and policy."[42]

The DOJ noted the significant participation of the Albuquerque community:

> We also thank community members for bringing relevant information to our attention and for sharing their experiences with us. We are encouraged by the many individuals who took an active interest in our investigation and who offered thoughtful recommendations. We appreciate those individuals who came forward to provide information about specific encounters with APD, even when

recounting such events was painful. We know that many residents care deeply about preventing the types of incidents described in this letter and have a genuine interest in supporting the many men and women of APD who uphold their oaths and keep Albuquerque safe.[43]

The city of Albuquerque presents an excellent case study of the durability of consent decrees. In November 2021, the DOJ held a meeting with city officials, the APD, the police unions, and the legal monitors when it was demonstrated that more than 198 violations of the consent decree were found by a specially formed External Force Investigation Team (EFIT) unit. Community groups had been pushing the DOJ to seek contempt of court violations against the APD. The district court had held hearings regarding the violations and the considerations of contempt. It was in the context of the hearings that the EFIT was created to enhance the monitoring and compliance of the APD.

The Ferguson, Missouri, Police Department[44]

As previously indicated, the DOJ commenced a pattern and practice investigation of the Ferguson, Missouri, Police Department and the city of Ferguson's municipal court in response to the shooting death of Michael Brown by Ferguson police officer Darren Wilson in August of 2014. As was widely reported, the shooting of Michael Brown and the manner of response to the shooting by the Ferguson Police and municipal authorities sparked weeks of demonstrations and police confrontations.

In March of 2016, the DOJ announced that it had completed a consent decree agreement that was filed in the U.S. District Court for the Eastern District of Missouri. The agreement covered:

- Community policing and engagement;
- Bias-free police and municipal court reform;
- Stops, searches, and arrests;
- Use of force and mental health crisis intervention;
- Officer supervision and accountability; and
- Civilian oversight, among other areas.

In announcing the consent decree, then U.S. Attorney General Loretta E. Lynch stated, "[t]he American people must be able to trust that their courts and law enforcement will uphold, protect and defend their constitutional rights. . . . The filing of this agreement marks the beginning of a process that the citizens of Ferguson have long awaited—the process of ensuring that they receive the rights and protections guaranteed to every American under the law."[45]

Ferguson, prior to the Brown shooting, was a predominately Black community with predominately white control. Today, four of six Ferguson City Council members are Black, compared to one before the Michael Brown shooting death and the DOJ's intervention. Both the mayor and the police chief are now Black, the police department is racially diverse and officers wear body cameras, and the city's residents no longer suffer from biased practices by its municipal court system. While there may be discussions as to whether Ferguson has, in fact, improved, the city no longer suffers from the violations that occurred prior to the Michael Brown shooting. In measuring the success of the consent decree, Ferguson is an example of how impactful a DOJ pattern or practice investigation and court-supervised consent decrees can be.[46]

Conclusion

Policing is a critical part of every community. Police departments are in every state, city, village, town, and hamlet in this nation. Police are intertwined into the workings of the communities where they exist. While many may believe that constitutional policing is a dream, few institutions in this nation are as critical to their communities as the police. Therefore, if we are to continue to grow as a nation and if we strive to ensure that every citizen is entitled to equal protection under the law, then our work as a nation is not complete until we know that our communities are being served and protected in a manner consistent with our nation's highest ideals. The true worth of a community can be determined by understanding its relationship with the police that work there.

148   *Constitutional Policing: Striving for a More Perfect Union*

As we have presented in this chapter, the federal government, through the Department of Justice, has extraordinary tools to work with communities and police departments to ensure respectful and secure environments. There are no tools on local and state levels that compare with the reach of pattern or practice investigations and resulting consent decrees or monitored settlements.

As the DOJ wrote in their findings regarding the Albuquerque Police Department:

> A well-functioning police department has the trust of the residents it protects, functions as a part of the community rather than insulated from it, and cultivates legitimacy when the public views it as engaging with them fairly and respecting the rule of law.[47]

These goals may be difficult, but they are by no means impossible.

One of the most successful recent efforts by community groups, social justice organizations, civil rights organizations, bar associations, national legislators, and the DOJ was working together to bring about President Joseph R. Biden, Jr.'s executive order on policing in America.[48] While the executive order will have significant impact, it is not a replacement for actual federal legislation on policing. The order will, however, "advance effective, accountable policing and criminal justice practices that will build public trust and strengthen public safety"[49]—efforts that will continue to ensure that constitutional policing happens.

Endnotes

1. Amber McKynzie, USC Gould School of Law, MSL '21, contributed significant research assistance to this article.

2. The DOJ has broad authority to investigate and prosecute criminal violations of federal law including the federal civil rights laws under 18 U.S.C. § 242 *et seq.* This chapter's focus is on the DOJ's civil prosecutions under its pattern or practice authority.

3. CRST Van Expedited, Inc. v. EEOC, 578 U.S. 419, 425–26 (2016).

4. Violent Crime Control and Law Enforcement Act of 1994, H.R. 3355, 103rd Cong. (1993–1994).

5. April J. Anderson, *Reforming Patterns of Unconstitutional Policing: Enforcement of 34 U.S.C. § 12601*, CONGRESSIONAL RESEARCH SERVICE (June 15, 2020), https://crsreports.congress.gov/product/pdf/LSB/LSB10494.

6. *Id.*

7. 42 U.S.C. § 1983; Bivens v. Six Unknown Name Federal Agents, 403 U.S. 388 (1971).

8. U.S. Const. art. III, Standing.

9. The Declaration of Independence.

10. U.S. Const.

11. Community Relations Services (CRS), *Toolkit for Policing: 2015*, https://www.justice.gov/crs/file/836486/download.

12. Office of Community-Oriented Policing Services, Department of Justice, Final Report of the President's Task Force on 21st Century Policing (May 2015), https://cops.usdoj.gov/pdf/taskforce/task force_finalreport.pdf.

13. Kyle Peyton et al., *A Field Experiment on Community Policing and Police Legitimacy*, 116(40) PNAS 19898 (2019).

14. *What is Community Policing*, Everbridge, https://www.everbridge.com/blog/what-is-community-policing/. *See also* Gayle Fisher-Stewart, Community Policing Explained: A Guide for Local Governments (U.S. Department of Justice Office of Community Oriented Policing Services 2007), https://cops.usdoj.gov/ric/Publications/cops-p136-pub.pdf.

15. *What is Community Policing*, Everbridge, https://www.everbridge.com/blog/what-is-community-policing/. *See also* Gayle Fisher-Stewart, Community Policing Explained: A Guide for Local Governments (U.S. Department of Justice Office of Community Oriented Policing Services 2007), https://cops.usdoj.gov/ric/Publications/cops-p136-pub.pdf.

16. 959 F. Supp. 2d 540, 556–57 (S.D.N.Y. 2013).

17. Department of Justice: Office of Public Affairs, Mar. 4, 2015, www.justice.gov/opa/speech/attorney-general-holder-delivers-update-investigations-ferguson-missouri.

18. Department of Justice: Office of Public Affairs, Apr. 21, 2021, www.justice.gov/opa/speech/attorney-general-merrick-b-garland-delivers-remarks-announcement-pattern-or-practice-investigation.

19. NLC (National League of Cities) Center for City Solutions, 2020, NLC2021_ReimaginingPolicing.pdf.

20. U.S. Department of Justice 2019. *Law Enforcement Best Practices: Lessons Learned from the Field* (Washington, D.C., Office of Community Oriented Policing Services).

21. *Civil Rights and Reimaging Politics*, 46(2) Human Rights Mag. (2021), https://www.americanbar.org/groups/crsj/publications/human_rights_magazine_home/civil-rights-reimagining-policing/.

22. *Matthew* 7:7.

23. 5 U.S.C.§ 552, as amended.

24. *The Civil Rights Division's Pattern and Practice Police Reform Work: 1994–Present*, U.S. Department of Justice (Jan. 2017), https://www.justice.gov/crt/file/922421/download.

25. *Fighting Police Abuse: A Community Action Manual*, ACLU, https://www.aclu.org/other/fighting-police-abuse-community-action-manual.

26. National Bar Association, Aug. 25, 2014, https://us7.campaign-archive.com/?u=b493e6c4d31beda32fdaf8e2d&id=70f5758f25.

27. *See generally* Firefighters v. City of Cleveland, 478 U.S. 501 (1986).

150   *Constitutional Policing: Striving for a More Perfect Union*

28. United States v. Armour & Co., 402 U.S. 673, 681–82 (1971).

29. United States v. Ward Baking Co., 376 U.S. 327 (1964).

30. Carson v. American Brands Inc., 450 U.S. 79, 88, n.14 (1981).

31. *See Firefighters*, 478 U.S. at 526–27.

32. Rufo v. Inmates of Suffolk Co. Jail, 502 U.S. 367, 391–92 (1992).

33. *See Firefighters*, 478 U.S. at 525.

34. Pacific R. Co. v. Ketchum, 11 Otto 289, 297, 101 U.S. 289, 297 (1880).

35. EEOC v. Safeway Stores Inc., 611 F.2d 795, 799 (CA10 1979), *cert. denied sub nom.*

36. *How Department of Justice Civil Rights Division Conducts Pattern-or-Practice Investigations*, U.S. DEPARTMENT OF JUSTICE, https://www.justice .gov/file/how-pp-investigations-work/download.

37. Jacob Schultz & Tia Sewell, *Pattern-or-Practice Investigations and Police Reform*, LAWFARE (Apr. 30, 2021), https://www.lawfareblog.com/pat tern-or-practice-investigations-and-police-reform.

38. *Id.*

39. *Justice Department Reaches Agreement with City of Springfield to Reform Police Department's Unconstitutional Practices*, U.S. DEPARTMENT OF JUSTICE (Apr. 13, 2022), https://www.justice.gov/opa/pr/justice-department-reac hes-agreement-city-springfield-reform-police-department-s.

40. *Id.*

41. https://www.justice.gov/usao-nm/pr/justice-department-releases -investigative-findings.

42. DOJ's 4/10/2014 letter to the City of Albuquerque, https://www .justice.gov/sites/default/files/usao-nm/legacy/2015/01/20/140410%20 DOJ-APD%20Findings%20Letter.pdf.

43. *Id.*

44. https://www.justice.gov/opa/pr/justice-department-and-city-ferg uson-missouri-resolve-lawsuit-agreement-reform-ferguson.

45. *Id.*

46. *'Nothing has changed': Ferguson grapples with legacy in wake of Floyd protests*, WASHINGTON POST (June 15, 2020), https://www.washingtonpost.com /national/nothing-has-changed-ferguson-grapples-with-legacy-in-wake -of-floyd-protests/2020/06/15/a559bc1c-abf9-11ea-a9d9-a81c1a491c52 _story.html.

47. U.S. Department of Justice, Civil Rights Division, 4/10/2014 letter to City of Albuquerque, https://www.justice.gov/sites/default/files/usa o-nm/legacy/2015/01/20/140410%20DOJ-APD%20Findings%20Letter .pdf, page 5 of letter.

48. *President Biden to Sign Historic Executive Order to Advance Effective, Accountable Policing and Strengthen Public Safety*, WHITE HOUSE (May 25, 2022), https://www.whitehouse.gov/briefing-room/statements-releases /2022/05/25/fact-sheet-president-biden-to-sign-historic-executive-order -to-advance-effective-accountable-policing-and-strengthen-public-safety/.

49. *Id.*

Chapter 7

Litigating Police-Civilian Encounters

William Harmening

Litigation in the area of police-citizen encounters, especially relating to the use of force, is contentious and at times downright ugly for the victims of police violence. There are some simple reforms that could more evenly stack the deck for these victims and their families. With a more balanced process, there is a greater likelihood that civil rights litigation will effect system-wide change and bring real consequences to the outcome. Three important reforms are needed: national police policy standards, the use of properly qualified experts in the courtroom, and more scrutiny of the science that is used to defend an officer's actions. In theory, the last two should not be in need of reform, but in reality, and mostly due to the highly organized efforts of those who defend the police no matter how wrong their actions, that need is stronger than ever. This chapter discusses the need for reform in the area of police litigation and the positive potential of these simple ideas.

Reform should follow litigation in a perfect world. In areas such as vehicle safety, tobacco, and pharmaceuticals, significant litigation seems to always result in industry-wide change. But in the area of policing, there is little connection between the two. I personally have participated as an expert witness in over 200 cases in 40 different states. These cases have resulted in jury awards and settlements of nearly $150 million, yet I cannot point to a single police department in the United States that has announced significant reforms following the disposition of their

152 *Constitutional Policing: Striving for a More Perfect Union*

case. These cases have involved questions surrounding body cameras, tasers, responding to the mentally ill, and shooting into moving vehicles, to name a few—all areas ripe for reform.

The reality is, based on my observations in nearly 40 years of policing, that jury awards and settlements are viewed by the police establishment as nothing more than a necessary inconvenience to be mostly ignored. Most of the officers I have been critical of in my cases were quickly cleared of any wrongdoing by their internal affairs unit, the assigned criminal investigators, and the local prosecutor's office. The outcome of any civil litigation is viewed as irrelevant. Imagine in the private sector an employee making a mistake that costs the company $10 million, for example. Chances are that employee will not be employed for long. But that does not happen in the police establishment. Consider the case of Tommy Le, a Vietnamese kid in Seattle, Washington, who was shot and killed in 2017 by a King County sheriff's deputy the night before his high school graduation. The deputy told investigators he feared that Tommy, who was in the throes of a mental health crisis, was about to attack him and his fellow officers with what turned out to be nothing more than an ink pen. The deputy shot Tommy in the back twice as Tommy moved past him and toward the other officers, some of whom were twice the size of Tommy's 126-pound frame. During the course of my investigation, which I conducted on behalf of Seattle attorney Jeffrey Campiche, I not only identified numerous inconsistencies in the officers' narratives but also identified evidence that had been tampered with, and still other evidence that had completely disappeared. In the end, the deputy's excessive use of force cost the county $5 million. Was the deputy terminated? Quite the contrary. He was promoted to detective.[1]

In another 2017 case in Missouri, a female deputy with the Jackson County Sheriff's Department shot and killed Donald Sneed III while she was working off-duty at a local Walmart. Sneed had shoplifted an item valued at less than $20. In this case, the entire incident was captured by security cameras, which meant that the sheriff and the local prosecutor had the same opportunity to watch the video and come to the same obvious conclusions I did—that the shooting was excessive and that the deputy was not telling the truth about what had transpired. Even before the civil complaint was filed by attorney Jermaine Wooten in St. Louis, Missouri, not only had the deputy been cleared of any wrongdoing but also the sheriff, in a very public ceremony, awarded her the department's medal of valor. The medal's luster quickly wore off, however. Within months, the same deputy shot an unarmed woman in the back during a foot pursuit and reported that the woman had taken her taser during a struggle. The evidence confirmed that the deputy was not telling the truth, and the local prosecutor had no choice but to file charges. She ultimately pled guilty and was given 180 days in jail and a suspended six-year prison term. Fortunately, her second victim survived the encounter and filed her own civil case. The county quickly settled both matters for undisclosed amounts.[2]

Even when significant police reform has happened, police officers seldom change their behavior but instead find ways to work around whatever new restrictions and limitations have been imposed on the way they do their jobs. To illustrate, with the U.S. Supreme Court's decision in *Tennessee v. Garner* (1985), for the first time the police were no longer allowed to shoot a fleeing felon in the back only because of the type of crime he or she was suspected of committing. Now the police needed an *imminent threat* of death or serious injury to themselves or others before deadly force could be used. The police simply adjusted their methods in a way that is best illustrated in an episode of the cartoon television show *South Park*, when Uncle Jimbo takes the boys hunting. When the group comes across an endangered species of bear off in the distance, Uncle Jimbo explains to the boys that the animal can be shot only if there is an imminent threat of danger. He then takes aim, yells out, "Watch out! He's coming right for us!" and fires. The fact that the bear was on a distant hill and posing no threat whatsoever was irrelevant. As Uncle Jimbo explained, the important thing was to always yell that out before shooting.

As funny as *South Park* can be at times, sadly there is very little daylight between Uncle Jimbo yelling "Watch out! He's coming right for us!" and a police officer, after shooting an unarmed kid in the back during a foot pursuit, telling investigators, "He was reaching for his waistband!" It is a popular workaround that is used every day by the police in America, and one that is difficult to overcome in the courtroom, especially when so many judges are willing to accept such an assertion as evidence of an imminent threat. The waistband defense, which has absolutely no basis in reality, is just one element of what I have described as the *deadly force script*. It is a collection of verbal tactics, gimmicks, and pseudoscientific research used by the police and their defenders in almost every criminal and civil case in which the police are accused of wrongdoing. Depending on the facts of the case, the officer may invoke the defense of *perceptual distortion*, describe the suspect as having a *thousand-yard stare* or *superhuman strength*, or justify their actions with the infamous *21-foot rule*,[3] to name a few tactics. None of these tactics are based in real science that can be generalized with any statistical certainty to a police-citizen encounter. Unfortunately, many judges have no awareness of the extent to which the deadly force script is used. If they did, they might consider limiting such arguments in their courtrooms.

To illustrate, consider the use of the *thousand-yard stare* defense.[4] It is used to help justify a shooting by portraying the suspect as an almost zombie-like figure, unpredictable and dangerous. In 2016, I was hired as the plaintiff's expert in the shooting death of Michael Brown in Ferguson, Missouri, nearly two years before. I fully expected to see in the various reports and transcripts that Officer Darren Wilson had invoked elements of the script. It is as predictable as the sunrise. Just prior to beginning my investigation, I had completed a report in the case of Dontre Hamilton in Milwaukee, Wisconsin, another high-profile police killing that led to unrest in the streets of that city. In that case, the officer who shot Hamilton stated to investigators and during a later deposition that Hamilton had demonstrated superhuman strength and had a thousand-yard stare in his eyes. Similarly, in the Michael Brown case, Officer Wilson testified before a St. Louis County grand jury that he felt like he was "a five-year-old holding onto Hulk Hogan" and that "I've never seen a look like that before. He seemed to look right through me."[5]

A simple Google search around the time of my report in the Brown case revealed the following press reports:

- Jamar Clark (killed by two Minneapolis police officers on November 15, 2015): "Minneapolis police officers Dustin Schwarze and Mark Ringgenberg described the unarmed Jamar Clark as having a 'thousand-yard stare' and 'this really weird stare,' respectively, before they killed him."[6]
- Terrence Crutcher (killed by a Tulsa, Oklahoma, police officer on September 16, 2016): "He had a very hollow look in his face, kind of a thousand-yard stare, so to speak, and would not communicate."[7]
- Laquon McDonald (killed by a Chicago police officer on October 20, 2014): "The officer stated that McDonald had a hundred-yard stare."[8] (Obviously, the officer was a bit confused in his description.)
- Che Taylor (killed by a Seattle police officer on February 21, 2016): "I recall him standing and giving us the, quote, unquote, thousand-yard stare as we move."[9]
- Michael Santiago (killed by a Brattleboro, Vermont, police officer on April 4, 2014): "Described as having a thousand-yard stare in his eyes and his face was completely emotionless."[10]
- Antonio Lopez (killed by San Jose State University police on February 21, 2014): "They said Lopez appeared catatonic, his face frozen in a thousand-yard stare."[11]

It was likely that none of the judges, juries, or family members in these cases had any awareness of the deadly force script or the extent to which such testimony, seemingly novel at the time, finds its way into civil rights cases across the United States. The sad fact is, if you ask ten police officers to define what the thousand-yard stare is, you may get ten different answers. In reality, it has been redefined by the law enforcement community to mean the exact opposite of its original usage. The term was coined during World War II to describe the condition known as *shell shock*. Physiologically speaking, it occurs when an individual is so overwhelmed by stress and fear that the parasympathetic nervous system is unable to return the body to a state of equilibrium. It is the final stage in the *fight, flight, or freeze* mechanism, when the person's ability to function simply shuts down, resulting in a catatonic-like state. The law enforcement community, especially those charged with training new officers, has redefined the term to mean a manifestation of a heightened state of agitation and fearlessness, resulting in an almost animal-like ferocity and indicating that an attack is imminent.[12] It is used to bolster an officer's state of mind defense and is particularly effective since it cannot be disproven.

National Policy Standards

It may surprise some to know that police departments in the United States are not legally mandated to even have policies and procedures, much less a set that is standardized across the country. Relating to the issue of force, arguably a department's most important policy, some police departments write their own policy; others simply copy the policy of another department. Some adopt a model policy authored by groups such as the International Association of Chiefs of Police, and still others purchase a model policy offered by some private entity that charges for its services. All have their own set of problems.

To illustrate the problem of non-standardized use of force policies, most police departments, but certainly not all, now have policies in place that prohibit their officers from shooting into a moving vehicle except under very limited circumstances, either in response to someone inside the vehicle shooting at them or if the vehicle itself is being used as a deadly weapon. Some departments prohibit even the latter if the officer can step out of the vehicle's path. These policies have been established due to the large number of innocent people, many of them children, who have been killed only because they had the misfortune of being inside a suspect's vehicle when the officer(s) chose to fire. Still other departments include no prohibition at all in their policies and leave it up to the officer's discretion. In fact, one popular provider of model police policies does not include such a prohibition unless the purchasing department chooses to add it. There is no national standard or law that mandates such a prohibition.

For the plaintiff's attorney who is litigating a case involving an officer firing into a moving vehicle and who must successfully make the case that the shooting was unreasonable, if the department already has a policy in place prohibiting it, then the attorney is already halfway to the goal line because the department itself has deemed it unreasonable by virtue of their policy. But in the case of a department that has no such policy, and thus no violation of policy by the officer, the attorney will have to take a longer route to establishing unreasonableness, a task made more difficult when the trier of fact considers that the officer violated no policy.

And this problem is not limited only to the act of shooting into moving vehicles. Some jurisdictions limit the number of taser cycles that can be deployed against a suspect to three (15 seconds total),[13] while others include no limitation at all in their policies. Some departments allow their officers to apply a vascular neck restraint—the classic sleeper hold—to restrain a struggling suspect, while other departments limit its use only to when deadly force is justified. And still others, including the Los Angeles Police Department (LAPD) and Miami-Dade Police Department, prohibit its use altogether. A few states, among them Washington and Minnesota, have now legislated a ban on the practice. Most states have remained silent on the issue. And finally, even the "force continuum," which shows the level of force that can be used against each level of threat, differs from department to department, especially across state lines. For example, some departments identify the taser as representing a minimal level of force that can be used merely to force compliance with an officer's command. Other departments describe it as an intermediate level of force that can be used only for defensive purposes when there is an active threat. There is not even agreement within the law enforcement community on what constitutes *passive* versus *active* resistance, a critical point that can limit or allow various forms of force. National policy standards would resolve these major inconsistencies in police practices from department to department.

Another important area where a national policy standard is needed relates to the use of police body cameras. Beginning in 1991 with the videotaped beating of Rodney King, the use of video cameras by the public and the police has become a great deal more widespread. Without cell phone videos we would not have seen Michael Brown's body lying on the hot pavement for nearly four hours. And more recently, we would never have known about the true length of time Officer Derek Chauvin had his knee on George Floyd's neck. Citizen videos have become extremely important in pursuing litigation against the police. And while early on the police establishment, and the legislators supporting them, took steps to prevent people from videotaping the police, those restrictions have all but disappeared from the statutes of most states. Now we have reached the point where the police in large part are videotaping themselves, not only with body cameras but also with dashboard cameras in their vehicles—some will show speed and direction of travel—and even cameras mounted on some of their weapons.

Those involved in police litigation, especially on the plaintiff's side, will tell you that police body cameras have had a positive impact on the litigation process. They will then likely tell you how many cases they have had where either the body camera did not work or the officer failed to strike the record button properly or forgot to activate it all. There are several different policies that police departments have adopted across the United States. Of course, many still do not use body cameras, and even in departments that do, most do not require their SWAT officers to use them under the guise of not wanting to disclose methods and tactics. Some departments will require their uniformed officers to activate their body cameras in every citizen encounter, while others leave it up to the officers' discretion by including a "when safe and feasible" provision in their policy. Even when officers intend to activate their body camera, there is no consensus on when they should do that.

There is a dirty little secret regarding body cameras that much of the public is unaware of. It relates to how they work. An officer's body camera is always recording and is constantly overwriting the prior 30 seconds. So, when the officer actually hits the record button, the buffer keeps the prior 30 seconds plus everything from there forward.[14] The benefit of this is that when something happens fast, the officers will still capture the event by activating their camera within 30 seconds. Of course, it also means that officers can activate the camera after the outcome is already known. If the officers know they just shot a suspect without justification, they need only wait 30 seconds before hitting the record button and the shooting will not be captured. They can then simply offer the "as soon as safe and feasible" argument and avoid a policy violation by having at least activated their body camera at some point.

The use of body cameras has been good for police litigation, and it has also been good for the law enforcement profession. Body cameras contribute to more professional and policy-adherent officers who are less willing to break the rules and communicate in unprofessional ways with the citizens they encounter. But body cameras are only as effective as policy demands them to be, and like many areas of policing, the policies need strengthening and standardizing. And certainly, there should be a national mandate that all police officers, including SWAT officers, use them.

The lack of national policy standards creates a huge gray area for the victims of police violence who choose to seek justice inside the courtroom. It creates a situation where officers may be able to argue that they were following proper procedure, or conversely, that there was no department policy prohibiting their actions. Once again, with this lack of uniformity, the cards are stacked in favor of the police from the get-go. What is desperately needed is a single set of legislated policy standards that will cover every officer in the United States and provide a single force continuum with clearly defined definitions. What is also needed are real consequences if a civil judge or jury rules in favor of a plaintiff in a civil rights case. No police officers in the United States who are alleged to have violated a person's constitutional rights should remain employed if the case against them is successful. It is as simple as that. With national policy standards, the opportunity for officers whose actions have been judged unreasonable to argue that they were following established department policy, or that there was no policy in place prohibiting their actions, will be greatly limited. Such standards will go a long way toward linking police litigation with police reform in a meaningful way.

Qualified Expert Witnesses

The area of expert witness testimony in police litigation can best be described as a complete free-for-all. Anyone can hang a shingle and call him- or herself a use of force or police practices expert. There is no standardized certification process or national court qualification standard. Experts must prove their level of expertise and qualifications in each and every case, even in the same judicial district. There is a real possibility that an expert may be qualified by one judge in a district only to be disqualified by another. The lack of real standards becomes burdensome for the truly qualified experts whose career may be in jeopardy if a judge for whatever reason bars their testimony. Conversely, the lack of standards benefits those who lack the proper credentials by increasing the odds that their testimony will be allowed.

Not only is there a deadly force *script*, as I have described it, but also there is an entire deadly force *industry* that has as its objective defending and exonerating police officers no matter how bad or unreasonable their actions. Even when an officer's unreasonable use of force is clearly seen on video, the wagons will still be circled, and the deadly force industry will move into action like a finely choreographed dance. It begins immediately following a questionable police action. It is not uncommon for an involved officer's union representative to arrive at the scene even before command staff and investigators. Within hours after the incident, a private attorney is engaged to represent the officer(s), oftentimes one recommended by the police union or even the department's insurance carrier. In my experience, those who maintain a practice of representing the police, a number of whom are former officers themselves, typically bring with them their own experts. This is where the deck is once again stacked in favor of the police. These pro-police experts may at times be little more than hired guns who will offer any theory or testimony needed to win their case. Very few of them are truly qualified to act as use of force experts. Most are little more than firearms experts, an area of knowledge that in no way qualifies them to testify about the complex behavioral dynamics inherent in any use of force encounter. I have been on the opposing side of supposed experts who have little more than a high school education and some police experience. Others provide in their CVs page after page of fancy-sounding police training and association memberships. If you peel away the layers, however, you will find that most police training occurs in a single day and is neither peer reviewed nor instructed by academically qualified individuals. And the associations, which number many, amount to little more than a newsletter, an annual conference, and some official-sounding letters that the members can put behind their name on a business card in return for a fee and an unverified application. I even came across one expert who belonged to an association related to police shooting investigations that appeared to have been started by the expert himself. I suspected he was probably its only member.

These questionable experts are able to act as experts because many judges, juries, and even plaintiffs' attorneys lack the knowledge to recognize a lack of qualifications when they see it. Law enforcement is a subculture with its own language, and they have been very effective at using that to their advantage in the courtroom. Pro-police experts almost always submit CVs that include credentials and training titles that civilians may have difficulty even translating into a meaningful subject they can comprehend. The routine is always to overpower their adversaries and the trier of fact with an inventory of credentials, memberships, and training that makes them appear beyond scrutiny. Does it work? In many cases, yes. I have yet to be involved in a case where the judge requested transcripts or written training modules to support an expert's represented knowledge and expertise. Likewise, I have seldom seen a plaintiff's attorney do the same, even when I recommended it. When experts are disclosed in a case, both sides should scrutinize their qualifications and education and accept nothing at face value. If they do, it will drive many of the unqualified pro-police experts out of the business or limit their opinions and testimony to specific areas. Eventually, this will lead to more qualified and independent experts participating on both sides.

162   *Constitutional Policing: Striving for a More Perfect Union*

A final word on the issue of independence. The deadly force industry is very good at window-dressing an expert's qualifications and expertise. Likewise, they are also good at keeping the curtain closed on the industry's rather incestuous network of relationships. Conflicts abound and oftentimes go unnoticed or unchallenged. One popular pro-police expert routinely testifies on the appropriateness of an officer's use of a particular weapon of force and always opines that the weapon could not have contributed to the victim's death. Peel back a few layers and you will discover that this particular expert sits on the board of directors of the company that manufactures the weapon. Members of a corporation's board have a fiduciary obligation to the corporation and its stockholders. They are precluded from publicly saying anything that could negatively impact the company or its stock value. This creates a huge conflict for the expert. If he were to opine that in certain situations the weapon can indeed kill or contribute significantly to an individual's death, this could cause police departments to pull away from its use, which in turn could negatively impact the company's revenue and stock value, exactly what happened with the PR-24 police baton in years past. If that connection is made, then the expert/board member may be held liable by both the corporation and the stockholders. As clear as this conflict is, this expert continues to testify and offer supposedly independent and unbiased opinions in cases where the weapon in question has been used, even inappropriately so.

The problem of independence, or a lack of, was laid bare at my feet in one deadly force case in California. In that case, two of the issues I addressed in my analysis were whether the officer's use of force was consistent with department policy and whether the policy itself was sufficiently written. In this case, the department used a model use of force policy written by a for-profit entity. The trial ended in a multi-million-dollar judgment for the plaintiff. It was after the trial when my curiosity compelled me to do some post-trial research, and I uncovered conflicts that caused my head to spin. First, the municipality's insurance carrier provided a discount for using the for-profit entity's policies. I then learned that the for-profit entity was founded and originally owned by the very defense attorney who had just spent seven hours grilling me on the stand. And finally, the most glaring conflict was that the supposedly independent and unbiased expert used by the attorney was also on the payroll of the for-profit entity as a policy writer! In my mind, that made both the attorney and the expert potential witnesses in the case if the policy—its creation, rationale, and genesis—were called into question.

Unfortunately, these are not isolated incidents. The most common conflict is when a former or retired officer is from the same department as the officer(s) involved in the litigation. I had one case where the expert was one of the academy training officers who trained the officer being sued. I had no expectations that the expert would testify to anything other than that the officer had been properly trained. The lack of independence in the expert witness business will only be remedied by scrutinizing and questioning experts' professional connections with the same level of intensity as their credentials and education.

So, what should it take to act as a use of force or police practices expert? By far, the more abused of the two is the former. To be able to present yourself as a true use of force expert, there are three areas of knowledge required—what I describe as the *when, how,* and *why* of force. Regarding the first, experts must have a comprehensive knowledge of when an officer can use various levels of force. This knowledge includes an understanding of *Tennessee v. Garner* (1985) and *Graham v. Connor* (1989), as well as the concept of the *reasonable officer*. They must understand the force continuum and its various related models. And they must understand how police officers are trained to know and understand when and at what level force can legally be used.

Regarding the *how* of force, experts must understand the various weapons available to an officer—including his or her own verbal interaction with a suspect—and how each is used. They must understand the taser, including how to read the various data reports available following a deployment. They must understand the effects of O.C. pepper spray and how an expandable baton is properly used. If the jurisdiction allows for the use of a vascular neck restraint, they must understand how it is properly applied and be able to relate that information to the facts of the case and the officer's statement. They must have a knowledge of positional/compressional asphyxiation as it relates to handcuffing and restraint, as well as the functionality of the various less lethal weapons the department may have at its disposal.

The final leg of knowledge, and the one most problematic for use of force experts, is a comprehensive knowledge of human behavior and the behavioral dynamics related to the use of force. Any use of force is first and foremost a psychological exchange between two or more adversaries. To act as an expert, the person must understand such concepts as perception, perceptual distortion, the effects of stress, human chronometry (reaction time), and the psychology of self-destruction (suicide by cop), to name just a few. This is where so many experts, especially on the side of the defense, overstep their expertise. Their reports will often be loaded with psychological concepts that include no citations or explanation. In a case I worked with Chicago attorney Brian Coffman involving an experienced Chicago Police Department detective who shot a kid in the back (fatally so) as he ran from the detective down a city street holding an iPhone box, the defense's expert offered the bold opinion that police officers often experience perceptual distortion under stress and misperceive other objects as guns. He offered no real research to support this, nor did he even explain the mechanisms of perceptual distortion or the factors that can mitigate this phenomenon. In the end, bolstered by my own affidavit, attorney Coffman filed the appropriate motion and nearly the entirety of the expert's report was excluded. The case was settled for $3 million.

The area of human behavior, with all its nuances and complexities, is the area of knowledge and expertise most lacking among expert witnesses. It is also the quickest conduit to getting a use of force expert excluded or greatly limited. When an expert's report is tendered, the opposing side should always have someone with an academic background in psychology or forensic psychology review the report for any use of psychological methods and constructs without the requisite academic background. It is not enough for experts to simply restate what they have read.

They must be able to articulate a knowledge of that subject that extends beyond their source. Multiple times I have come across experts offering an opinion on a particular psychological concept only to discover that their source was the very first item returned in a Google search.

Science in the Courtroom

The third area of reform that is desperately needed goes hand in hand with the second, and that is a return to allowing only legitimate science in the courtroom. Unfortunately, the waters have become so muddied by non-peer-reviewed pseudoscientific research published in non-peer-reviewed police publications that the trier of fact is faced with a challenging task in trying to separate the wheat from the chaff. Not only does the deadly force industry include experts ready to roll into action and support accused officers no matter how unreasonable their actions, but also those experts have a briefcase full of mostly reverse-engineered or fatally flawed research to bolster their efforts. And if that is not enough, they will conduct their own experiments, always with the outcome predetermined, and then portray them as scientific.

One of the more comical experiments I have seen was offered by a pro-police expert who was hired by a district attorney to review the case of a Wisconsin officer who shot and killed a suspect during a foot pursuit after the suspect purportedly turned and threatened the officer with nothing more than an empty five-gallon plastic bucket, hardly a deadly weapon.[15] This did not deter the supposed expert. He conducted an experiment showing a rather large actor breaking a board with the same bucket and concluded that it was in fact a deadly weapon. There were so many problems with this exercise in absurdity, not the least of which was the fact that when some viewers recognized dust flying out of the bucket when it struck the board, the expert was forced to admit that he put dry concrete in it. No one until I came along recognized the other major problem. The expert had pulled the same trick martial artists do when they break boards and bricks with their hands. He had elevated the board with blocks on each end, thereby guaranteeing that the full force of the strike would move to the middle and cause the board to break much easier. Even if he had tried to do it properly, the expert made no effort to control for such things as bone density and strength compared to wood.

In the end, even with the expert offering what amounted to a fraudulent piece of research to support his conclusion, the district attorney claimed that the officer's use of deadly force was justified. Even worse, when the same expert was used in the civil case, minus the bucket experiment, the judge accepted his report, along with another absurd experiment involving an 80-pound floor jack, and granted qualified immunity to the officer, bringing an end to the family's case.

Unfortunately, it is not uncommon for pro-police experts to offer supposed scientific research like the above, nor is it uncommon for judges to accept it as science. Even when research that has an air of legitimacy is offered, mostly conducted by pro-police academicians, care must be taken to scrutinize the research for any "confounding" variables, or those variables that are not readily apparent that will skew the research in one direction or the other. One of the often-used elements of the deadly force script by pro-police experts is the *perceptual distortion* defense. It allows officers to argue that they did not see something that was right in front of them or that they did see something that was not. It is a popular defense in cases where the police shoot an unarmed suspect. I have had cases where the officer, typically after meeting with his or her union representative, argues that he or she misperceived a cell phone, a set of keys, and even a pair of sunglasses for a gun. To support this defense, the expert who works on the officer's behalf will almost always use the same piece of research that was carried out by a professor (and former LAPD officer) in Missouri. In his study,[16] which provides only anecdotal evidence, less than 100 officers involved in deadly force encounters described whether they experienced perceptual distortion, and if so, what type (visual, auditory, passage of time, etc.). Not surprisingly, a significant number stated that they did, leading the researcher to conclude that it is understandable when an officer under stress shoots an unarmed suspect.

The above research sounds reasonable but for one fatal flaw, a confounding variable. Every police officer is aware of the statute of limitations on murder and civil rights violations in his or her state. No police officers involved in a recent deadly force encounter will see much to gain by telling a researcher that they perceived their circumstances during the shooting with perfect clarity. Conversely, they will likely see little risk in telling the researcher that they experienced perceptual distortion during the encounter. Aside from this fatal flaw, the researcher also failed to control for the officers' level of experience or the amount of stress they reported feeling. Unfortunately, this piece of research continues to routinely find its way into the courtroom and be accepted by judges as legitimate research.

One need only look at the 1999 shooting of Amadou Diallo by four NYPD detectives to see this defense in play. Diallo, who was mistaken for a recent rape suspect and who was holding his wallet in an attempt to hand over his ID, was shot 19 times after the four detectives fired a total of 41 bullets at him. The officers were indicted and eventually acquitted after arguing a perceptual distortion defense. The case also illustrated another phenomenon—*contagious shooting*—the existence of which the law enforcement community to this day denies.[17] Not surprisingly, when such a circumstance is alleged, pro-police experts will have more pseudoscientific research relating to that phenomenon ready to cite in their report and conclusions.

Conclusion

Litigation and reform should be inextricably linked, with the former demanding and defending the latter. But that has not been the case in the area of police litigation. For example, in one judicial district the trier of fact may conclude that the use of a taser in the manner it was used caused or contributed to the person's death. Yet not a single police department, not in that or any other district, nor even the department named in the lawsuit, will change their taser policies to avoid such a tragedy from repeating itself. And such a conclusion will have no bearing on other cases with similar circumstances. Pro-police experts will still testify that the taser is a perfectly safe weapon that has never caused or contributed to anyone's death and will use questionable science to support their opinions. In recent years, I have worked many compressional/positional asphyxiation cases across the United States, yet still, even after the case of George Floyd in Minneapolis, a case I worked on behalf of Chicago attorney Anthony Romanucci, I still listen in disbelief as pro-police experts routinely testify that compressional/positional asphyxiation is a myth. I also find it appalling that so many police departments in the United States still allow their officers to use a vascular neck restraint after a few hours of training and in situations where no lethal threat is present, oftentimes on a person who is in the throes of a mental health crisis.

We are in a time of transition in policing, and the law enforcement community will be resistant to change. Until there are real consequences that accompany police misconduct that extend beyond the occasional criminal conviction, a change of attitude will be difficult to achieve. For starters, it is my belief that in any litigation where a civil rights violation is alleged, if the trier of fact rules in favor of the plaintiff, then the officer(s) involved should immediately forfeit their ability to ever again serve as a police officer in the United States. While many departments will quietly "terminate" such officers, they will typically negotiate a voluntary resignation, which is then reported as such to the state's Peace Officer Standards and Training organization. By checking that box, as opposed to "for cause," it allows the officer to simply go to another department. And given that an experienced officer will not need academy training, something that can seriously strain a small department's budget, most are quickly rehired. This circumstance points to another area of needed reform.

Until reform happens in the courtroom, real reform on the street will be difficult to achieve. This will require that unqualified experts and pseudoscientific and even fraudulent research be eliminated from the process. That will happen when plaintiffs' attorneys become better at scrutinizing and challenging the deadly force industry at every turn with well-written and scientifically based motions to exclude or disqualify. It will also change when reformers push the idea of a national court certification, perhaps through the U.S. Department of Justice, of anyone who intends to testify as an expert in the areas of police practices and use of force. Short of that, a set of standards to guide a judge's evaluation of an expert and his or her science would be of benefit. The court could also be required or petitioned to engage its own expert to provide opinion on the qualifications and conclusions of the designated experts on both sides of the case.

One thing is for certain: reform cannot be a knee-jerk political reaction apart from the legal process. Case in point is the George Floyd case. Afterward, politicians across the country pushed for a ban on chokeholds. But of course, most police officers quietly snickered because there has ALWAYS been a ban on chokeholds unless deadly force is justified. What was and still is needed, and what a few cities, counties, and states astutely concluded, is a ban on the vascular neck restraint and any other type of restraint that compresses the neck when deadly force is not justified. Long before George Floyd, civil litigation all over the United States involving cases of compressional/positional asphyxiation had already resulted in many multi-million-dollar settlements and jury awards, yet on May 25, 2020, the Minneapolis Police Department's policies still allowed for the use of the vascular neck restraint and had no specific prohibition on compressing an individual's neck with a knee or otherwise. Perhaps the outcome in that case, both the civil and criminal, was a foregone conclusion, but in similar matters across the United States since, cases with nearly identical circumstances and little or no publicity, the deadly force industry has continued to circle the wagons and argue that the vascular neck restraint and neck compression are mostly safe—even bringing in one of a handful of medical doctors in the United States who are willing to offer such testimony in spite of a significant body of research to the contrary—and that the victim could not have been choking since he or she was still able to speak. Thus, the department's ban on chokeholds was never violated. Even a lengthy prison term for Officer Chauvin and a $27 million settlement has had limited effect, mostly because there is no nationally mandated policy standard that simply bans all neck compression in any form unless deadly force is justified. Without it, such unnecessary tragedies will only continue, and the officers' actions will be aggressively defended in the courtroom by unqualified experts using questionable or even fraudulent science. Sadly, it is a predictable drama that plays out daily in America's courtrooms.

Endnotes

1. Mike Carter, *King County Sheriff's Office will pay $5 million settlement in deputy's fatal shooting of Tommy Le*, SEATTLE TIMES (Mar. 24, 2021), https://www.seattletimes.com/seattle-news/king-county-sheriffs-office-will-pay-5-million-settlement-in-deputys-fatal-shooting-of-tommy-le/ (accessed Apr. 18, 2022).

2. Brian Dulle & Sean McDowell, *Former Jackson County deputy sentenced to 180 days in jail as shock time for 2019 shooting*, FOX4 KANSAS CITY (Mar. 25, 2021), https://fox4kc.com/news/former-jackson-county-deputy-sentenced-to-180-days-in-jail-for-august-2019-midtown-shooting-of-woman/ (accessed Apr. 18, 2022).

3. William L. Sandel et al., *A scientific examination of the 21-foot rule*, 22(3) POLICE PRACTICE AND RESEARCH 1314 (2021).

4. Jason Sole & Rachel Warnaka, *On police, black men and the 'thousand yard stare,'* MINN. POST (May 19, 2016), https://www.minnpost.com/community-voices/2016/05/police-black-men-and-thousand-yard-stare/ (accessed Apr. 18, 2022).

5. State of Missouri v. Darren Wilson. Wilson testimony on September 16, 2014, before a St. Louis County grand jury. Pgs. 212–24.

6. Sole & Warnaka, *supra* note 4.

7. *North Carolina Shooting Sparks Protests; New Discovery in Tulsa Shooting*, CBN NEWS (Sept. 21, 2016), https://www1.cbn.com/cbnnews/us/2016/september/north-carolina-shooting-sparks-protests-new-discovery-in-tulsa-shooting (accessed Apr. 18, 2022).

8. Paige Fry & Madeline Buckley, *Chicago Police Department slow to make reform progress since the shooting of Laquon McDonald, and still in need of cultural change, experts say*, CHICAGO TRIBUNE (Jan. 31, 2022), https://www.chicagotribune.com/news/breaking/ct-jason-van-dyke-release-police-reform-20220131-sb3joci7ijcxdfjnx3go3aia2q-story.html (accessed Apr. 18, 2022).

9. Rick Anderson, *Did Che Taylor Have to Die?*, SEATTLE WEEKLY (Sept. 14, 2016), https://www.seattleweekly.com/news/an-inquest-jury-next-week-will-ask-did-che-taylor-have-to-die/ (accessed Apr. 18, 2022).

10. Bob Audette, *Police report in Santiago shooting released*, Brattleboro Reformer (July 22, 2014), https://www.reformer.com/local-news/police-report-in-santiago-shooting-released/article_07e3644f-17f4-5f1b-96bb-cf7f68b5a259.html (accessed Apr. 18, 2022).

11. Jennifer Wadsworth, *DA Clears Officer in San Jose State Shooting*, San Jose Inside (May 27, 2015), https://www.sanjoseinside.com/news/da-clears-officer-in-san-jose-state-shooting/ (accessed Apr. 18, 2022).

12. *Let's review the pre-attack indicators*, Police1 (Sept. 8, 2014), https://www.police1.com/officer-safety/articles/lets-review-the-pre-attack-indicators-xS5lghHPRkWg9VRN/ (accessed Apr. 18, 2022).

13. This in fact has been the standard established by the U.S. Department of Justice since 2011.

14. *See* Axon Body Camera User Manual, Chapter 4, *Buffering Mode*.

15. This was the 2015 case of Aaron Siler, who was shot and killed by a Kenosha, Wisconsin, police officer following a foot pursuit when Siler purportedly threatened the officer with an empty five-gallon plastic bucket. The officer was cleared of any wrongdoing.

16. David Klinger & Rod K. Brunson, *Police officers' perceptual distortions during lethal force situations: Informing the reasonableness standard*, 8(1) Criminology & Public Policy 117 (2009).

17. Chuck Joyner, *Fighting the contagious fire phenomenon*, Police1 (Jan. 29, 2010), https://www.police1.com/police-products/firearms/articles/fighting-the-contagious-fire-phenomenon-5JYTjrb0SPXtNbbI/ (accessed Apr. 19, 2022).

Chapter 8

Transforming Policing: Lessons from New York City[1]

Donna Lieberman, with Johanna Miller,
Lee Rowland, Chris Dunn, Michael Sisitzky,
and Jared Trujillo

Police officers are increasingly present in our daily lives. They are on our streets, at our schools, and at protests with increasing authority and scope. Troublingly, they are responsible for being first responders to issues that law enforcement personnel are fundamentally unsuited for: public health needs, dispute resolution, mental health crises, and even routine school discipline and operating metal detectors at the schoolhouse door—issues that are often exacerbated by police officers' training to see everyone as a potential suspect.[2] Out of the 10.3 million arrests made per year, only 5 percent involve allegations of violence. Most of the remaining 95 percent are acts that are considered crimes but do not have to be (for example, marijuana possession) or offenses that stem from poverty, mental illness, and drug addiction.[3] As a result, many minor conflicts and potential harms that have little or no connection to crime—and many people, particularly in high-policing communities—are viewed with suspicion and met with a police-first, lock-'em-up response.[4]

As police reach expands, so too does their size and budget. The New York City Police Department (NYPD) is the largest municipal police department in the country with approximately 35,000 uniformed officers and another 10,000 civilian employees.[5] The School Safety Division of the NYPD maintains a headcount that makes it the fifth-largest police department in the country, employing more officers to patrol New York City public schools than the entire cities of Las Vegas, San Francisco, or Washington, D.C.[6]

While the power, responsibility, and resources of police departments have grown, their oversight and accountability have continued to be inadequate. Police officers are rarely held accountable when they harm—and even kill—the people they are supposed to protect.

In a decades-long effort to achieve justice and equity for New Yorkers, especially New Yorkers of color, who are most impacted by over-policing, the New York Civil Liberties Union (NYCLU) identified several areas of deep concern with the NYPD.[7] We at the NYCLU have undertaken extensive research, litigaton, and advocacy about police policies and practices and their racially disparate impact on New Yorkers, especially young Black men. We were instrumental in the establishment and ongoing monitoring of the New York City Civilian Complaint Review Board (CCRB); achieving and analyzing public data on "broken windows" tactics such as stop and frisk and marijuana enforcement; the criminalization of school discipline; accountability for wrongdoing, including civil rights violations and deaths; and challenging police abuse and over-policing in a range of contexts, including low-level offenses, school discipline, political protest, and the vice squad. The recommendations below are drawn from the NYCLU's extensive institutional knowledge, understanding, and ongoing work on these issues, particularly in New York City.

Here are six things policy makers can do to limit the excessive power and scope of police departments:

1. Achieve police-free schools.
2. Remove police as first responders to mental health crises. Public health professionals should be the first responders, and police should be available as emergency backup.
3. End militarized, "command-and-control" policing of protests.
4. End broken windows policing.
5. Eliminate vice squads.
6. Ensure transparency about policing practices and discipline.

Achieve Police-Free Schools

Walk into any public school in America and you will most likely be greeted by a security guard, police officer, or surveillance camera. The presence of police, police tactics, and police equipment in schools has become almost as commonplace as student artwork in the hallways.

Although many people point to the 1999 Columbine High School shooting as the beginning of the securitization of schools, the relationship between the police and education began much earlier and has an indelible connection to racial integration and the civil rights movement. In 1948, the city of Los Angeles established a school police force to protect school property after schools were integrated;[8] in 1957, the National Guard first attempted to block the "Little Rock Nine" from entering Central High School before being deployed to protect them; and in 1967, Philadelphia police in riot gear responded when Black students staged a walkout to demand access to African-American studies.[9] Today, approximately 58 percent of schools in the United States report having a sworn law enforcement officer on campus at least one day a week.[10] For high schools, that number rises to almost 70 percent.[11]

Millions of state and federal dollars are available to hire school police. In New York City, for example, almost half a billion dollars is spent on the NYPD's School Safety operations each year.[12] At the same time, across the country, school budgets are under intense pressure[13] with many having never recovered to pre-recession numbers. This has resulted in a system where educators rely on police to fill staffing gaps, improperly viewing them as ad hoc teachers, disciplinarians, guidance counselors, school nurses, and school social workers.[14] A 2018 report by the American Civil Liberties Union (ACLU) found that 14 million American children attend a school with police officers but zero counselors, nurses, psychologists, or social workers on staff.[15]

Police are assumed to be essential to school safety, particularly with regard to gun violence. Yet, tragically, gun violence has occurred in dozens of schools that employ a police officer. In nearly all incidents, the shooting was over before the officer intervened.[16]

Keeping kids safe at school is, of course, a paramount responsibility of communities and school leaders. But relying on police as the only or primary mechanism for safety misses the root causes of student conflict and makes school deeply unsafe for any kid viewed as a problem.

Often, school police take over the role of maintaining traditional school discipline. As a result, behavior that may have once resulted in a walk to the principal's office—such as shoving matches, disrespectful behavior, tardiness, and dress code violations—can result in a walk to the precinct. Police in schools sometimes operate with Immigration and Customs Enforcement, endangering immigrant youth and families.[17] They may use facial recognition software, metal detectors, and surveillance cameras at school entrances (sometimes barring parents and students themselves) and turning the morning arrival experience into a stressful series of delays, suspicion, fear, and even conflict. And far too often, they use unnecessary force and physical restraints on students, including children as young as five.[18]

The impacts of modern school policing are most dire for students of color. Despite making up only 39 percent of student enrollment nationwide, Black and Latinx students represent 58 percent of school arrests, and nearly always for minor misbehavior.[19] In New York City, the nation's largest school district, approximately 100,000 children walk through a school metal detector every day, and more than 90 percent of them are Black and Latinx.[20] For children growing up in communities of color, police officers are often associated with feelings of fear, intimidation, and trauma, not a welcoming school environment.[21]

It is time for America's schools to move toward a vision of police-free education. Achieving this will require serious investment in school climate and increasing the number of educators and support staff in school buildings. A generation of teachers may well need professional development resources to reboot their approaches to classroom and conflict management. And schools must employ trained educators, counselors, and paraprofessionals in proper ratios to meet students' needs in resolving conflict, healing trauma, and living with disabilities. Many schools serving vulnerable populations have already successfully integrated restorative practices for conflict resolution, clinical counseling, and unarmed safety monitors with ties to the local community into their safety protocols.[22]

School district budgets can be read as community values statements. Unfortunately, too many communities are investing huge sums into school police while starving school budgets of what they need to thrive. By divesting from school police, communities can free up funds to hire teachers, counselors, and other supports that help students learn and thrive. In 2020, Senator Chris Murphy and Congresswoman Ayanna Pressley introduced the Counselors Not Criminalization in Schools Act, a bill that would pause federal funding for school police while simultaneously making more funds available for support staff such as counselors.[23] This legislation would begin to turn the tide on decades of overinvestment in school policing.

School districts across the country have begun to recognize the ways overinvesting in school police have harmed their students. In the early 2020s, Columbus, Madison, Seattle, Minneapolis, Oakland, Denver, and Rochester all ended or suspended contracts with local police. These districts are an important vanguard for a new era of school safety and should be viewed as models for the police-free classrooms of the future.

Replace Police with Public Health Professionals as First Responders to Mental Health Crises

In March 2020, Daniel Prude was experiencing an acute mental health crisis in Rochester, New York, when his family called 911 for help. He was naked in the street and posed no risk to any other person. Yet, Rochester police responded in force, handcuffed him, placed a hood over his head, and held him face down until he stopped breathing. Daniel Prude was a man experiencing an obvious mental health crisis, and he deserved care and dignity—but he was denied both. Instead, police killed him.

Daniel Prude's death is not an outlier. Studies show that up to one-half of people who become victims of police violence have a disability—and overwhelmingly, a mental health disability.[24] For too many communities, 911 has become the only option for seeking help in a mental health crisis. And police often arrive at the scene armed with deadly weapons, a lack of mental health training, and an inability to de-escalate the personal crisis.

In most cities, police are the first to respond to the scene of someone in a mental health crisis, and many transport individuals to an emergency room, jail, or psychiatric hospital. But police are not mental health counselors or social workers. Their lack of comprehensive training and skills and their approach of treating everyone as a potential criminal do not result in safe and appropriate responses to people in distress.[25]

Moreover, the presence of armed police officers too frequently escalates crisis situations. In fact, people with untreated mental illness are 16 times more likely to be killed during a police encounter than others approached or stopped by an officer.[26] The *Washington Post* found that 20 to 25 percent of fatal police shootings killed a person with mental illness, and that approximately 92 percent of people killed by police while holding some sort of weapon (ranging from a toy weapon to a knife or a gun) were people with mental illness. However, those numbers only represent individuals "perceived to be mentally ill *at the time of* the shooting," which means the true numbers may be much higher.[27] One study found close to one-third of those killed by police were people with disabilities,[28] and individual jurisdictions and other studies have reported numbers as high as 57[29] and 81 percent.[30] In no other medical emergency do we expect the patient to communicate with, work with, and navigate help from a person carrying a gun.

Transforming the role of police in our society must include an end to our over-reliance on police as first responders in every crisis. When our friends or neighbors or fellow community members are experiencing a mental health crisis, they deserve to be treated with compassion, expert care, and understanding—not with threats of violence and jail.

To that end, cities and states should create systems that treat mental health crises as a public health concern rather than an inherent public safety problem for the criminal justice system to solve. There are three pillars that should be core to any crisis intervention model:

1. A mental health crisis should be treated as a public health issue, not a public safety threat. Professionals who have experience working with individuals with mental health and drug use problems and people with disabilities should set the rules for responding to a mental health crisis. They should also lead development of training and protocols for calls to dispatch and responses to mental health emergencies. These protocols and training should be fully integrated into existing 911 and other emergency dispatch services, existing emergency medical technician (EMT) response, local mental health providers, and local police response.

2. Crisis response should center on consensual, community-informed care and de-escalating crisis. New crisis intervention models should be overseen by government agencies explicitly dedicated to the goals of providing trauma-informed and culturally competent care, de-escalation, and avoiding unnecessary contact with the criminal system. And every model should be informed and staffed by peers with lived experience in mental health and substance use, who can ensure that people in crisis receive care and support that reflects a deep understanding of their individual needs.

3. Mental health professionals should be the first responders to mental health crises. Local mental health response units should be trained and designed to respond to people in crisis, de-escalate these situations, and connect people with the care they need. These mobile teams should respond without law enforcement accompaniment unless the crisis team determines that a safety threat requires law enforcement assistance.

Programs replacing police with social workers, mental health counselors, and medical staff have been in operation for at least a year in Austin, Eugene, Olympia, and Edmonton.[31] These programs

180   *Constitutional Policing: Striving for a More Perfect Union*

all focus on providing more effective and appropriate services and reducing government spending. Other cities have recently begun or approved crisis response programs of their own.[32]

A report[33] by the Albany Government Law Center notes that, while the programs vary in design, there are certain critical takeaways for local governments attempting to reform and implement a crisis response program. Based on a review of pilot programs and early models, the center identified elements that are key to a proven and successful crisis intervention model: a focus on building community trust and including key stakeholders in program design, establishing a capable administrative body with adequate funding, clear and consistent training for dispatch and responders, enabling flexible referral options for people in crisis, and continually evaluating the system's policies in light of emergency dispatch call data and outcomes.[34] We know these systems can work—and save lives.

If structured thoughtfully and fully funded, a new crisis intervention model promises a bold new vision for community safety that starts with removing police as the default solution to serving individuals with mental health needs.

End Militarized "Command-and-Control" Policing of Protests

The May 2020 murder of George Floyd in Minneapolis prompted months of protests across the country decrying discriminatory and violent policing. All too often, those protests were met by excessive and destructive police responses, ranging from intimidation to outright violence.[35] And while some police leaders acknowledged that police killings of Black people like George Floyd must stop, they closed ranks when it came to critiques of the policing of the Floyd demonstrations.

At the heart of the policing problems that the Floyd protests targeted and at the heart of the police responses to those protests lies a key fact: policing in the United States is controlled and commanded almost entirely by the police themselves. When it comes to policing, elected officials and the public have virtually no say in how the police operate.

The NYPD, the largest municipal police department in the country with approximately 35,000 sworn members and another 10,000 civilian employees, provides a useful example. Its commissioner exercises complete control over the department, including over operations and personnel. Although the New York City Council must approve the NYPD's multi-billion-dollar budget, the budget presented to members is devoid of detail. All of the command staff are appointed by the commissioner and come from inside the NYPD. The department's disciplinary process is run inside the NYPD and overseen by commissioner-appointed administrative law judges hearing cases in courtrooms actually located inside NYPD headquarters; the police commissioner alone has final authority to decide discipline. The NYPD has its own internal law department, which represents the agency in many disputes and insulates its leaders from the city's Office of Corporation Counsel. And the department is notoriously hostile to public-records requests, thereby severely curtailing the important accountability that comes with transparency.

To be sure, the commissioner is appointed by the elected mayor, and various external agencies have oversight responsibility. But the NYPD has an enormous amount of unchecked power. Take, for example, how the NYPD handles claims of police mistreatment. The New York CCRB, which is the largest civilian-oversight agency in the country, is authorized to receive and investigate civilian complaints of police misconduct directed at civilians. And it can even prosecute some cases, albeit inside the NYPD court. But it has no power to find officers guilty of misconduct or to impose any discipline or other punishment; rather, it can do nothing more than make recommendations to the police commissioner.

While different models of command and control exist across the country, the NYPD illustrates how most policing in the United States is run by the police for the police. This creates enormous problems, both for the public and for police departments themselves. And this has become an even greater problem as police departments have been given, or taken, responsibility for regulating more and more of daily life that has less and less to do with crime.

A good starting point for accountability of police officials is transparency. In far too many jurisdictions, police secrecy surrounding budgets, technologies, personnel, and civilian encounters makes it impossible for elected officials, external oversight agencies, and members of the public to weigh in on key policy decisions about policing. If police officials had to provide detailed budgets, disclose invasive technologies, seek community input on important personnel decisions, and report on problematic police-civilian interactions, their power would naturally be reduced.

A second important step would be to take away key responsibilities from police officials. Discipline for officer mistreatment of civilians, for instance, should be handled entirely by investigators and adjudicators outside police departments in settings freely open to the public. The lack of accountability for officers who abuse the people they are supposed to protect is long-standing, and history reveals that the police simply are not going to police themselves.

Another important reform for lessening police control would be to get the police out of the business of regulating protests. Most protests present little more than crowd-control and traffic-management challenges that other agencies are more than capable of handling. But in place after place, the police are deeply embedded in the regulation of protests, starting with permit schemes and ending with vast numbers of armed officers appearing at demonstrations, inherently escalating situations.

Law enforcement agencies have become increasingly more powerful and unchecked, leading to the dangerous situation in which law enforcement officials have far too much authority over their own oversight and discipline. Through a range of sensible reforms, police can be held accountable when they harm the people they are charged with protecting.

End Broken Windows Policing of Black and Brown Communities

For nearly three decades, a central pillar of policing has been an aggressive crackdown on minor offenses on the theory that it will drive down more serious crime. The "broken windows" theory of policing—so named because of its premise that when signs of disorder and neglect, such as broken windows, are visible in a neighborhood, it encourages more dangerous criminal activity[36]—was the driving force behind New York City's aggressive prosecution of so-called quality of life offenses that began with the administration of Rudy Giuliani in 1994 and NYPD Commissioner William Bratton.[37]

The city's answer to violent crime was to aggressively target minor offenses such as having an open container of alcohol in public, public urination, and possession of marijuana. As stops, summonses, and arrests for quality of life offenses skyrocketed and more serious crime rates declined, supporters of broken windows policing proclaimed that correlation equaled causation.[38] Despite the fact that there was little empirical evidence to support those claims, even Mayor Bill de Blasio, whose first mayoral campaign was centered on ending the tale of two cities that was sustained, in part, by the broken windows policy of stop and frisk, appointed Bratton as his first police commissioner and remained steadfast in his defense of broken windows policing.[39]

Nowhere were the racial disparities of broken windows policing more apparent than in marijuana enforcement. For decades, the war on drugs has had a devastating and disproportionate impact on communities of color. Even though New York partially decriminalized possession of small amounts of marijuana in 1977, the NYPD has since made hundreds of thousands of low-level marijuana arrests, overwhelmingly impacting Black and Brown men.[40] Low-level possession persisted as one of the most frequently charged offenses in New York, leading some to describe the city as the "marijuana arrest capital of the world."[41] These arrests have had devastating and far-reaching consequences: people have lost their jobs, their homes, custody of their children, and their ability to remain in the country.

Through it all, it was almost exclusively communities of color who suffered the consequences of broken windows enforcement. Despite the fact that white and Black people have been found to use marijuana at roughly the same rate,[42] in 2011, 86 percent of people arrested in New York City on low-level marijuana offenses were Black or Latinx.[43] By 2020, the disparities were even more appalling, with Black and Latinx people making up 93 percent of people arrested and more than 93 percent of people ticketed by the NYPD.[44]

Despite the continued embrace of broken windows policing in New York City and in police departments across the state, there has been some progress. In 2016, the New York City Council passed legislation to create and prioritize civil alternatives to some of the most commonly enforced low-level violation offenses. Since then, the number of criminal summonses has indeed decreased, although the racial disparities in enforcement have stubbornly persisted and have carried over into the civil enforcement realm as well.[45]

In 2020, the state legislature passed the Police STAT Act to bring greater transparency to violation and misdemeanor enforcement statewide, including demographic information on people subject to broken windows enforcement.[46] The Office of Court Administration began publishing this data in December 2020,[47] and New Yorkers should now be able to better assess policing practices in their communities.

In March 2021, a major blow against broken windows policing in New York came with the passage of the state's Marijuana Regulation and Taxation Act (MRTA). In addition to legalizing possession and use of cannabis by adults, the law provides a framework for repairing harms and reinvesting in communities that have long been devastated by aggressive and discriminatory policing. It includes provisions that repeal the very offenses that drove broken windows summons and arrest activity, expunges records of prior convictions, and requires the reinvestment of substantial amounts of funding into the communities that bore the brunt of hyper-aggressive enforcement in the racist war on drugs.[48] After decades of overinvestment in aggressive policing and criminalization, the MRTA will instead put resources where they have belonged all along: in communities.

While marijuana legalization removes one of the primary drivers of broken windows enforcement in New York, the tactic remains stubbornly embedded in policing strategies across the state. From the continued use of police to remove people experiencing homelessness from public spaces to cracking down on crimes of poverty such as turnstile jumping to the presence of police in schools, we continue to rely on police as a one-size-fits-all answer to quality of life issues. To bring an end to broken windows policing, we must acknowledge that quality of life policing dramatically worsens the quality of life for the communities that are targeted.

As we call for an end to the era of this excessive enforcement, we should look to the MRTA as a model and prioritize necessary investments in areas such as public health, education, and housing to actually address the root causes of quality of life issues.

Eliminate Vice Squads

Vice units are divisions of police departments that enforce laws concerning a broad range of morality crimes, which often include prostitution, the use of alcohol and narcotics, and gambling. These units began in the early 20th century, when governments sought to criminalize so-called quality of life offenses.[49] Today, vice officers use their badges to bully, molest, exploit, and harass marginalized communities for behaviors that often should not be criminalized. To reduce inequities in policing, jurisdictions should eliminate vice units and reallocate their funding to services and organizations that serve the marginalized communities vice currently harms.

While the specific offenses vice units enforce vary by jurisdiction, almost all focus on offenses involving prostitution, which is the focus of this section. Importantly, sex work is the consensual trade of sexual services for remuneration between adults. It does not refer to sex trafficking where coercion is involved. Leading non-governmental organizations (NGOs) such as the World Health Organization and scientists recognize decriminalizing sex work as the most effective way to reduce exploitation, reduce sexually transmitted diseases, and enable sex workers to use harm reduction tools.[50] Yet vice squads continue to arrest sex workers and non-abusive clients, merely pushing the trade deeper into the shadows and making it more difficult for workers to access services.

There are stark racial disparities in the enforcement of sex work–related crimes. In New York, approximately 90 percent of those charged with purchasing or selling sex are people of color (POC).[51] Disproportionate treatment is even more prevalent for POC with intersecting identities, such as non-citizens and LGBTQ+ people. In New York City, transgender women of color are over-policed for street-based sex work, while over 95 percent of those arrested for unlicensed massage are Asian women, particularly non-citizens.[52]

Workers from these groups often trade sex because they cannot secure other employment or essential support services.[53] Criminal records exacerbate barriers to employment, housing, childcare, and other necessities. Sex workers who would like to leave the trade often cannot because their criminal records make it more difficult to find formal employment.[54] As a result, rather than reduce prostitution, vice policing and prosecution can perpetuate it.

Most offenses that vice units enforce are considered "crimes involving moral turpitude," which can have dire immigration consequences.[55] The threat of harsh collateral consequences makes marginalized sex workers more vulnerable to exploitation and coercion.

The structure of vice policing invites corruption and predation. Vice officers often operate undercover, which helps them evade discipline.[56] While sexual misconduct is the second most common form of police misconduct, it often goes unreported due to fear of reprisals.[57] For sex workers and trafficking survivors, these fears are magnified.

This is certainly true of New York City's vice squad. Attorneys for sex workers and other advocates have long complained about the lack of transparency for the department's practices. Sex workers report that arresting officers often unnecessarily fondle them or coerce sexual favors. In a recent *ProPublica* report, a former vice sergeant noted how "humorous" it was for an officer to arrest a "crack prostitute [*sic*] on the street for a hamburger and fries."[58] Another former sergeant gleefully recounted "the undercover can have a nice, cold beer and watch a girl take off her clothes—and he's getting paid for it."[59] In the same report, vice officers admit that they falsely arrested men for patronizing who showed no interest in soliciting the undercover officer. In 2017, a former vice detective was caught coercing sex from non-citizen sex workers only to arrest them afterward, and another vice officer was accused of raping a massage worker at gunpoint.[60] Two years later, eight current and former vice officers—approximately 4 percent of the unit—were indicted for running a $2 million prostitution ring.[61]

Mere reform will not create meaningful change because the entire mission of vice units—to criminalize sex work—increases exploitation and harm. In disbanding vice squads, it is imperative that police departments do not create units with similar functions that perpetrate the same harms. Policy makers should work with marginalized sex workers, massage workers, trafficking survivors, and other key stakeholders to determine how resources should be reallocated. It is also critical to repeal offenses and vacate convictions for quality of life offenses currently enforced by vice. District attorneys should decline to prosecute cases involving the consensual sale or purchase of sex between adults. Further, DAs should support advocacy efforts to move money for sex worker programs from compulsory programs tied to the legal system to non-compulsory peer-led providers.

In New York City, the New York Civil Liberties Union works with directly impacted community members and other partners to achieve these policy goals. It has launched a campaign urging the city to reinvest money spent policing sex workers and survivors of trafficking into NGOs and economic empowerment programing for LGBTQ+ youth, expand language access for services, and increase funding for legal and housing assistance for sex workers and survivors.

Additionally, the NYCLU and partners coordinated successful legislative campaigns to legalize marijuana, to create a process to vacate convictions for survivors of sex and labor trafficking, and repeal Loitering for the Purpose of Prostitution.[62] Repealing these statutes took away tools for vice to target marginalized people, while also providing a path for community members to expunge prior convictions under these repealed laws. The NYCLU is currently working on campaigns to decriminalize sex work and automatically vacate prior sex-work related convictions.

Finally, the NYCLU and other advocates work with DAs to develop policies that reduce the functions of vice and reinvest resources for those targeted by vice away from the carceral system. As a result, in the past year, some DAs have stopped prosecuting some prostitution-related offenses, and thousands of warrants have been vacated.[63]

Ensure Transparency about Policing Practices and Discipline

Secrecy is and always has been a hallmark of law enforcement agencies. While few government agencies welcome scrutiny, law enforcement has elevated secrecy to an essential element of its culture and operations. This has been possible because law enforcement agencies have been able to invoke "public safety" as an almost unassailable justification for operating in secrecy.

In truth, extreme law enforcement secrecy benefits no one, including police agencies. To be sure, important aspects of law enforcement—for instance, ongoing criminal investigations—can and should be kept from the public. But vast portions of law enforcement operations, such as disciplinary practices, can be disclosed without harming legitimate interests.

Perhaps the most dramatic example of legislative police transparency reform came out of New York. Since the 1970s, New York Civil Rights Law § 50-a exempted from public-records requests the disciplinary records of police officers (as well as correction officers and firefighters). Despite decades of objections, legislative efforts, and litigation challenging the exemption, it had stood—a testament to the power of the police unions and their "safety" narrative.

That all changed in the tumult of the George Floyd protests. Within weeks the state legislature repealed the exemption. And shortly thereafter unprecedented amounts of disciplinary information—including hundreds of thousands of records about NYPD officers—became available as a result of requests under New York's revised Freedom of Information Law.[64]

Important as this reform was, it highlights one of the greatest flaws in the approach to transparency across the country. At both the federal level, as reflected in the Freedom of Information Act (FOIA), and the counterpart statutes enacted by states and localities, public access to information about policing depends on someone having to formally request information from police agencies. Agencies have almost unfettered ability to reject the request, and requestors are then left having to file lawsuits to obtain records.

Anyone familiar with public agencies and the courts will readily recognize the enormous barriers this system creates. First, formulating and filing a request can be a challenge for people unfamiliar with (often hidden) agency record-request procedures. Second, agencies routinely respond with denials or with acknowledgments stating only that they will respond many weeks, or even months, later. Third, for requests denied (or, as too often is the case, ignored), requestors typically have to file administrative appeals providing a basis for challenging the initial action, a step that further screens out many requestors who lack the necessary time, patience, or resources. Finally, those who file administrative appeals that agencies deny are left having to bring a lawsuit, which is an option only for requestors with significant resources.

Thus, while the prevailing legal regime of public records laws like FOIA sounds good in theory, in practice, it creates nearly insurmountable impediments to transparency. And law enforcement agencies are particularly bad when it comes to honoring both the letter and the spirit of public-records laws.

The direct solution to this problem lies in the enactment of legal mandates requiring government agencies, including law enforcement ones, to affirmatively disclose information independent of any request from a member of the public. Rather than a system in which agencies field, process, and contest voluminous individual requests for information, this approach would have agencies devote their time and attention to making information available on an ongoing basis. And in an era when so much government information is contained in readily accessible databases and can be made available online, such a system promises enormous efficiencies for government agencies.

To be sure, agencies would still need to accommodate individual requests for information not included in broader affirmative disclosures. But when it comes to transparency for broad aspects of policing of greatest public concern, a system of regular affirmative disclosure would mark an enormous step forward in curtailing police secrecy.

Conclusion

To transform policing in service of safety, equity, and justice, police departments can learn from our experiences in New York City and work toward:

- Achieving police-free schools;
- Removing police as first responders to mental health crises; public health professionals should be the first responders and police should be available as emergency backup;
- Ending militarized "command-and-control" policing of protests;
- Ending broken windows policing;
- Eliminating vice squads; and
- Ensuring transparency about policing practices and discipline.

Every community has its own needs and culture that must be reflected in its approach to law enforcement. While principles of equity and justice are universal, and the experiences in New York City are instructive, these recommendations must be tailored to each community.

Endnotes

1. This chapter is authored by Donna Lieberman and co-authored by Johanna Miller (section titled *Achieve Police-Free Schools*), Lee Rowland (section titled *Replace Police with Public Health Professionals as First Responders to Mental Health Crises*), Chris Dunn (sections titled *End Militarized "Command and Control" Policing of Protests* and *Ensure Transparency about Policing Practices and Discipline*), Michael Sisitzky (section titled *End Broken Windows Policing of Black and Brown Communities*), and Jared Trujillo (section titled *Eliminate Vice Squads*).

2. Rosa Brooks, Tangled Up in Blue 124 (Penguin Press 2021).

3. *Transformational Public Safety: Reducing the Roles, Resources, and Power of Police*, ACLU (June 2021), https://www.aclu.org/news/topic/transform ational-public-safety-reducing-the-roles-resources-and-power-of-police.

4. Brooks, *supra* note 2, at 181–83.

5. NYCLU and ACLU, Criminalizing the Classroom (2007), https://www.nyclu.org/sites/default/files/publications/nyclu_pub_criminalizing_the_classroom.pdf.

6. Alex Zimmerman, *Activists Demand Removing the NYPD From Schools. De Blasio Plans to Give School Police More Money*, The City (June 5, 2020), https://www.thecity.nyc/education/2020/6/5/21281680/activists-demand-removing-the-nypd-from-schools-de-blasio-plans-to-give-school-police-more-money.

7. From 2000 to 2022, this work was done under the leadership of Donna Lieberman, first as Interim Director and then as Director of the NYCLU. For detailed information about the NYCLU's work see generally https://www.nyclu.org.

8. Megan French-Marcelin & Sarah Hinger, *Bullies in Blue: The Origins and Consequences of School Policing*, ACLU (Apr. 2017), https://www.aclu.org/report/bullies-blue-origins-and-consequences-school-policing.

9. Ron Whitehorne, *1967: African American Students Strike, Survive Police Riot to Force Change*, The Notebook (Sept. 25, 2002), https://philadelphia.chalkbeat.org/2002/9/25/22185400/1967-african-american-students-strike-survive-police-riot-to-force-change.

10. Chelsea Connery, *The Prevalence and the Price of Police in Schools*, UConn Center for Education Policy Analysis (Oct. 27, 2020), https://education.uconn.edu/2020/10/27/the-prevalence-and-the-price-of-police-in-schools/#.

11. Constance A. Lindsay et al., *The prevalence of police officers in US schools*, Urban Institute (June 21, 2018), https://www.urban.org/urban-wire/prevalence-police-officers-us-schools.

12. *NYC School Safety Spending*, Children's Defense Fund New York (2019), https://www.cdfny.org/wp-content/uploads/sites/3/2019/09/NYPD-School-Safety-Budget-Explainer.pdf.

13. Michael Leachman et al., *A Punishing Decade for School Funding*, Center on Budget and Policy Priorities (Nov. 29, 2017), https://www.cbpp.org/research/state-budget-and-tax/a-punishing-decade-for-school-funding.

14. Melinda D. Anderson, *The Importance of Examining Schooling Policing in the Aftermath of McKinney and Ahmed Mohamed*, The Atlantic (Sept. 21, 2015), https://www.theatlantic.com/education/archive/2015/09/when-schooling-meets-policing/406348/.

15. Amir Whitaker et al., *Cops But No Counselors*, ACLU (2018), https://www.nyclu.org/sites/default/files/field_documents/030119-acluschooldisciplinereport.pdf.

16. John Woodrow Cox & Stephen Rich, *Scarred by School Shootings*, Washington Post (Mar. 25, 2018), https://www.washingtonpost.com/graphics/2018/local/us-school-shootings-history/.

17. Irma Solis & JP Perry, *Why Stopping the School-to-Deportation Pipeline Will Make Schools Safer for Everyone*, NYCLU (Feb. 13, 2019), https://www.nyclu.org/en/news/why-stopping-school-deportation-pipeline-will-make-schools-safer-everyone; JP Perry & Simon McCormack, *How This NY County Is Helping ICE Trap Teens*, NYCLU (June 20, 2019), https://www.nyclu.org/en/news/how-ny-county-helping-ice-trap-teens.

18. *See, e.g.*, NBC News, *Florida School Resource Officer Slams Student to the Ground* (Jan. 27, 2021), https://www.google.com/url?sa=t&rct=j&q=&esrc=s&source=web&cd=&cad=rja&uact=8&ved=2ahUKEwjg4ryuw4HzAhXFTN8KHQ14BKoQwqsBegQIAhAB&url=https%3A%2F%2Fwww.nbcnews.com%2Fvideo%2Fvideo-shows-florida-school-resource-officer-slamming-student-to-the-ground-100115525859&usg=AOvVaw1zVkaq9NQu1taSn1SZrFdK; CBS Mornings, *School Resource Officer in North Carolina Slams Student to the Ground* (Dec. 16, 2019), https://www.youtube.com/watch?v=56_zQ8a4IUc; NBC News, *Video Shows Cop Body-Slamming High School Girl in SC* (Oct. 27, 2015), https://www.nbcnews.com/news/us-news/video-appears-show-cop-body-slamming-student-s-c-classroom-n451896; NBC News, *Video Shows Maryland Police Handcuffing, Berating Five-Year-Old Boy* (Mar. 27, 2021), https://www.nbcnews.com/news/us-news/video-shows-maryland-police-handcuffing-berating-5-year-old-boy-n1262262.

19. *Policing America's Schools*, EDUCATION WEEK (2017), https://www.edweek.org/which-students-are-arrested-most-in-school-u-s-data-by-school#/overview.

20. *A Look at School Safety*, NYCLU, https://www.nyclu.org/en/school-prison-pipeline-look-new-york-city-school-safety.

21. Jocelyn Smith Lee, *That's My Number One Fear in Life. It's the Police": Examining Young Black Men's Exposures to Trauma and Loss Resulting From Police Violence and Police Killings*, 45(3) JOURNAL OF BLACK PSYCHOLOGY 143 (July 30, 2019), https://journals.sagepub.com/doi/pdf/10.1177/0095798419865152.

22. Kalyn Belsha, *Canada's Largest School District Ended Its Police Program. Now, Toronto May Be an Example for US Districts Considering the Same*, CHALKBEAT (June 19, 2020), https://www.chaalkbeat.org/2020/6/19/21297248/toronto-canada-ended-school-police-program-example-for-united-states-school-district.s

23. S.4360/H.R. 7848, 116th Cong. (2019–2020).

24. Abigail Abrams, *Black, Disabled, and at Risk: The Overlooked Problem of Police Violence Against Americans with Disabilities*, TIME (June 25, 2020), https://time.com/5857438/police-violence-black-disabled/; Ryan W. Miller & Grace Hauck, *It's working in Eugene, Olympia, Denver: More cities are sending civilian responders, not police, on mental health calls*, USA TODAY (Apr. 5, 2021), https://www.usatoday.com/in-depth/news/nation/2021/04/05/george-floyd-daniel-prude-911-mental-health-response/6819744002/.

25. Police have limited options, all grounded in traditional policing models of command, control, and coercion principles, when responding to a person in crisis. They may arrest the individual; refer the person to mental health services or transport the person for an involuntary psychiatric evaluation; resolve the situation informally, for example, by asking the individual to leave the scene; or if the individual is a crime victim, take a report and perhaps provide assistance.

26. *See, e.g.*, D. CHAPPELL, POLICING AND THE MENTALLY ILL (2013) (referenced in TREATMENT ADVOCACY CENTER, OVERLOOKED IN THE UNDERCOUNTED, https://www.treatmentadvocacycenter.org/storage/documents/overlooked-in-the-undercounted.pdf).

27. *Fatal Force Database*, Washington Post, updated as of Mar. 28, 2021, https://www.washingtonpost.com/graphics/investigations/police-shoot ings-database/ (italics added).

28. David M. Perry & Lawrence Carter-Long, *The Ruderman White Paper on Media Coverage of Law Enforcement Use of Force and Disability*, Ruderman Family Foundation (Mar. 2016), https://rudermanfoundation.org/wp -content/uploads/2017/08/MediaStudy-PoliceDisability_final-final.pdf; *see also* Kate Mather & James Queally, *More than a third of people shot by L.A. police last year were mentally ill, LAPD report finds*, Los Angeles Times, Mar. 1, 2016, http://www.latimes.com/local/lanow/la-me-ln-lapd-use-of-force -report-20160301-story.html.

29. Alex Emslie & Rachael Bale: *Half of those Killed by SFPD are Mentally Ill*, KQED, Sept. 30, 2014, https://www.kqed.org/news/147854/half -of-those-killed-by-san-francisco-police-are-mentally-ill.

30. *See* Perry & Carter-Long, *supra* note 28. Studies range from 27 percent (a low number focusing only on mental illness) to 81 percent (a high number lumping together mental illness and substance abuse).

31. *See* Matt DeLaus, *Alternatives to Police as First Responders: Crisis Response Programs*, Albany Law School (Nov. 16, 2020), https://www.alb anylaw.edu/government-law-center/alternatives-police-first-responders -crisis-response-programs. "Eugene's program has operated since 1989, and in 2019 responded to 20% (24,000) of all 911 calls, with a police backup request rate of 0.625% (160)."

32. *Id.*, noting:

> Cities with non-police crisis response programs in operation less than a year include Portland, Oregon, and Denver, Colorado. *See* https://www.usatoday.com/story/news /nation/2020/06/22/defund-police-what-means-black- lives-matter/3218862001/. Oakland, California, decided to fund a crisis response program, but it is not yet in operation. See https://www.kron4.com/news/bay-area/mobile -response-unit-coming-to-oakland-to-help-with-non -violent-911-calls. Local governments that have decided to fund a crisis response program since George Floyd's killing include Los Angeles, California (https://www.cnn.com /2020/10/14/us/los-angeles-unarmed-crisis-response- teams-911-calls/index.html); Miami-Dade County, Florida (http://www.miamidade.gov/govaction/legistarfiles/Mat ters/Y2020/201239_Analysis.pdf; http://www.miamidade .gov/govaction/legistarfiles/Matters/Y2020/201239. pdf); Philadelphia, Pennsylvania (https://philadelphia.pa .networkofcare.org/mh/news-article-detail.aspx?id =116033); Rochester, New York (https://www.rochester first.com/news/local-news/watch-live-mayor-warren -to-announce-crisis-intervention-program/); Salt Lake City, Utah; Albuquerque, New Mexico; Hartford, Connecticut; Durham, North Carolina (https://www.prainc.com/wp -content/uploads/2020/08/PoliceReformAcrossUS508.pdf

at 2); and San Francisco, California (https://www.usatoday.com/story/news/nation/2020/06/22/defund-police-what-means-black-lives-matter/3218862001/). Many other locales are exploring the possibility. *See, e.g.,* https://www.prainc.com/wp-content/uploads/2020/08/PoliceReformAcrossUS508.pdf."

33. *Id.*

34. *Id.*

35. *E.g., "Kettling" Protesters in the Bronx,* HUMAN RIGHTS WATCH (Sept. 30, 202), https://www.hrw.org/report/2020/09/30/kettling-protesters-bronx/systemic-police-brutality-and-its-costs-united-states (last visited May 24, 2022).

36. Shankar Vedantam, et al., *How a Theory of Crime and Policing was Born, and Went Terribly Wrong,* WBUR, Nov. 1, 2016, https://www.wbur.org/npr/500104506/broken-windows-policing-and-the-origins-of-stop-and-frisk-and-how-it-went-wrong.

37. *Id.*

38. *Id.*

39. Emma Whitford, *De Blasio Calls Broken Windows "Right Approach" as Commissioner Bratton Steps Down,* GOTHAMIST, Sept. 16, 2016, https://gothamist.com/news/de-blasio-calls-broken-windows-right-approach-as-commissioner-bratton-steps-down.

40. Harry G. Levine & Deborah Peterson Small, *Marijuana Arrest Crusade: Racial Bias and Police Policy, 1997–2007,* NEW YORK CIVIL LIBERTIES UNION, Apr. 2008, http://marijuana-arrests.com/docs/MARIJUANA-ARREST-CRUSADE.pdf.

41. Phillip Smith, *DPA Study: New York City Remains the World's Marijuana Arrest Capital, and It's Still Mainly Black and Brown People Getting Popped,* SALON, Aug. 13, 2017, https://www.salon.com/2017/08/13/dpa-study-new-york-city-remains-the-worlds-marijuana-arrest-capital-and-it-is-still-mainly-black-and-brown-people-getting-popped_partner/.

42. Dayna Bowen Matthew & Richard V. Reeves, *Trump Won White Voters, but Serious Inequities Remain for Black Americans,* BROOKINGS INSTITUTE, Jan. 13, 2017, https://www.brookings.edu/blog/social-mobility-memos/2017/01/13/trump-won-white-voters-but-serious-inequities-remain-for-black-americans/.

43. Ben Yakas, *Vast Majority Arrested for Pot are Black or Latino,* GOTHAMIST, Feb. 13, 2011, https://gothamist.com/news/vast-majority-arrested-for-pot-are-black-or-latino.

44. Jake Offenhartz, *NYPD's Enforcement of Marijuana Laws Still Plagued by Extreme Racial Disparities,* GOTHAMIST, Mar. 10, 2021, https://gothamist.com/news/nypds-enforcement-marijuana-laws-still-plagued-extreme-racial-disparities.

45. Samar Khurshid, *NYPD Continues Move Away from Criminal Penalties for Low-Level Offenses, but Racial Disparities Remain,* GOTHAM GAZETTE, Sept. 4, 2019, https://www.gothamgazette.com/city/8768-nypd-fewer-criminal-penalties-for-low-level-offenses-racial-differences-remain.

46. *The Police STAT Act is Now in Effect,* WIVB, Dec. 14, 2020, https://www.wivb.com/news/new-york/the-police-stat-act-is-now-in-effect/.

47. *OCA-STAT Act Report*, New York State Office of Court Administration, https://ww2.nycourts.gov/oca-stat-act-31371.

48. Luis Ferré-Sadurní, *New York Legalizes Recreational Marijuana, Tying Move to Racial Equity*, N.Y. Times, Mar. 31, 2021, https://www.nytimes.com/2021/03/31/nyregion/cuomo-ny-legal-weed.html.

49. Albert Reiss, Jr., *Police Organization in the Twentieth Century*, 15 Crime & Just. 51, 74 (1992).

50. Elizabeth Nolan Brown, *Science-Based Policy Means Decriminalizing Sex Work, Say Hundreds of Researchers*, Reason, Mar. 3, 2021, https://reason.com/2021/03/03/science-based-policy-means-decriminalizing-sex-work-say-hundreds-of-researchers; Erin Albright & Kate D'Adamo, *Decreasing Human Trafficking through Sex Work Decriminalization*, AMA J. Ethics (2017), https://journalofethics.ama-assn.org/article/decreasing-human-trafficking-through-sex-work-decriminalization/2017-01.

51. Joshua Kaplan & Joaquin Sapien, *NYPD Cops Cash In on Sex Trade Arrests with Little Evidence, while Black and Brown New Yorkers Pay the Price*, ProPublica, July 12, 2021, https://www.propublica.org/article/nypd-cops-cash-in-on-sex-trade-arrests-with-little-evidence-while-black-and-brown-new-yorkers-pay-the-price.

52. Meredith Dank, Jennifer Yahner & Lilly Yu, *Consequences of Policing Prostitution: An Analysis of Individuals Arrested and Prosecuted for Commercial Sex in New York City*, Urban Institute, Apr. 5, 2017, https://www.urban.org/research/publication/consequences-policing-prostitution.

53. Meredith Dank et al., *Surviving the Streets of New York: Experiences of LGBTQ Youth, YMSM, and YWSW Engaged in Survival Sex*, Urban Institute, Feb. 2015, https://www.urban.org/sites/default/files/publication/42186/2000119-Surviving-the-Streets-of-New-York.pdf; A Red Canary Song, Massage Parlor Outreach Project, Butterfly, Bowen Public Affairs & Brown University Center for the Study of Slavery and Justice, *Un-Licensed: Asian Migrant Massage Licensure and the Racist Policing of Poverty*, Feb. 2022, https://static1.squarespace.com/static/5e4835857fcd934d19bd9673/t/6218d9316e93a74b051c9f00/1645795656006/2022_Un-Licensed.pdf.

54. *State Report Cards: Grading Criminal Record Relief Laws For Survivors of Human Trafficking*, POLARIS, Mar. 2019, https://polarisproject.org/wp-content/uploads/2019/03/Grading-Criminal-Record-Relief-Laws-for-Survivors-of-Human-Trafficking.pdf.

55. INA 101(f) (3); CFR 316.10(b)(2).

56. *See* Kaplan & Sapien, *supra* note 51.

57. Andrea Ritchie, *How Some Cops Use the Badge to Commit Sex Crimes*, Washington Post, Jan. 12, 2018, https://www.washingtonpost.com/outlook/how-some-cops-use-the-badge-to-commit-sex-crimes/2018/01/11/5606fb26-eff3-11e7-b390-a36dc3fa2842_story.html.

58. Kaplan & Sapien, *supra* note 51.

59. *Id.*

60. Vice Detective Michael Golden coerced several non-citizen sex workers to have sex with him while he was on duty. He arrested many of them. Matt Tracy, NYPD Resists Calls for Vice Squad Probe, Gay City News, Apr. 19, 2019, https://www.gaycitynews.com/nypd-resists-calls-for-vice-squad-probe; Yang Song, a 38-year-old immigrant that worked as a masseuse and

a sex worker in Queens, jumped nearly 40 feet to her death during a vice raid. Yang Song confided in her mother and her attorney that she had been sexually assaulted by a vice officer who made threats and wielded a gun and his badge. Melissa Gira Grant & Emma Whitford *Family, Former Attorney Of Queens Women Who Fell to Her Death in a Vice Sting Say She Was Sexually Assaulted, Pressured to Become An Informant*, THE APPEAL, Dec. 15, 2017, https://theappeal.org/family-former-attorney-of-queens-woman-who -fell-to-her-death-in-vice-sting-say-she-was-sexually.

61. Former Vice Detective Ludwig Paz was convicted of running an illegal prostitution and gambling business, worth $2 million, alongside seven other vice officers. He used his knowledge of the operations of the unit to avoid detection James Baron, *Ex-Detective Admits to Running Brothels in the Worst NYPD Scandal in Years*, NEW YORK TIMES, Mar. 22, 2019, https://www .nytimes.com/2019/05/22/nyregion/nypd-detective-brothel.

62. The Marijuana Regulation and Taxation Act (S854A/A1248) and the bill to repeal loitering for the purpose of engaging in prostitution (S1351/ A3355) both passed the New York legislature and were signed by Governor Andrew Cuomo in 2021. The later bill repealed an offense colloquially referred to as the "Walking While Trans" ban. These were the first two statutes in New York's history to qualify for automatic expungement of old convictions.

63. Otilla Steadman *More Than 1000 Open Prostitution Cases in Brooklyn Are Going to Be Wiped from the Files*, BUZZFEED, Jan. 28, 2021, https:// www.buzzfeed.com/article/otillasteadman/prostitution-loitering-cases-brooklyn; Jonah Bromwich, *Manhattan to Stop Prosecuting Prostitution, Part of Nationwide Shift*, NEW YORK TIMES, Apr. 21, 2021, https://www.nytimes .com/2021/04/21.nyregion/Manhattan-to-stop-prosecuting-prostitution .html.

64. Laws of 2020, Chapter 96 (effective June 12, 2020) (repealing Civil Rights Law section 50-a and amending New York's Freedom of Information Law).

Afterword

The Most Perfect Union Protects and Serves Us All

Jelani Jefferson Exum

Constitutional Policing: Striving for a More Perfect Union. The title of this book draws from our societal expectation of police and our Constitution's Preamble to inspire those doing the difficult work of advocating for police reform. As the book chapters detail, improving police practices and repairing police-community relationships require an understanding of several issues, from qualified immunity to police as employees. However, in addition to offering practical ways to move forward, the chapters also reveal the difficulty of moving past decades of laws, practices, and policies that have shored up our current system of policing.[1] Overcoming those difficulties is worth the considerable effort it will take to effect systemic change. The success of police reforms is a matter of life and death for certain populations in America. Native Americans are more likely than any other ethnic group to be killed in a police encounter.[2] For the last several years, police killings of unarmed Black people in this country were three times higher than those of whites.[3] And, in many parts of the United States, Hispanics are disproportionately killed by police as well.[4] Achieving a more perfect union in which police truly protect and serve all people and all communities equitably requires us to constantly assess our progress and to possess a willingness to break free from traditional conceptions of policing.[5] Despite the weaknesses in our system highlighted within the chapters of this book, we can draw hope from the direction in the book's title and the information with which contributing authors equip us. We can move toward a more perfect union in which police protect and serve. Doing so requires that readers take from the information presented in this text the understanding that lasting, transformative police reform requires promoting an inclusive view of the general welfare and must demand system accountability.

As highlighted in this book, one necessary aspect of achieving lasting police reform that protects the welfare of all communities is a redistribution of power that will allow for traditionally marginalized groups to have a voice in reform. The history of the book's inspiring subtitle—*Striving for a More Perfect Union*—highlights the need for a such power shift. Our Constitution opens with the following virtuous words:

> We the People of the United States, in Order to form a more perfect Union, establish Justice, insure domestic Tranquility, provide for the common defence, promote the general Welfare, and secure the Blessings of Liberty to ourselves and our Posterity, do ordain and establish this Constitution for the United States of America.

The history of this aspirational prose highlights the very questions that police reformers face: Who are *the people* who will have a voice in reform? What are *our goals*? Initially, the Constitution's Preamble was drafted with a much less poetic approach. The first draft read:

> We the People of the States of New-Hampshire, Massachusetts, Rhode-Island and Providence Plantations, Connecticut, New-York, New-Jersey, Pennsylvania, Delaware, Maryland, Virginia, North-Carolina, South-Carolina, and Georgia, do ordain, declare and establish the following Constitution for the Government of Ourselves and our Posterity.[6]

The eventual changes to the Preamble came once the draft Constitution was sent to the Committee of Style, led by Gouverneur Morris, who deleted the list of states, leaving the opening as the now famous "We the People of the United States."[7] He then also added the six famous purposes for the Constitution: to form a more perfect union, establish justice, insure domestic tranquility, provide for the common defense, promote the general welfare, and secure the blessings of liberty.[8] In its final form, the Preamble tells us that "We the People of the United States" established the Constitution to achieve the aforementioned goals for "ourselves" and "our posterity." Of course, the obvious shortcoming is that when these words were penned in 1787, the people who made up the "ourselves" and the "our" did not include all groups of people actually present in the country at the time.[9] Studies of systemic racism reveal that it is no coincidence that the excluded groups happen to be the same groups that disproportionately bear the brunt of societal injustices today—including the disproportionate use of force by police.[10] As is the case today, being excluded from the "we" in 1787 was extremely consequential. This sobering fact was made evident by the ratification debates that zeroed in on the Preamble's new language. When Anti-Federalist Patrick Henry of Virginia questioned removing the individual states from the Preamble, Edmund Pendleton replied in defense,"[W]ho but the people can delegate powers?"[11] James Wilson contended that "all authority is derived from the people" and that "the people have a right to do what they please with regard to the government."[12] Undoubtedly, being included in the people meant being included in the power. Today, being included in the power means having the power to shape the state's control over your daily life. The chapters of this book offer several ways to include more voices in police reform in ways that can give more communities the power to have a say in the way policing will feel in their communities. Whether that change comes through administrative complaints, civilian oversight, or another approach, opening the reform process to more individuals means sharing the power to determine what would ultimately constitute a more perfect union.[13]

Another crucial aspect of true police reform—reform that will increase safety for all communities—is rethinking the mechanisms for defining appropriate police behavior while enforcing accountability. The phrase "to protect and serve" has become a famous refrain to both praise and criticize police officers and departments.[14] The expression was originally developed as a motto for the Los Angeles Police Department in 1955, but it was ultimately adopted by police departments and in common parlance across the country.[15] However genuine the intent behind this sentiment may have been, courts have made it clear that police officers do not have a general duty to provide protection.[16] Without the legal imposition on police to carry out their duty in this protective manner, society must depend upon policies and practices that can give substance to this policing ideal.

This book sets forth the concept of constitutional policing as "policing in which humanity is at the forefront of law enforcement as they perform their duties to 'Protect and Serve.'"[17] Holding police officers and departments accountable for straying from an approach to policing that recognizes the humanity of all human beings[18]—regardless of the neighborhood in which they reside—requires building avenues for contesting unacceptable police behavior.

Whether this goal is enforced through pattern and practice consent decrees or litigating police-citizen encounters as discussed in this text, it is clear that lawyers are an important part of creating systemic change through their work. Although litigating in the area of policing can be onerous for the attorney who wants to effectuate change, this book has offered valuable information to begin the work of shifting power and creating systems of accountability. Each effort in this regard gets us closer to transform policing in the ways proposed by the chapter authors.[19] Each effort moves us closer to the most perfect union, in which police protect and serve us all.

Endnotes

1. For instance, in Chapter 2, Rita McNeil Danish points out the need to improve public trust of police. Likewise, in Chapter 5, Sharon R. Fairley explains that fatal police shootings have occurred even in jurisdictions with some form of civilian oversight of police.

2. Teran Powel, *Native Americans Most Likely to Die From Police Shootings, Families Who Lost Loved Ones Weigh In*, WUWM 89.7 FM (June 2, 2021), https://www.wuwm.com/2021-06-02/native-americans-most-likely-to-die-from-police-shootings-families-who-lost-loved-ones-weigh-in (reporting that "Native American people are killed in police encounters more than any other ethnic group, according to the Centers for Disease Control & Prevention.").

3. See *Fatal Force*, WASHINGTON POST, https://www.washingtonpost.com/graphics/investigations/police-shootings-database/ (logging every fatal police shooting since 2015).

4. *Id.*

5. For an example of this approach, *see* Jalila Jefferson-Bullock & Jelani Jefferson Exum, *That's Enough Punishment: Situating Defunding the Police within Antiracist Sentencing Reform*, 48 FORDHAM URB. L.J. 625 (2021).

6. 2 THE RECORDS OF THE FEDERAL CONVENTION OF 1787, at 177 (Max Farrand ed., 1966).

7. *See* CARL VAN DOREN, THE GREAT REHEARSAL: THE STORY OF THE MAKING AND RATIFYING OF THE CONSTITUTION OF THE UNITED STATES 160 (1948); *see also* RICHARD BROOKHISER, GENTLEMAN REVOLUTIONARY: GOUVERNEUR MORRIS, THE RAKE WHO WROTE THE CONSTITUTION 90 (2003).

8. THE RECORDS OF THE FEDERAL CONVENTION OF 1787, *supra* note 6, at 590.

9. In the 1857 case *Dred Scott v. Sanford*, the U.S. Supreme Court confirmed that the framers of the Constitution did not intend for Blacks to have the privileges of American citizenship. 60 U.S. 393 (1857). Further, Native Americans, although already on the soil claimed as the original colonies and the eventual first states in the country, were not given birthright citizenship until 1924 with the passage of the Indian Citizenship Act, Public Law 68-175, 43 STAT 253, which authorized the Secretary of the Interior to issue certificates of citizenship to Indians. 06/02/1924; Enrolled Acts and Resolutions of Congress, 1789–1996; General Records of the U.S. Government; Record Group 11; National Archives.

10. For a brief explanation, *see* N'dea Yancey-Bragg, *What is systemic racism? Here's what it means and how you can help dismantle it*, USA TODAY (June 15, 2020), https://www.usatoday.com/story/news/nation/2020/06/15/systemic-racism-what-does-mean/5343549002/.

11. JONATHAN ELLIOT, 3 ELLIOT'S DEBATES ON THE FEDERAL CONSTITUTION 22, 37 (2d. ed. 1996).

12. *Id.* at 434–35.

13.*See* Rita McNeil Danish, *Administrative Complaints against Police*; Sharon R. Fairley, *Contemporary Civilian Oversight of Law Enforcement*.

14. *See, e.g.*, Marleina Ubel, *To Protect and Serve: Investing in Public Safety Beyond Policing*, NEW JERSEY POLICY PERSPECTIVE (Oct. 13, 2021), https://www.njpp.org/publications/report/to-protect-and-serve-investing-in-public-safety-beyond-policing/; *see also* titles such as G. GAMBLER & C. CLARK, TO SERVE AND PROTECT: A TRIBUTE TO AMERICAN LAW ENFORCEMENT (1995), referenced by the U.S. Department of Justice Office of Justice Programs at https://www.ojp.gov/ncjrs/virtual-library/abstracts/serve-and-protect-tribute-american-law-enforcement.

15. See explanation on LAPD website, https://www.lapdonline.org/lapd-motto/.

16. *See* Warren v. District of Columbia, 444 A.2d 1 (Dist. of Columbia Court of Appeals 1981); DeShaney v. Winnebago County Department of Social Services, 489 U.S. 189 (1989); Castle Rock v. Gonzales, 455 U.S. 748 (2005).

17. Royce Russell, *Constitutional* Policing.

18. For an approach to human dignity in policing, *see* Jelani Jefferson Exum, *The Death Penalty on the Streets: What the Eighth Amendment Can Teach Us about Regulating Police Force*, 80 MISSOURI L. REV. 987 (Fall 2015).

19. Donna Lieberman, *Transforming Policing: Lessons from New York City*.

Index

accountability
  civil rights protections and, 58–64
  civil service protections and, 61–64
  collective bargaining and, 54–58
  constitutional policing and, 133
  contract terms and, 46–48
  disciplinary actions and, 58–60
  freedom of association and, 38–39
  freedom of speech and, 38
  grievability of disciplinary action and, 51–54
  paid leave and, 49–50
  public employment and, 37–45
  unions and, 45–54
ACLU. *See* American Civil Liberties Union (ACLU)
administrative review. *See* complaints, administrative
Aitchison, Will, 52
Albuquerque, New Mexico, 145–146
American Civil Liberties Union (ACLU), 140–141

Americans with Disabilities Act, 58
Armour & Co, United States v., 141–142
association, freedom of, 38–39
audit model, of independent agency review, 28

Biden, Joseph, 144
bills of rights, with public employees, 41–42, 45, 47–48
Black Lives Matter, 15. *See also* Floyd, George
broken-windows policing, 182–185
Brown, Michael, 95, 146–147, 154, 158

cannabis legalization, 184–185
Castro, Julian, 14
CCRB. *See* Civilian Complaint Review Board (CCRB) (New York)
Charles v. City of New York, 79
Chauvin, Derek, 14–15, 99
chiefs, police, civilian oversight and employment of, 122–123
chokeholds, 157, 163–164, 169

City of Ontario v. Quon, 40
civil rights. *See also*
    employment, public
    accountability and, 58–64
    disciplinary actions and,
    58–60
Civil Rights Act of 1866, 4
Civil Rights Act of 1875, 4–5
Civil Rights Act of 1964, 58, 60,
    130
civil service protections, 61–64
Civilian Complaint Review
    Board (CCRB) (New
    York), 72, 75, 174
Civilian Complaint Review
    Board (CCRB) (Newark,
    New Jersey), 104–107
Civilian Office of Police
    Accountability (COPA)
    (Chicago), 108–111
civilian oversight. *See*
    oversight, civilian
Civilian Police Accountability
    Council (CPAC), 109
Civilian Review Board
    (Atlanta), 121–122
Clark, Jamar, 155
Clarke, Kristen, 145
classism, 74–86
"clearly established," 8–9
Coffman, Brian, 164
collaboration, 134
collective bargaining. *See also*
    unions
    accountability and, 54–58
    arbitration and, 57–58
    civil service protections
    and, 63–64

disciplinary actions and, 48
duty of fair representation
    and, 45–46
as give and take, 55–56
grievability of disciplinary
    action and, 51
internal affairs review and,
    23–24, 26
paid leave and, 49–50
as private, 54–55
procedural rights of public
    employees and, 41–42
property rights and, 40
statutory impasse and,
    56–57
transparency and, 26
Weingarten rights and, 43
Colorado Law Enforcement
    Integrity and
    Accountability Act, 15–16
command-and-control
    policing, of protests,
    180–182
Communications Decency Act,
    39
Community Commission
    for Public Safety and
    Accountability (Chicago),
    108–109
Community Oriented Policing
    Services (COPS), 138
community policing, 69–70
Community Relations Service
    (CRS), 133–134
complaints, administrative
    as alternative to litigation,
    21
    audit model with, 28

independent agency review
with, 27–34
internal affairs review and,
23–26
investigation model with,
29
monitor model with, 27–28
oversight model with, 28–29
successful model with,
31–34
consent decrees, 141–147
Constitution, 198–199. *See also*
employment, public;
specific amendments
constitutional policing
accountability and, 133
community engagement
and, 86–87
community in, 138–141
community policing and,
69–70
defined, 69
equal justice and, 87–89
freedom of speech and,
71–72
law enforcement trends
and, 74–76
litigators in, 138–141
mental health and, 80–81
pattern or practice
investigations and,
132–138
positive steps toward, 86–90
power and, 75–83
quota policing and, 73–74
social justice and, 89–90
transparency and, 133
contagious shooting, 167

contract terms, accountability
and, 46–48
COPA. *See* Civilian Office of
Police Accountability
(COPA) (Chicago)
COPS. *See* Office of
Community Oriented
Policing Services (COPS)
CPAC. *See* Civilian Police
Accountability Council
(CPAC)
CRS. *See* Community Relations
Service (CRS)
Crutcher, Terrence, 155
cultural competence, 134
Cunningham, Terrence M., 138

defamation, public employees
and, 41
defense
financial support for, from
unions, 50–51
qualified immunity as, 6–7
demophobia, 103
Department of Justice (DOJ),
129–130, 133–134,
139–141, 143–144
Diallo, Amadou, 167
disciplinary action
accountability and, 58–60
arbitration and, 60
civil rights and, 58–60
civil service protections
and, 61–63
court review of, 58–60
grievability of, 51–54
insurance settlements and,
61

disciplinary action *(continued)*
   internal affairs review and,
      23–26
   protection against
      disclosure of, 42–43
   supervisors in, union and,
      48–49
   transparency with, 188–190
   unions and, 45–46
diversity, internal, 134
DOJ. *See* Department of Justice
   (DOJ)
due process, paid leave and, 26
duty of fair representation,
   45–46

Electronic Communications
   Act, 39
Emanuel, Rahm, 108
Employee Polygraph
   Protection Act, 58
employment, public
   accountability and, 37–45
   bills of rights with, 41–42,
      45, 47–48
   defamation and, 41
   disciplinary action
      disclosure protections
      and, 42–43
   Fourth Amendment and,
      39–40
   freedom of association and,
      38–39
   freedom of speech and, 38
   Garrity warning with, 44–45
   liberty interests protected
      in, 38–40
   personal interests protected
      in, 40–41

   procedural rights with,
      41–42
   property rights and, 40–41
   search and seizure and,
      39–40
   unions and, 45–54
   Weingarten rights and, 43–44
End Qualified Immunity Act
   (H.R. 7085), 15
expert witnesses, 160–165
External Force Investigation
   Team (EFIT)
   (Albuquerque), 146

Fair Credit Reporting Act, 58
Ferguson, Missouri, 95,
   146–147
Fifth Amendment, 26, 40, 44,
   58
Fighting Police Abuse: A
   Community Action
   Manual (ACLU), 141
First Amendment, 38–39, 58,
   70–72, 78–80
Floyd, George, 14–15, 85, 88,
   99, 109, 115, 118, 136–137,
   168–169, 180, 188
Floyd v. City of New York,
   135–136
FOIA. *See* Freedom of
   Information Act (FOIA)
force continuum, 157, 159, 163
Fourteenth Amendment, 4, 40,
   58, 88
Fourth Amendment, 74, 88, 144
   public employees and,
      39–40
   qualified immunity and,
      10–11, 16

freedom of association, 38–39
Freedom of Information Act
    (FOIA), 140, 189
freedom of speech, 38, 70–72

GAPA. *See* Grassroots Alliance
    for Police Accountability
    (GAPA)
Garland, Merrick B., 144
Garrity warning, 44–45
Genetic Information
    Nondiscrimination Act,
    58
George Floyd Justice in
    Policing Act of 2020
    (H.R. 7120), 15
Golden, Michael, 195n60
Graham, Ramarley, 84
Graham v. Connor, 163
Grassroots Alliance for Police
    Accountability (GAPA),
    109
grievability, of disciplinary
    action, 51–54

Hamilton, Dontre, 154
Harlow v. Fitzgerald, 7
health professionals, police *vs.*,
    177–180
Holder, Eric, 135

independence
    of civilian oversight,
        111–115
    of expert witnesses, 162–163
independent agency review
    with administrative
        complaints, 27–34
    audit model with, 28

challenges with, 29–31
investigation model with,
    29
monitor model with, 27–28
oversight model with, 28–29
successful model with,
    31–34
insurance settlements, 61
internal affairs review, 23–26
investigation model, of
    independent agency
    review, 29
investigations, pattern or
    practice, 130–138
investigative powers, of
    civilian oversight, 122
investigators, internal affairs,
    23–24

Jim Crow, 4–5
jurisdiction, civilian oversight
    and, 110–111

King, Rodney, 157–158
Ku Klux Klan, 3
Ku Klux Klan Act (KKK Act),
    3, 5

Law Enforcement Integrity
    and Accountability Act
    (Colorado), 15–16
law enforcement officer bill of
    rights (LEOBOR), 42, 45,
    47–48
Le, Tommy, 152
leave, paid administrative, 26,
    49–50
legalization, of marijuana,
    184–185

Leija, Johnny, 9–10
LEOBOR. *See* law enforcement
officer bill of rights
(LEOBOR)
litigation
administrative complaints
vs., 22–23
of civilian-police
encounters, 151–170
in constitutional policing,
138–141
expert witnesses in,
160–165
insurance settlements *vs.*, 61
national policy standards
and, 156–159
reform and, 151–152
science in, 165–167
Lopez, Antonio, 155

marijuana legalization,
184–185
McDonald, Laquan, 99–100,
108, 155
McDonnell Douglas Corp. v.
Green, 60
mental health, 80–81, 177–180
Monell claim, 17
monitor model, of
independent agency
review, 27–28
Monroe v. Pape, 3
Murphy, Chris, 177

New Mexico Civil Rights Act,
16
New York Police Department
(NYPD), 173–190. *See*

also Civilian Complaint
Review Board (CCRB)
(New York)
NLRB v. Weingarten, 43–44

Obama, Barack, 95, 123
Office of Community Oriented
Policing Services (COPS),
138
Office of Police Accountability
and Transparency (OPAT)
(Boston), 121
Omnibus Crime Control and
Safe Streets Act of, 39
OPAT. *See* Office of Police
Accountability and
Transparency (OPAT)
(Boston)
oversight, civilian
agencies, shift to, 119–121
characteristics of successful,
109–118
contemporary, 95–124
entities, 101–102
example, 104–109
flourishing of, despite
evidence for, 99–101
future of, 119–123
growth of, 97–99
independence of, 111–115
as influencing *vs.*
controlling, 121–123
investigative powers of, 122
jurisdictional scope of,
110–111, 122
neutrality of, 116–117
patience and perseverance
with, 102–104

police chief employment
and, 122–123
Presidential Task Force
recommendations on,
95–97, 123
prevalence of, 101
professionalism in, 116–117
representativeness, 117–118
resources for, 115–116
transparency with, 117
oversight model, of
independent agency
review, 28–29

paid leave, 26, 49–50
pattern or practice
investigations, 130–141,
144–147
Paz, Ludwig, 196n61
Pearson v. Callahan, 8
perceptual distortion, 154, 164,
166
Plessey v. Ferguson, 5
power, 75–83
Pregnancy Discrimination Act,
58
President's Task Force on 21st
Century Policing, 95–97,
123
Pressley, Ayanna, 177
Pride, Daniel, 177–178
private attorney general
statute, 3–4
private right of action, 132
procedural rights, with public
employees, 41–42
Proceedings of the National
Academy of Sciences

of the United States of
America (PNAS), 134–135
professional growth, 134
property rights, public
employment and, 40–41
protests, command-and-
control policing of,
180–182
public employment. *See*
employment, public
public health professionals,
177–180

qualified immunity
"clearly established" in, 8–9
criticism of, by Supreme
Court, 11–14
decency and, 9–11
evolution of standard, 7–8
examples of application of,
9–11
excessive force and, 10–11
inroads against, 15–16
interest groups around,
14–15
Jim Crow and, 4–5
as legal defense, 6–7
origins of, 5
rational conduct and, 9–11
Reconstruction and, 4–5
quota policing, 73–74

racial prejudice, 14–15, 74–75,
81–86
Reconstruction, 4–5
Reeves, Carleton W., 13–14
representation, duty of fair,
45–46

representativeness, in civilian oversight, 117–118
right of action, private, 132
Riley v. California, 40
Romanucci, Anthony, 168

Santiago, Michael, 155
Saucier v. Katz, 8
Scheindlin, Shira A., 135
schools, police-free, 175–177
search and seizure. *See also* Fourth Amendment
public employees and, 16
Section 12601, 131–132
shell shock, 155–156
sleeper hold, 157, 163–164, 169
Sneed, Donald, III, 152
social justice, 89–90
South Park (television show), 153–154
speech, freedom of, 38, 70–72
Springfield, Massachusetts, 144–145
Stored Wire Communications Act, 39

Taylor, Breonna, 88, 100, 118
Taylor, Che, 155
Taylor v. Riojas, 16
Tennessee v. Garner, 153, 163
Thirteenth Amendment, 4
Thomas, Clarence, 11–12
thousand-yard stare, 154–156
Torres v. Madrid, 88
transparency, 26, 34, 117, 133, 188–190

Trawick, Kawaski, 83–84
Trump, Donald, 89
Turner v. Driver, 78–79

Uniformed Services Employment and Reemployment Act, 58
unions. *See also* collective bargaining
accountability and, 45–54
duty of fair representation with, 45–46
failure to represent employee by, 46
financial support for defense and, 50–51
grievability of disciplinary action and, 51–54
paid leave and, 49–50
police as members of, 45–54
supervisors and, 48–49

Vaca v. Sipes, 45
Van Dyke, Jason, 99, 108
vascular neck restraint, 157, 163–164, 169
vice squads, 185–188, 195n60

Weingarten rights, 43–44
Wilson, Darren, 154
Wiretap Act, 40
witnesses, expert, 160–165
Wooten, Jermaine, 153
Wright, Daunte, 88
Wynn, James A., 12–13